Java Threads™

THE JAVA™ SERIES

Exploring Java™

Java™ Threads

Java™ Network Programming

Java™ Virtual Machine

Java™ AWT Reference

Java™ Language Reference

Java™ Fundamental Classes Reference

Database Programming with JDBC™ and Java™

Java™ Distributed Computing

Developing Java Beans™

Java™ Security

Java™ Cryptography

Java™ Swing

Java™ Servlet Programming

Also from O'Reilly

Java™ in a Nutshell

Java™ in a Nutshell, Deluxe Edition

Java™ Examples in a Nutshell

Java™ Threads

Second Edition

Scott Oaks and Henry Wong

O'REILLY®

Beijing · Cambridge · Farnham · Köln · Paris · Sebastopol · Taipei · Tokyo

Java™ Threads, Second Edition
by Scott Oaks and Henry Wong

Copyright © 1999, 1997 O'Reilly & Associates, Inc. All rights reserved.
Printed in the United States of America.

Published by O'Reilly & Associates, Inc., 101 Morris Street, Sebastopol, CA 95472.

Editor: Mike Loukides

Production Editor: Madeleine Newell

Printing History:

January 1997:	First Edition.
January 1999:	Second Edition.

ISBN: 1-56592-418-5
[M]

[6/00]

Table of Contents

Preface

When Sun Microsystems released the first alpha version of Java™ in the winter of 1995, developers all over the world took notice. There were many features of Java that attracted these developers, not the least of which were the set of buzzwords Sun used to promote Java: Java was, among other things, robust, safe, architecture-neutral, portable, object oriented, simple, and multithreaded. For many developers, these last two buzzwords seemed contradictory: how could a language that is multithreaded be simple?

It turns out that Java's threading system is simple, at least relative to other threading systems. This simplicity makes Java's threading system easy to learn, so that even developers who are unfamiliar with threads can pick up the basics of thread programming with relative ease. But this simplicity comes with trade-offs: some of the advanced features that are found in other threading systems are not present in Java. However, these features can be built by the Java developer from the simpler constructs Java provides. And that's the underlying theme of this book: how to use the threading tools in Java to perform the basic tasks of threaded programming, and how to extend them to perform more advanced tasks for more complex programs.

Who Should Read This Book?

This book is intended for programmers of all levels who need to learn to use threads within Java programs. The first few chapters of the book deal with the issues of threaded programming in Java, starting at a basic level: no assumption is made that the developer has had any experience in threaded programming. As the chapters progress, the material becomes more advanced, in terms of both the information presented and the experience of the developer that the material assumes. For developers who are new to threaded programming, this sequence should provide a natural progression of the topic.

This progression mimics the development of Java itself as well as the development of books about Java. Early Java programs tended to be simple, though effective: an animated image of Duke dancing on a web page was a powerful advertisement of Java's potential, but it barely scratched the surface of that potential. Similarly, early books about Java tended to be complete overviews of Java with only a chapter or two dedicated to Java's threading system.

This book belongs to the second wave of Java books: because it covers only a single topic, it has the luxury of explaining in deeper detail how Java's threads can be used. It's ideally suited to developers targeting the second wave of Java programs—more complex programs that fully exploit the power of Java's threading system.

Though the material presented in this book does not assume any prior knowledge of threads, it does assume that the reader has a knowledge of other areas of the Java API and can write simple Java programs.

Versions Used in This Book

Writing a book on Java in the age of Internet time is hard: the sand on which we're standing is constantly shifting. But we've drawn a line in that sand, and the line we've drawn is at the JDK™ 2 from Sun Microsystems. It's likely that versions of Java that postdate Java 2 will contain some changes to the threading system not discussed in this version of the book. We will also point out the differences between Java 2 and previous versions of Java as we go, so that developers who are using earlier releases of Java will also be able to use this book.

Some vendors that provide Java—either embedded in browsers or as a development system—are contemplating releasing extensions to Java that provide additional functionality to Java's threading system (in much the same way as the examples we provide in Chapters 5 through 8 use the basic techniques of the Java threaded system to provide additional functionality). Those extensions are beyond the scope of this book: we're concerned only with the reference JDK 2 from Sun Microsystems. The only time we'll consider platform differences is in reference to an area of the reference JDK that differs on Unix platforms and Windows platforms: these platforms contain some differences in the scheduling of Java threads, a topic we'll address in Chapter 6.

Organization of This Book

Here's an outline of the book, showing the progression of the material we present. The material in the appendixes is generally either too immature to present fully or is mostly of academic interest, although it may be useful in rare cases.

Chapter 1, *Introduction to Threading*
   This chapter introduces the concept of threads and the terms we use in the book.

Chapter 2, *The Java Threading API*
   This chapter introduces the Java API that allows the programmer to create threads.

Chapter 3, *Synchronization Techniques*
   This chapter introduces the simple locking mechanism that Java developers can use to synchronize access to data and code.

Chapter 4, *Wait and Notify*
   This chapter introduces the other Java mechanism that developers use to synchronize access to data and code.

Chapter 5, *Useful Examples of Java Thread Programming*
   This chapter summarizes the techniques presented in the previous chapters. Unlike the earlier chapters, this chapter is solutions oriented: the examples give you an idea of how to put together the basic threading techniques that have been presented so far, and provide some insight into designing effectively using threads.

Chapter 6, *Java Thread Scheduling*
   This chapter introduces the Java API that controls how threads are scheduled by the virtual machine, including a discussion of scheduling differences between different implementations of the virtual machine.

Chapter 7, *Java Thread Scheduling Examples*
   This chapter provides examples that extend Java's scheduling model, including techniques to provide round-robin scheduling and thread pooling.

Chapter 8, *Advanced Synchronization Topics*
   This chapter discusses various advanced topics related to data synchronization, including designing around deadlock and developing some additional synchronization classes, including synchronization methods from other platforms that are not directly available in Java.

Chapter 9, *Parallelizing for Multiprocessor Machines*
   This chapter discusses how to design your program to take advantage of a machine with multiple processors.

Chapter 10, *Thread Groups*
   This chapter discusses Java's ThreadGroup class, which allows a developer to control and manipulate groups of threads. Java's security mechanism for threads is based on this class and is also discussed in this chapter.

Appendix A, *Miscellaneous Topics*

> This appendix presents a few methods of the Java API that are of limited interest: methods that deal with the thread's stack and the ThreadDeath class.

Appendix B, *Exceptions and Errors*

> This appendix presents the details of the exceptions and errors that are used by the threading system.

Conventions Used in This Book

Constant width font is used for:

- Code examples:

```
public void main(String args[]) {
    System.out.println("Hello, world");
}
```

- Method, variable, and parameter names within the text, as well as keywords

Bold constant width font is used for:

- Presenting revised code examples as we work through a problem:

```
public void main(String args[]) {
    System.out.println("Hello, world");
}
```

- Highlighting a section of code for discussion within a longer code example

Italic font is used for URLs and filenames, and to introduce new terms.

Examples of the programs in this book may be retrieved online from:

> *http://www.oreilly.com/catalog/jthreads2*

Feedback for Authors

We've attempted to be complete and accurate throughout this book. Changes in releases of the Java specification as well as differing vendor implementations across many platforms and underlying operating systems make it impossible to be completely accurate in all cases (not to mention the possibility of our having made a mistake somewhere along the line). This book is a work in progress, and as Java continues to evolve, so, too, will this book. Please let us know about any errors you find, as well as your suggestions for future editions, by writing to:

O'Reilly & Associates, Inc.
101 Morris Street
Sebastopol, CA 95472
1-800-998-9938 (in the U.S. or Canada)
1-707-829-0515 (international/local)
1-707-829-0104 (FAX)

You can also send us messages electronically. To be put on the mailing list or request a catalog, send email to:

info@oreilly.com

To ask technical questions or comment on the book, send email to:

bookquestions@oreilly.com

We have a web site for the book, where we'll list examples, errata, and any plans for future editions. You can access this page at:

http://www.oreilly.com/catalog/jthreads2/

For more information about this book and others, see the O'Reilly web site:

http://www.oreilly.com

The authors welcome your feedback about this book, especially if you spot errors or omissions that we have made. You can contact us at *scott.oaks@sun.com* and *henry.wong@sun.com.*

Acknowledgments

As readers of prefaces are well aware, writing a book is never an effort undertaken solely by the authors who get all the credit on the cover. We are deeply indebted to the following people for their help and encouragement: Michael Loukides, who believed us when we said that this was an important topic and who shepherded us through the creative process; David Flanagan, for valuable feedback on the drafts; Hong Zhang, for helping us with Windows threading issues; and Reynold Jabbour and Wendy Talmont, for supporting us in our work.

Mostly, we must thank our respective families. To James, who gave Scott the support and encouragement necessary to see this book through (and to cope with his continual state of distraction), and to Nini, who knew to leave Henry alone for the ten percent of the time when he was creative, and encouraged him the rest of the time: Thank you for everything!

Finally, we must thank the many readers of the first edition of this book who sent us invaluable feedback. We have tried our best to answer every concern that they have raised. Keep those cards and letters coming!

1

Introduction to Threading

This is a book about using threads in the Java programming language and the Java virtual machine. The topic of threads is very important in Java—so important that many features of a threaded system are built into the Java language itself, while other features of a threaded system are required by the Java virtual machine. Threading is an integral part of using Java.

The concept of threads is not a new one: for some time, many operating systems have had libraries that provide the C programmer with a mechanism to create threads. Other languages, such as Ada, have support for threads embedded into the language, much as support for threads is built into the Java language. Nonetheless, the topic of threads is usually considered a peripheral programming topic, one that's only needed in special programming cases.

With Java, things are different: it is impossible to write any but the simplest Java program without introducing the topic of threads. And the popularity of Java ensures that many developers who might never have considered learning about threading possibilities in a language like C or C++ need to become fluent in threaded programming.

Java Terms

We'll start by defining some terms used throughout this book. Many terms surrounding Java are used inconsistently in various sources; we'll endeavor to be consistent in our usage of these terms throughout the book.

Java

First is the term *Java* itself. As we know, Java started out as a programming language, and many people today think of Java as being simply a programming language. But Java is much more than just a programming language: it's also an API specification and a virtual machine specification. So when we say Java, we mean the entire Java platform: a programming language, an API, and a virtual machine specification that, taken together, define an entire programming and runtime environment. Often when we say Java, it's clear from context that we're talking specifically about the programming language, or parts of the Java API, or the virtual machine. The point to remember is that the threading features we discuss in this book derive their properties from all the components of the Java platform taken as a whole. While it's possible to take the Java programming language, directly compile it into assembly code, and run it outside of the virtual machine, such an executable may not necessarily behave the same as the programs we describe in this book.

Virtual machine, interpreters, and browsers

The Java *virtual machine* is another term for the Java *interpreter*, which is the code that ultimately runs Java programs by interpreting the intermediate byte-code format of the Java programming language. The Java interpreter actually comes in three popular forms: the interpreter for developers (called *java*) that runs programs via the command line or a file manager, the interpreter for end users (called *jre*) that is a subset of the developer environment and forms the basis of (among other things) the Java plug-in, and the interpreter that is built into many popular web browsers such as Netscape Navigator, Internet Explorer, HotJava™, and the appletviewer that comes with the Java Developer's Kit. All of these forms are simply implementations of the Java virtual machine, and we'll refer to the Java virtual machine when our discussion applies to any of them. When we use the term *Java interpreter*, we're talking specifically about the command-line, standalone version of the virtual machine (including those virtual machines that perform just-in-time compilation); when we use the term *Java-enabled browser* (or, more simply, *browser*), we're talking specifically about the virtual machine built into web browsers.

For the most part, virtual machines are indistinguishable—at least in theory. In practice, there are a few important differences between implementations of virtual machines, and one of those differences comes in the world of threads. This difference is important in relatively few circumstances, and we'll discuss it in Chapter 6.

Programs, applications, and applets

This leads us to the terms that we'll use for things written in the Java language. Generically, we'll call such entities *programs*. But there are two types of programs a typical Java programmer might write: programs that can be run directly by the Java interpreter and programs designed to be run by a Java-enabled browser.* Much of the time, the distinction between these two types

---

* Though it's possible to write a single Java program so that it can be run both by the interpreter and by a browser, the distinction still applies at the time the program is actually run.

of Java programs is not important, and in those cases, we'll refer to them as programs. But in those cases where the distinction is important, we'll use the term *applets* for programs running in the Java-enabled browser and the term *applications* for standalone Java programs. In terms of threads, the distinction between an applet and an application manifests itself only in Java's security model; we'll discuss the interaction between the security model and Java threads in Chapter 10.

Thread Overview

This leaves us only one more term to define: what exactly is a thread? The term *thread* is shorthand for *thread of control*, and a thread of control is, at its simplest, a section of code executed independently of other threads of control within a single program.

Thread of Control

Thread of control sounds like a complicated technical term, but it's really a simple concept: it is the path taken by a program during execution. This determines what code will be executed: does the `if` block get executed, or does the `else` block? How many times does the `while` loop execute? If we were executing tasks from a "to do" list, much as a computer executes an application, what steps we perform and the order in which we perform them is our path of execution, the result of our thread of control.

Having multiple threads of control is like executing tasks from two lists. We are still doing the tasks on each "to do" list in the correct order, but when we get bored with the tasks on one of the lists, we switch lists with the intention of returning at some future time to the first list at the exact point where we left off.

Overview of Multitasking

We're all familiar with the use of multitasking operating systems to run multiple programs simultaneously. Each of these programs has at least one thread within it, so at some level, we're already comfortable with the notion of a thread in a single process. The single-threaded process has the following properties, which, as it turns out, are shared by all threads in a program with multiple threads as well:

- The process begins execution at a well-known point. In programming languages like C and C++ (not to mention Java itself), the thread begins execution at the first statement of the function or method called `main()`.

- Execution of the statements follows in a completely ordered, predefined sequence for a given set of inputs. An individual process is single-minded in this regard: it simply executes the next statement in the program.

- While executing, the process has access to certain data. In Java, there are three types of data a process can access: *local* variables are accessed from the thread's stack, *instance* variables are accessed through object references, and *static* variables are accessed through class or object references.

Now consider what happens when you sit at your computer and start two single-threaded programs: a text editor, say, and a file manager. You now have two processes running on your computer; each process has a single thread with the properties just outlined. Each process does not necessarily know about the other process, although, depending on the operating system running on your computer, there are several ways in which the processes can send each other various messages. A common behavior is that you can drag a file icon from the file manager into the text editor in order to edit the file. Each process thus runs independently of the other, although they can cooperate if they so choose. The typical multitasking environment is shown in Figure 1-1.

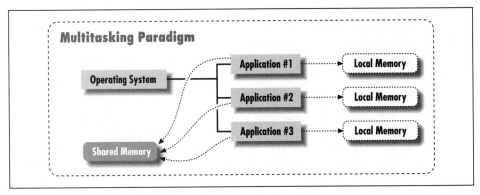

Figure 1-1. Processes in a multitasking environment

From the point of view of the person using the computer, these processes often appear to execute simultaneously, although many variables can affect that appearance. These variables depend on the operating system: for example, a given operating system may not support multitasking at all, so that no two programs appear to execute simultaneously. Or the user may have decided that a particular process is more important than other processes and hence should always run, shutting out the other processes from running and again affecting the appearance of simultaneity.

Finally, the data contained within these two processes is, by default, separated: each has its own stack for local variables, and each has its own data area for objects and other data elements. Under many operating systems, the programmer can make arrangements so that the data objects reside in memory that can be shared between the processes, allowing both processes to access them.

Overview of Multithreading

All of this leads us to a common analogy: we can think of a thread just as we think of a process, and we can consider a program with multiple threads running within a single instance of the Java virtual machine just as we consider multiple processes within an operating system, as we show in Figure 1-2.

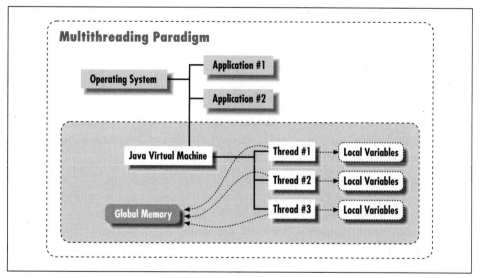

Figure 1-2. Multitasking versus threading

So it is that within a Java program, multiple threads have these properties:

- Each thread begins execution at a predefined, well-known location. For one of the threads in the program, that location is the main() method; for the rest of the threads, it is a particular location the programmer decides on when the code is written. Note that this is true of an applet as well, in which case the main() method was executed by the browser itself.

- Each thread executes code from its starting location in an ordered, predefined (for a given set of inputs) sequence. Threads are single-minded in their purpose, always simply executing the next statement in the sequence.

- Each thread executes its code independently of the other threads in the program. If the threads choose to cooperate with each other, there are a variety of mechanisms we will explore that allow that cooperation. Exploiting those methods of cooperation is the reason why programming with threads is such a useful technique, but that cooperation is completely optional, much as the user is never required to drag a file from the file manager into the text editor.

- The threads appear to have a certain degree of simultaneous execution. As we'll explore in Chapter 6, the degree of simultaneity depends on several factors—programming decisions about the relative importance of various threads as well as operating system support for various features. The potential for simultaneous execution is the key thing you must keep in mind when threading your code.

- The threads have access to various types of data. At this point, the analogy to multiple processes breaks down somewhat, depending on the type of data the Java program is attempting to access.

  Each thread is separate, so that local variables in the methods that the thread is executing are separate for different threads. These local variables are completely private; there is no way for one thread to access the local variables of another thread. If two threads happen to execute the same method, each thread gets a separate copy of the local variables of that method. This is completely analogous to running two copies of the text editor: each process would have separate copies of the local variables.

  Objects and their instance variables, on the other hand, can be shared between threads in a Java program, and sharing these objects between threads of a Java program is much easier than sharing data objects between processes in most operating systems. In fact, the ability to share data objects easily between threads is another reason why programming with threads is so useful. But Java threads cannot arbitrarily access each other's data objects: they need permission to access the objects, and one thread needs to pass the object reference to the other thread.

  Static variables are the big exception to this analogy: they are automatically shared between all threads in a Java program.

Don't panic over this analogy: the fact that you'll be programming with threads in Java doesn't mean you'll necessarily be doing the system-level type of programming you'd need to perform if you were writing the multitasking operating system responsible for running multiple programs. The Java Thread API is designed to be simple and requires little specialized skill for most common tasks.

Why Threads?

The notion of threading is so ingrained in Java that it's almost impossible to write even the simplest programs in Java without creating and using threads. And many of the classes in the Java API are already threaded, so that often you are using multiple threads without realizing it.

Historically, threading was first exploited to make certain programs easier to write: if a program can be split into separate tasks, it's often easier to program the algorithm as separate tasks or threads. Programs that fall into this category are typically specialized and deal with multiple independent tasks. The relative rareness of these types of programs makes threading in this category a specialized skill. Often, these programs were written as separate processes using operating-system-dependent communication tools such as signals and shared memory spaces to communicate between processes. This approach increased system complexity.

The popularity of threading increased when graphical interfaces became the standard for desktop computers because the threading system allowed the user to perceive better program performance. The introduction of threads into these platforms didn't make the programs any faster, but it did create an illusion of faster performance for the user, who now had a dedicated thread to service input or display output.

Recently, there's been a flurry of activity regarding a new use of threaded programs: to exploit the growing number of computers that have multiple processors. Programs that require a lot of CPU processing are natural candidates for this category, since a calculation that requires one hour on a single-processor machine could (at least theoretically) run in half an hour on a two-processor machine, or 15 minutes on a four-processor machine. All that is required is that the program be written to use multiple threads to perform the calculation.

While computers with multiple processors have been around for a long time, we're now seeing these machines become cheap enough to be very widely available. The advent of less expensive machines with multiple processors, and of operating systems that provide programmers with thread libraries to exploit those processors, has made threaded programming a hot topic, as developers move to extract every benefit from these new machines. Until Java, much of the interest in threading centered around using threads to take advantage of multiple processors on a single machine.

However, threading in Java often has nothing at all to do with multiprocessor machines and their capabilities; in fact, the first Java virtual machines were unable to take advantage of multiple processors on a machine, and many implementations of the virtual machine still follow that model. However, there are also implementations of the virtual machine that do take advantage of the multiple processors that the computer may have. A correctly written program running in one of those virtual machines on a computer with two processors may indeed take roughly half the time to execute that it would take on a computer with a single processor. If you're looking to use Java to have your program scale to many processors, that is indeed possible when you use the correct virtual machine. However, even if your Java program is destined to be run on a machine with a single CPU, threading is still very important.

The major reason threading is so important in Java is that Java has no concept of asynchronous behavior. This means that many of the programming techniques you've become accustomed to using in typical programs are not applicable in Java; instead, you must learn a new repertoire of threading techniques to handle these cases of asynchronous behavior.

This is not to say there aren't other times when threads are a handy programming technique in Java; certainly it's easy to use Java for a program that implements an algorithm that naturally lends itself to threading. And many Java programs implement multiple independent behaviors. The next few sections cover some of the circumstances in which Java threads are a required component of the program, due to the need for asynchronous behavior or to the elegance that threading lends to the problem.

Nonblocking I/O

In Java, as in most programming languages, when you try to get input from the user, you execute a read() method specifying the user's terminal (System.in in Java). When the program executes the read() method, the program will typically wait until the user types at least one character before it continues and executes the next statement. This type of I/O is called *blocking I/O*: the program blocks until some data is available to satisfy the read() method.

This type of behavior is often undesirable. If you're reading data from a network socket, that data is often not available when you want to read it: the data may have been delayed in transit over the network, or you may be reading from a network server that sends data only periodically. If the program blocks when it tries to read from the socket, then it's unable to do anything else until the data is actually available. If the program has a user interface that contains a button and the user presses the button while the program is executing the read() method, nothing will happen: the program will be unable to process the mouse events and execute the event-processing method associated with the button. This can be very frustrating for the user, who thinks the program has hung.

Traditionally, there are three techniques to cope with this situation:

I/O multiplexing
> Developers often take all input sources and use a system call like select() to
> notify them when data is available from a particular source. This allows input
> to be handled much like an event from the user (in fact, many graphical tool-

kits use this method transparently to the user, who simply registers a callback function that is called whenever data is available from a particular source).

Polling

Polling allows a developer to test if data is available from a particular source. If data is available, the data can be read and processed; if it is not, the program can perform another task. Polling can be done either explicitly—with a system call like `poll()`—or, in some systems, by making the `read()` function return an indication that no data is immediately available.

Signals

A file descriptor representing an input source can often be set so that an asynchronous signal is delivered to the program when data is available on that input source. This signal interrupts the program, which processes the data and then returns to whatever task it had been doing.

In Java, none of these techniques is directly available. There is limited support for polling via the `available()` method of the FilterInputStream class, but this method does not have the rich semantics that polling typically has in most operating systems. To compensate for the lack of these features, a Java developer must set up a separate thread to read the data. This separate thread can block when data isn't available, and the other thread(s) in the Java program can process events from the user or perform other tasks.

While this issue of blocking I/O can conceivably occur with any data source, it occurs most frequently with network sockets. If you're used to programming sockets, you've probably used one of these techniques to read from a socket, but perhaps not to write to one. Many developers, used to programming on a local area network, are vaguely aware that writing to a socket may block, but it's a possibility that many of them ignore because it can only happen under certain circumstances, such as a backlog in getting data onto the network. This backlog rarely happens on a fast local area network, but if you're using Java to program sockets over the Internet, the chances of this backlog happening are greatly increased; hence the chance of blocking while attempting to write data onto the network is also increased. So in Java, you may need two threads to handle the socket: one to read from the socket and one to write to it.

Alarms and Timers

Traditional operating systems typically provide some sort of timer or alarm call: the program sets the timer and continues processing. When the timer expires, the program receives some sort of asynchronous signal that notifies the program of the timer's expiration.

In Java, the programmer must set up a separate thread to simulate a timer. This thread can sleep for the duration of a specified time interval and then notify other threads that the timer has expired.

Independent Tasks

A Java program is often called on to perform independent tasks. In the simplest case, a single applet may perform two independent animations for a web page. A more complex program would be a calculation server that performs calculations on behalf of several clients simultaneously. In either case, while it is possible to write a single-threaded program to perform the multiple tasks, it's easier and more elegant to place each task in its own thread.

The complete answer to the question "Why threads?" really lies in this category. As programmers, we're trained to think linearly and often fail to see simultaneous paths that our program might take. But there's no reason why processes that we've conventionally thought of in a single-threaded fashion need necessarily remain so: when the Save button in a word processor is pressed, we typically have to wait a few seconds until we can continue. Worse yet, the word processor may periodically perform an autosave, which invariably interrupts the flow of typing and disrupts the thought process. In a threaded word processor, the save operation would be in a separate thread so that it didn't interfere with the work flow. As you become accustomed to writing programs with multiple threads, you'll discover many circumstances in which adding a separate thread will make your algorithms more elegant and your programs better to use.

Parallelizable Algorithms

With the advent of virtual machines that can use multiple CPUs simultaneously, Java has become a useful platform for developing programs that use algorithms that can be parallelized. Any program that contains a loop is a candidate for being parallelized; that is, running one iteration of the loop on one CPU while another iteration of the loop is simultaneously running on another CPU. Dependencies between the data that each iteration of the loop needs may prohibit a particular loop from being parallelized, and there may be other reasons why a loop should not be parallelized. But for many programs with CPU-intensive loops, parallelizing the loop will greatly speed up the execution of the program when it is run on a machine with multiple processors.

Many languages have compilers that support automatic parallelization of loops; as yet, Java does not. But as we'll see in Chapter 9, parallelizing a loop by hand is often not a difficult task.

Summary

The idea of multiple threads of control within a single program may seem like a new and difficult concept, but it is not. All programs have at least one thread already, and multiple threads in a single program are not radically different from multiple programs within an operating system.

A Java program can contain many threads, all of which may be created without the explicit knowledge of the developer. For now, all you need to consider is that when you write a Java application, there is an initial thread that begins its operation by executing the `main()` method of your application. When you write a Java applet, there is a thread that is executing the callback methods (`init()`, `actionPerformed()`, etc.) of your applet; we speak of this thread as the applet's thread. In either case, your program starts with what you can consider as a single thread. If you want to perform I/O (particularly if the I/O might block), start a timer, or do any other task in parallel with the initial thread, you must start a new thread to perform that task. In the next chapter, we'll examine how to do just that.

2

The Java Threading API

In this chapter, we will create our own threads. As we shall see, Java threads are easy to use and well integrated with the Java environment.

Threading Using the Thread Class

In the last chapter, we considered threads as separate tasks that execute in parallel. These tasks are simply code executed by the thread, and this code is actually part of our program. The code may download an image from the server or may play an audio file on the speakers or any other task; because it is code, it can be executed by our original thread. To introduce the parallelism we desire, we must create a new thread and arrange for the new thread to execute the appropriate code.

Let's start by looking at the execution of a single thread in the following example:

```
public class OurClass {
    public void run() {
        for (int I = 0; I < 100; I++) {
            System.out.println("Hello");
        }
    }
}
```

In this example, we have a class called OurClass. The OurClass class has a single public method called `run()` that simply writes a string 100 times to the Java console or to the standard output. If we execute this code from an applet as shown here, it runs in the applet's thread:

```
import java.applet.Applet;

public class OurApplet extends Applet {
```

```
    public void init() {
        OurClass oc = new OurClass();
        oc.run();
    }
}
```

If we instantiate an OurClass object and call its run() method, nothing unusual happens. An object is created, its run() method is called, and the "Hello" message prints 100 times. Just like other method calls, the caller of the run() method waits until the run() method finishes before it continues. If we were to graph an execution of the code, it would look like Figure 2-1.

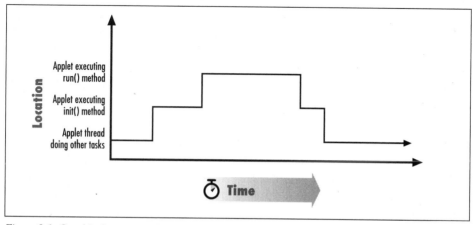

Figure 2-1. Graphical representation of nonthreaded method execution

What if we want the run() method of OurClass to execute in parallel with the init() and other methods of the applet? In order to do that, we must modify the OurClass class so that it can be executed by a new thread. So the first thing we'll do is make OurClass inherit from the Thread (java.lang.Thread) class:

```
public class OurClass extends Thread {
    public void run() {
        for (int I = 0; I < 100; I++) {
            System.out.println("Hello");
        }
    }
}
```

If we compile this code and run it with our applet, everything works exactly as before: the applet's init() method calls the run() method of the OurClass object and waits for the run() method to return before continuing. The fact that this example compiles and runs proves that the Thread class exists. This class is our first look into the Java threading API and is the programmatic interface for starting and stopping our own threads. But we have not yet created a new thread of control; we have simply created a class that has a `run()` method. To continue, let's modify our applet like this:

```
import java.applet.Applet;

public class OurApplet extends Applet {
    public void init() {
        OurClass oc = new OurClass();
        oc.start();
    }
}
```

In this second version of our applet, we have changed only one line: the call to the `run()` method is now a call to the `start()` method. Compiling and executing this code confirms that it still works and appears to the user to run exactly the same way as the previous example. Since the `start()` method is not part of the OurClass class, we can conclude that the implementation of the `start()` method is part of either the Thread class or one of its superclasses. Furthermore, since the applet still accomplishes the same task, we can conclude that the `start()` method causes a call, whether directly or indirectly, to the `run()` method.

Upon closer examination, this new applet actually behaves differently than the previous version. While it is true that the `start()` method eventually calls the `run()` method, it does so in another thread. The `start()` method is what actually creates another thread of control; this new thread, after dealing with some initialization details, then calls the `run()` method. After the `run()` method completes, this new thread also deals with the details of terminating the thread. The `start()` method of the original thread returns immediately. Thus, the `run()` method will be executing in the newly formed thread at about the same time the `start()` method returns in the first thread, as shown in Figure 2-2.

Here are the methods of the Thread class that we've discussed so far:

Thread()

    Constructs a thread object using default values for all options.

void run()

    The method that the newly created thread will execute. Developers should override this method with the code they want the new thread to run; we'll show the default implementation of the `run()` method a little further on, but it is essentially an empty method.

void start()

    Creates a new thread and executes the `run()` method defined in this thread class.

To review, creating another thread of control is a two-step process. First, we must create the code that executes in the new thread by overriding the `run()` method

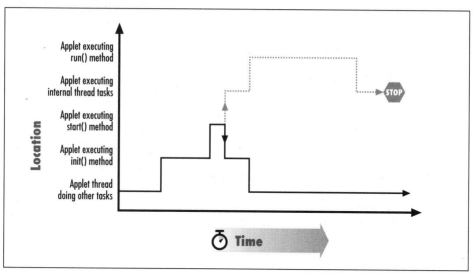

Figure 2-2. Graphical representation of threaded method execution

in our subclass. Then we create the actual subclassed object using its constructor (which calls the default constructor of the Thread class in this case) and begin execution of its `run()` method by calling the `start()` method of the subclass.

---

run() Versus main()

In essence, the `run()` method may be thought of as the `main()` method of the newly formed thread: a new thread begins execution with the `run()` method in the same way a program begins execution with the `main()` method.

While the `main()` method receives its arguments from the `argv` parameter (which is typically set from the command line), the newly created thread must receive its arguments programmatically from the originating thread. Hence, parameters can be passed in via the constructor, static instance variables, or any other technique designed by the developer.

Animate Applet

Let's see a more concrete example of creating a new thread. When you want to show an animation in your web page, you do so by displaying a series of images (frames) with a time interval between the frames. This use of a timer is one of the most common places in Java where a separate thread is required: because there are no asynchronous signals in Java, you must set up a separate thread, have the thread sleep for a period of time, and then have the thread tell the applet to paint the next frame.

An implementation of this timer follows:

```
import java.awt.*;

public class TimerThread extends Thread {
    Component comp;              // Component that needs repainting
    int timediff;               // Time between repaints of the component
    volatile boolean shouldRun; // Set to false to stop thread

    public TimerThread(Component comp, int timediff) {
        this.comp = comp;
        this.timediff = timediff;
        shouldRun = true;
    }

    public void run() {
        while (shouldRun) {
            try {
                comp.repaint();
                sleep(timediff);
            } catch (Exception e) {}
        }
    }
}
```

In this example, the TimerThread class, just like the OurClass class, inherits from the Thread class and overrides the run() method. Its constructor stores the component on which to call the repaint() method and the requested time interval between the calls to the repaint() method.

What we have not seen so far is the call to the sleep() method:

static void sleep (long milliseconds)
Puts the currently executing thread to sleep for the specified number of milliseconds. This method is static and may be accessed through the Thread class name.

static void sleep (long milliseconds, int nanoseconds)
Puts the currently executing thread to sleep for the specified number of milliseconds and nanoseconds. This method is static and may be accessed through the Thread class name.

The sleep() method is part of the Thread class, and it causes the current thread (the thread that made the call to the sleep() method) to pause for the specified amount of time in milliseconds. The try statement in the code example is needed due to some of the exceptions that are thrown from the sleep() method. We'll discuss these exceptions in Appendix B; for now, we'll just discard all exceptions.

The easiest description of the task of the sleep() method is that the caller actually sleeps for the specified amount of time. This method is part of the Thread class because of how the method accomplishes the task: the current (i.e., calling) thread is placed in a "blocked" state for the specified amount of time, much like the state it would be in if the thread were waiting for I/O to occur. See Appendix A for a discussion of the volatile keyword.

---

sleep(long) and sleep(long, int)

The Thread class provides a version of the sleep() method that allows the developer to specify the time in terms of nanoseconds. Unfortunately, most operating systems that implement the Java virtual machine do not support a resolution as small as a nanosecond. For those platforms, the method simply rounds the number of nanoseconds to the nearest millisecond and calls the version of the sleep() method that only specifies milliseconds. In fact, most operating systems do not support a resolution of a single millisecond, so that the milliseconds are in turn rounded up to the smallest resolution that the platform supports.

For the developer, we should note that support of nanoseconds may never be available in all versions of the Java virtual machine. As a matter of policy, one should not design programs that require support of nanoseconds (or even exact timing of milliseconds) in order to function correctly.

To return to step 2 of the two-step process: let's take a look at the Animate applet that uses our TimerThread class:

```
import java.applet.*;
import java.awt.*;

public class Animate extends Applet {
    int count, lastcount;
    Image pictures[];
    TimerThread timer;

    public void init() {
        lastcount = 10; count = 0;
        pictures = new Image[10];
        MediaTracker tracker = new MediaTracker(this);
        for (int a = 0; a < lastcount; a++) {
            pictures[a] = getImage (
                getCodeBase(), new Integer(a).toString()+".jpeg");
            tracker.addImage(pictures[a], 0);
        }
        tracker.checkAll(true);
    }
```

```
public void start() {
    timer = new TimerThread(this, 1000);
    timer.start();
}

public void stop() {
    timer.shouldRun = false;
    timer = null;
}

public void paint(Graphics g) {
    g.drawImage(pictures[count++], 0, 0, null);

    if (count == lastcount)
        count = 0;
}
}
```

Here we create and start the new thread in the applet's start() method. This new thread is responsible only for informing the applet when to redraw the next frame; it is still the applet's thread that performs the redraw when the applet's paint() method is called. The init() method in this case simply loads the image frames from the server.

Stopping a Thread

When the stop() method of the applet is called, we need to stop the timer thread, since we do not need repaint() requests when the applet is no longer running. To do this, we relied on the ability to set the shouldRun variable of the TimerThread class to notify that class that it should return from its run() method. When a thread returns from its run() method, it has completed its execution, so in this case we also set the timer instance variable to null to allow that thread object to be garbage collected.

This technique is the preferred method for terminating a thread: threads should always terminate by returning from their run() method. It's up to the developer to decide how a thread should know when it's time to return from the run() method; setting a flag, as we've done in this case, is typically the easiest method to do that.

Setting a flag means that my thread has to check the flag periodically. Isn't there a cleaner way to stop the thread? And isn't there a way to terminate the thread immediately, rather than waiting for it to check some flag? Well, yes and no. The Thread class does contain a stop() method that allows you to stop a thread immediately: no matter what the thread is doing, it will be terminated. However, the stop() method is very dangerous. In Java 2, the stop() method is deprecated; however, the reasons that led it to become deprecated actually exist in all versions of Java, so you should avoid using the stop() method in any release of Java. We'll discuss the motivation for this in Chapter 6 after we understand a little more about the details of threaded programming; for now, you'll have to accept our word that using the stop() method is a dangerous thing. In addition, calling the stop() method will sometimes result in a security exception, as we'll explain in Chapter 10, so you cannot rely on it always working.

The start() and stop() Methods of the Applet Class

It is unfortunate that both the Applet and the Thread classes have a start() and a stop() method, and that they have the same signature in both classes. This may be a source of confusion when implementing or debugging threaded applets.

These methods serve different purposes and are not directly related to each other.

For the record, here is the definition of the stop() method:

void stop() (deprecated in Java 2)
   Terminates an already running thread.

What does returning from the run() method (or calling the stop() method) accomplish? As we mentioned, when the run() method completes, the thread automatically handles the cleanup process and other details of terminating the thread. The stop() method simply provides a way of prematurely terminating the run() method. The thread will then, as usual, automatically handle the cleanup process and other details of terminating the thread. Details of how the stop() method actually works are given in Appendix A.

Threading Using the Runnable Interface

As simple as it is to create another thread of control, there is one problem with the technique we've outlined so far. It's caused by the fact that Java classes can inherit their behavior only from a single class, which means that inheritance itself can be considered a scarce resource, and is therefore "expensive" to the developer.

In our example, we are threading a simple loop, so this is not much of a concern. However, if we have a complete class structure that already has a detailed inheritance tree and want it to run in its own thread, we cannot simply make this class structure inherit from the Thread class as we did before. One solution would be to create a new class that inherits from Thread and contains references to the instances of the classes we need. This level of indirection is an annoyance.

The Java language deals with this lack of multiple inheritance by using the mechanism known as *interfaces*.* This mechanism is supported by the Thread class and simply means that instead of inheriting from the Thread class, we can implement the Runnable interface (java.lang.Runnable), which is defined as follows:

```
public interface Runnable {
    public abstract void run();
}
```

The Runnable interface contains only one method: the run() method. The Thread class actually implements the Runnable interface; hence, when you inherit from the Thread class, your subclass also implements the Runnable interface. However, in this case we want to implement the Runnable interface without actually inheriting from the Thread class. This is achieved by simply substituting the phrase "implements Runnable" for the phrase "extends Thread"; no other changes are necessary in step 1 of our thread creation process:

```
public class OurClass implements Runnable {
    public void run() {
        for (int I = 0; I < 100; I++) {
            System.out.println("Hello, from another thread");
        }
    }
}
```

Step 2 of our thread creation processes has some other changes. Since an instance of the OurClass class is no longer a Thread object, it cannot be treated as one. So in order to create a separate thread of control, an instance of the Thread class is still needed, but it will be instantiated with a reference to our OurClass object. In other words, its usage is slightly more complicated:

```
import java.applet.Applet;

public class OurApplet extends Applet {
    public void init() {
        Runnable ot = new OurClass();
        Thread th = new Thread(ot);
        th.start();
    }
}
```

---

* It can be argued that interfaces cannot accomplish everything that multiple inheritance can, but that is a debate for a different book.

As before, we have to create an instance of the OurClass class. However, in this new version, we also need to create an actual thread object. We create this object by passing our runnable OurClass object reference to the constructor of the thread using a new constructor of the Thread class:

Thread(Runnable target)

Constructs a new thread object associated with the given Runnable object.

The new Thread object's `start()` method is called to begin execution of the new thread of control.

The reason we need to pass the runnable object to the thread object's constructor is that the thread must have some way to get to the `run()` method we want the thread to execute. Since we are no longer overriding the `run()` method of the Thread class, the default `run()` method of the Thread class is executed; this default `run()` method looks like this:

```
public void run() {
    if (target != null) {
        target.run();
    }
}
```

Here, `target` is the runnable object we passed to the thread's constructor. So the thread begins execution with the `run()` method of the Thread class, which immediately calls the `run()` method of our runnable object.

Interestingly, since we can use the Runnable interface instead of inheriting from the Thread class, we can merge the OurClass class into the applet itself. This is a common technique for spinning off a separate thread of control for the applet. Since the applet itself is now runnable, instance variables of the applet thread and the `run()` method in this newly spun-off thread are the same:

```
import java.applet.Applet;

public class OurApplet extends Applet implements Runnable {
    public void init() {
        Thread th = new Thread(this);
        th.start();
    }

    public void run() {
        for (int I = 0; I < 100; I++) {
            System.out.println("Hello, from another thread");
        }
    }
}
```

This technique can also be used with our Animate class:

```
import java.applet.*;
import java.awt.*;

public class Animate extends Applet implements Runnable {
    int count, lastcount;
    Image pictures[];
    Thread timer;

    public void init() {
        lastcount = 10; count = 0;
        pictures = new Image[10];
        MediaTracker tracker = new MediaTracker(this);
        for (int a = 0; a < lastcount; a++) {
            pictures[a] = getImage (
                getCodeBase(), new Integer(a).toString()+".jpeg");
            tracker.addImage(pictures[a], 0);
        }
        tracker.checkAll(true);
    }

    public void start() {
        if (timer == null) {
            timer = new Thread(this);
            timer.start();
        }
    }

    public void paint(Graphics g) {
        g.drawImage(pictures[count++], 0, 0, null);
        if (count == lastcount) count = 0;
    }

    public void run() {
        while (isActive()) {
            try {
                repaint();
                Thread.sleep(1000);
            } catch (Exception e) {}
        }
        timer = null;
    }
}
```

After merging the classes, we now have a direct reference to the applet, so we can call the `repaint()` method directly. Because the Animate class is not of the Thread class, its `run()` method cannot call the `sleep()` method directly. Fortunately, the `sleep()` method is a static method, so we can still access it using the Thread class specifier.

As can be seen from this example, the threading interface model allows classes that already have fixed inheritance structures to be threaded without creating a new class. However, there is still one unanswered question: when should you use the Runnable interface and when should you create a new subclass of Thread?

The isActive() Method

We used the `isActive()` method in the last example instead of stopping the thread explicitly. This shows another technique you can use to stop your threads; the benefit of this technique is that it allows the `run()` method to terminate normally rather than through the immediate termination caused by the `stop()` method. This allows the `run()` method to clean up after itself before it terminates.

The `isActive()` method is part of the Applet class and determines if an applet is active. By definition, an applet is active between the periods of the applet's `start()` and `stop()` methods. Don't confuse this method with the `isAlive()` method of the Thread class, which we'll discuss later.

Does threading by the Runnable interface solve a problem that cannot be solved through threading by inheritance or vice versa? At this point, there do not seem to be any significant differences between the two techniques. It is easier to use one technique for certain tasks and the other technique for other tasks. For example, our last Animate class saved us the need to have an extra class definition, via its use of the Runnable interface in the Applet class. In the earlier example, having a separate TimerThread definition may have been both easier to understand and to debug. But these differences are relatively minor, and there do not seem to be any tasks that cannot be solved by either technique.

At this point, we will not worry about the difference between the two techniques. We will use one technique or the other based on personal preference and the clarity of the solution. As we develop examples throughout this book, we hope that you will learn to use either technique on a case-by-case basis.

This is all there is to writing simple threaded Java programs. We have a class that allows us to define a method that will be executed in a separate thread; this thread can be initiated via its `start()` method, and it should stop by returning from its `run()` method. However, as we have seen in the previous chapter, it is not just the ability to have different threads that makes the threaded system a powerful tool; it

---

Inheritance or Interfaces?

As noted, we will choose threading with inheritance or interfaces based on personal preference and the clarity of the solution. However, those of you who are object-oriented purists could argue that unless we are enhancing the Thread class, we should not inherit from the Thread class.

Theorists could insert an entire chapter on this issue. Our main concern is for the clarity of the code; any other reasons for choosing between threading by inheritance or interfaces are beyond the scope of this book.

---

is that these threads can communicate easily with each other by invoking methods on objects that are shared between the threads.

The Life Cycle of a Thread

So far, we have a simple knowledge of working with threads: we know how to use the start() method to start a thread, and how to terminate a thread by arranging for its run() method to complete. We'll now look at two techniques that provide us more information about the thread during its life cycle.

The isAlive() Method

There is a period of time after you call the start() method before the virtual machine can actually start the thread. Similarly, when a thread returns from its run() method, there is a period of time before the virtual machine can clean up after the thread; and if you use the stop() method, there is an even greater period of time before the virtual machine can clean up after the thread.

This delay occurs because it takes time to start or terminate a thread; therefore, there is a transitional period from when a thread is running to when a thread is not running, as shown in Figure 2-3. After the run() method returns, there is a short period of time before the thread stops. If we want to know if the start() method of the thread has been called—or, more usefully, if the thread has terminated—we must use the isAlive() method. This method is used to find out if a thread has actually been started and has not yet terminated:

boolean isAlive()

> Determines if a thread is considered alive. By definition, a thread is considered alive from sometime before a thread is actually started to sometime after a thread is actually stopped.

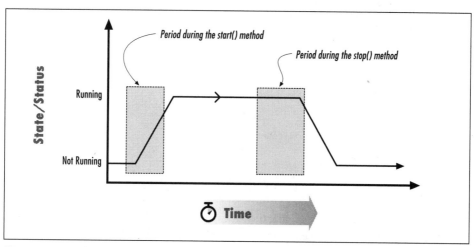

Figure 2-3. Graphical representation of the states of the thread

Let's modify our Animate class to wait until the timer thread stops before finishing:

```java
import java.applet.*;
import java.awt.*;

public class Animate extends Applet {
    int count, lastcount;
    Image pictures[];
    TimerThread timer;

    public void init() {
        lastcount = 10; count = 0;
        pictures = new Image[10];
        MediaTracker tracker = new MediaTracker(this);
        for (int a = 0; a < lastcount; a++) {
            pictures[a] = getImage(
                getCodeBase(), new Integer(a).toString()+".jpeg");
            tracker.addImage(pictures[a], 0);
        }
        tracker.checkAll(true);
    }

    public void start() {
        timer = new TimerThread(this, 1000);
        timer.start();
    }

    public void stop() {
        timer.shouldRun = false;
```

```
        while (timer.isAlive()) {
            try {
                Thread.sleep(100);
            } catch (InterruptedException e) {}
        }
        timer = null;
    }

    public void paint(Graphics g) {
        g.drawImage(pictures[count++], 0, 0, null);

        if (count == lastcount) count = 0;
    }
}
```

Just because a thread has been started does not mean it is actually running, nor that it is able to run—the thread may be blocked, waiting for I/O, or it may still be in the transitional period of the start() method. For this reason, the isAlive() method is more useful in detecting whether a thread has stopped running. For example, let's examine the stop() method of this applet. Just like the earlier versions, we have a TimerThread object that is started and stopped when the applet is started and stopped. In this newer version, the applet's stop() method does more than just stop the TimerThread: it also checks to make sure the thread actually has stopped.

In this example, we don't gain anything by making sure the timer thread has actually stopped. But if for some reason we need to deal with common data that is being accessed by two threads, and it is critical to make sure the other thread is stopped, we can simply loop and check to make sure the thread is no longer alive before continuing.

There is another circumstance in which a thread can be considered no longer alive: if the stop() method is called, the thread will be considered no longer alive a short time later. This is really the same case: the isAlive() method can be used to determine if the run() method has completed, whether normally or as a result of the stop() method having been called.

Joining Threads

The isAlive() method can be thought of as a crude form of communication. We are waiting for information: the indication that the other thread has completed. As another example, if we start a couple of threads to do a long calculation, we are then free to do other tasks. Assume that sometime later we have completed all other secondary tasks and need to deal with the results of the long calculation: we need to wait until the calculations are finished before continuing on to process the results.

We could accomplish this task by using the looping isAlive() technique we've just discussed, but there are other techniques in the Java API that are more suited to this task. This act of waiting is called a *thread join*. We are "joining" with the thread that was "forked" off from us earlier when we started the thread. So, modifying our last example, we have:

```
import java.applet.Applet;

public class Animate extends Applet {
    ...
    public void stop() {
        t.shouldRun = false;
        try {
            t.join();
        } catch (InterruptedException e) {}
    }
}
```

The Thread class provides the following join() methods:

void join()

Waits for the completion of the specified thread. By definition, join() returns as soon as the thread is considered "not alive." This includes the case in which the join() method is called on a thread that has not been started.

void join(long timeout)

Waits for the completion of the specified thread, but no longer than the timeout specified in milliseconds. This timeout value is subject to rounding based on the capabilities of the underlying platform.

void join(long timeout, int nanos)

Waits for the completion of the specified thread, but no longer than a timeout specified in milliseconds and nanoseconds. This timeout value is subject to rounding based on the capabilities of the underlying platform.

When the join() method is called, the current thread will simply wait until the thread it is joining with is no longer alive. This can be caused by the thread not having been started, or having been stopped by yet another thread, or by the completion of the thread itself. The join() method basically accomplishes the same task as the combination of the sleep() and isAlive() methods we used in the earlier example. However, by using the join() method, we accomplish the same task with a single method call. We also have better control over the timeout interval, and we don't waste CPU cycles by polling.

Another interesting point about both the isAlive() method and the join() method is that we are actually not affecting the thread on which we called the method. That thread will run no differently whether the join() method is called or not; instead, it is the calling thread that is affected. The `isAlive()` method simply returns the status of a thread, and the `join()` method simply waits for a certain status on the thread.

---

join(), isAlive(), and the Current Thread

The concept of a thread calling the `isAlive()` or the `join()` method on itself does not make sense. There is no reason to check if the current thread is alive since it would not be able to do anything about it if it were not alive. As a matter of fact, `isAlive()` can only return `true` when it checks the status of the thread calling it. If the thread were stopped during the `isAlive()` method, the `isAlive()` method would not be able to return. So a thread that calls the `isAlive()` method on itself will always receive `true` as the result.

The concept of a thread joining itself does not make sense, but let's examine what happens when one tries. It turns out that the `join()` method uses the `isAlive()` method to determine when to return from the `join()` method. In the current implementation, it also does not check to see if the thread is joining itself. In other words, the `join()` method returns when and only when the thread is no longer alive. This will have the effect of waiting forever.

Thread Naming

The next topic we will examine concerns the thread support methods that are used mainly for thread "bookkeeping." First, it is possible to assign a String name to the Thread object itself:

void setName(String name)
    Assigns a name to the Thread instance.

String getName()
    Gets the name of the Thread instance.

The Thread class provides a method that allows us to attach a name to the thread object and a method that allows us to retrieve the name. The system does not use this string for any specific purpose, though the name is printed out by the default implementation of the `toString()` method of the thread. The developer who assigns the name is free to use this string for any purpose desired. For example, let's assign a name to our TimerThread class:

```
import java.awt.*;

public class TimerThread extends Thread {
    Component comp;                        // Component that needs repainting
```

```
        int timediff;                  // Time between repaints of the component
        volatile boolean shouldRun;    // Set to false to stop thread

    public TimerThread(Component comp, int timediff) {
        this.comp = comp;
        this.timediff = timediff;
        shouldRun = true;
        setName("TimerThread(" + timediff + " milliseconds)");
    }

    public void run() {
        while (shouldRun) {
            try {
                comp.repaint();
                sleep(timediff);
            } catch (Exception e) {}
        }
    }
}
```

In this version of the TimerThread class, we assigned a name to the thread. The name that is assigned is simply "TimerThread" followed by the number of milliseconds used in this timer thread. If the getName() method is later called on this instance, this string value will be returned.

Uses for a Thread Name?

Using the thread name to store information is not too beneficial. We could just as easily have added an instance variable to the Thread class (if we're threading by inheritance) or to the Runnable type class (if we're threading by interfaces) and achieved the same results. The best use of this name is probably for debugging. With an assigned name, the debugger and the toString() method display thread information in terms of a "logical" name instead of a number.

By default, if no name is assigned, the Thread class chooses a unique name. This name is generally "Thread-" followed by a unique number.

The naming support is also available as a constructor of the Thread class:

Thread(String name)

Constructs a thread object with a name that is already assigned. This constructor is used when threading by inheritance.

Thread(Runnable target, String name)

> Constructs a thread object that is associated with the given Runnable object and is created with a name that is already assigned. This constructor is used when threading by interfaces.

Just like the `setName()` method, setting the name via the thread constructor is simple. One constructor is provided for threading by inheritance and another for threading by interfaces. In our TimerThread example, since we are setting the name in the constructor, we could just as easily have used the thread constructor instead of the `setName()` method:

```java
import java.awt.*;

public class TimerThread extends Thread {
    Component comp;                  // Component that needs repainting
    int timediff;                    // Time between repaints of the component
    volatile boolean shouldRun;      // Set to false to stop thread

    public TimerThread(Component comp, int timediff) {
        super("TimerThread(" + timediff + " milliseconds)");
        this.comp = comp;
        this.timediff = timediff;
        shouldRun = true;
    }

    public void run() {
        while (shouldRun) {
            try {
                comp.repaint();
                sleep(timediff);
            } catch (Exception e) {}
        }
    }
}
```

Thread Access

Next, we'll look into several methods that show us information about specific threads.

The Current Thread

First, we'll examine the `currentThread()` method:

static Thread currentThread()

> Gets the Thread object that represents the current thread of execution. The method is static and may be called through the Thread class name.

This is a static method of the Thread class, and it simply returns a Thread object that represents the current thread; the current thread is the thread that called the `currentThread()` method. The object returned is the same Thread object first created for the current thread.

But why is this method important? The Thread object for the current thread may not be saved anywhere, and even if it is, it may not be accessible to the called method. For example, let's look at a class that performs socket I/O and stores the data it reads into an internal buffer. We'll show the full implementation of this class in the next chapter, but for now, we're interested only in its interface:

```
public class AsyncReadSocket extends Thread {
    StringBuffer result;

    public AsyncReadSocket(String host, int port) {
    // Open a socket to the given host.
    }

    public void run() {
    // Read data from a socket into the result string buffer.
    }

    // Get the string already read from the socket so far.
    // Only allows "Reader" threads to execute this method.
    public String getResult() {
        String reader = Thread.currentThread().getName();
        if (reader.startsWith("Reader")) {
            String retval = result.toString();
            result = new StringBuffer();
            return retval;
        } else {
            return "";
        }
    }
}
```

To retrieve the data that has been read by this class, you must call the `getResult()` method, but we've coded the `getResult()` method such that only reader threads are allowed actually to retrieve the stored data. For our example, we are assuming that reader threads are threads whose names start with "Reader." This name could have been assigned by the `setName()` method earlier or when the threads are constructed. To obtain a name, we need simply to call the `getName()` method. However, since we do not have the Thread object reference of the caller, we must call the `currentThread()` method to obtain the reference. In this case, we are using the name of the thread, but we could just as easily have used the thread reference for other purposes. Other uses of the thread reference could be priority control or thread groups; these and other services are described in upcoming chapters.

Note that there is a very subtle thing going on here. The getName() method is a method of the Thread class, and we might have called it directly in our code. That would return the name of the AsyncReadSocket thread itself. Instead, what we're after is the name of the thread that has called the getResult() method, which is probably not the AsyncReadSocket thread. Typically, we'd use the AsyncRead-Socket class like this:

```
public class TestRead extends Thread {
    AsyncReadSocket asr;
    public static void main(String args[]) {
        AsyncReadSocket asr = new AsyncReadSocket("myhost", 6001);
        asr.start();
        new TestRead(asr).start();
    }

    public TestRead(AsyncReadSocket asr) {
        super("ReaderThread");
        this.asr = asr;
    }

    public void run() {
        // Do some other processing, and allow asr to read data.
        System.out.println("Data is " + asr.getResult());
    }
}
```

There are three threads of interest to us in this example: the thread that the virtual machine started for us that is executing the main() method, the asr thread, and the TestRead thread. Since the TestRead thread is executing the getResult() method, it will actually receive the data, as its name begins with "Reader." If another thread in this example were to call the getResult() method, it would receive merely an empty string.

This can be a common source of confusion: methods in subclasses of the thread class may be executed by the thread object itself, or they may—like the get-Result() method in this example—be executed by another thread object. Don't assume that the code in a thread object is only being executed by the specific thread that the object represents.

Enumerating Threads in the Virtual Machine

Also provided with the Thread class are methods that allow you to obtain a list of all the threads in the program:

static int enumerate(Thread threadArray[])
> Gets all the thread objects of the program and stores the result into the thread array. The value returned is the number of thread objects stored into the array. The method is static and may be called through the Thread class name.

static int activeCount()

> Returns the number of threads in the program. The method is static and may be called through the Thread class name.

This list is retrieved with the `enumerate()` method. The developer simply needs to create a Thread array and pass it as a parameter. The `enumerate()` method stores the thread references into the array and returns the number of thread objects stored; this number is the size of the array parameter or the number of threads in the program, whichever is smaller.

In order to size the array for the `enumerate()` method, we need to determine the number of threads in the program. The `activeCount()` method can determine the number of threads and size the thread array accordingly. For example, we could add a support method to our Animate applet that prints all the threads in the applet, as follows:

```
import java.applet.*;
import java.awt.*;

public class Animate extends Applet {
// Instance variables and methods not shown

    public void printThreads() {
        Thread ta[] = new Thread[Thread.activeCount()];

        int n = Thread.enumerate(ta);
        for (int i = 0; i < n; i++) {
            System.out.println("Thread " + i + " is " +
                    ta[i].getName());
        }
    }
}
```

In this example, we are instantiating a Thread array; the size of the array is determined by the `activeCount()` method of the Thread class. Once we have an active count, we call the `enumerate()` method to obtain references to all the thread objects in our applet. In the rest of the method, we simply print the name assigned to each thread by calling the `getName()` method on the thread reference.

Note that we've been careful in this section to say "all the threads in the program" rather than "all the threads in the virtual machine." That's because at the level of the Thread class, the `enumerate()` method shows us only the threads that our program has created, plus (possibly) the main and GUI threads of an application or applet that the virtual machine has created for us. It will not show us other threads of the virtual machine (e.g., the garbage collection thread), and in an applet, it will not show us other threads in other applets. We'll see how to examine all these other threads in Chapter 10.

Trivia: When Is a Thread Active?

When is a thread active? At first glance, this seems to be a simple question. Using the `isAlive()` method, a thread is considered alive during the period between the call to the `start()` method and a short time period after the `stop()` method is called. We might consider a thread active if it is alive.

However, if the definition of an active thread is a thread whose thread reference appears in the active count returned by the `activeCount()` method, we would have a different definition of active. A thread reference first appears in the thread array returned by the `enumerate()` method, and is counted by the `activeCount()` method, when the thread object is first constructed and not when the thread is started.

The thread is removed from the thread array either when the thread is stopped or when the `run()` method has completed. This means that if a thread object is constructed but is not started, the thread object will not be removed from the enumeration list, even if the original reference to the object is lost.

More on Starting, Stopping, and Joining

Consider this revision to the Animate example:

```
import java.applet.Applet;

public class Animate extends Applet {
    TimerThread t;
    public void start() {
        if (t == null)
            t = new TimerThread(this, 500);
        t.start();
    }

    public void stop() {
        t.shouldRun = false;
        try {
            t.join();
        } catch (InterruptedException e) {}
        // t = null;
    }
}
```

In our last version of the Animate applet (see "The Life Cycle of a Thread," earlier in this chapter), the `start()` method of the applet created a new TimerThread object and started it. But what if we had only created the TimerThread once? In

the example just shown, we once again create a new TimerThread in the `start()`
method of the applet; however, since we know the thread will be stopped in the
`stop()` method, we try to restart the stopped thread in the `start()` method. In
other words, we create the TimerThread only once and use this one thread object
to start and stop the animation. By starting and stopping a single TimerThread, we
do not need to create a new instance of TimerThread every time the applet is
started, and the garbage collector will not need to clean up the TimerThread
instance that's left when the applet is stopped and the TimerThread dereferenced.

But will this work? Unfortunately, the answer is no. It turns out that when a thread
is stopped, the state of the thread object is set so that it is not restartable. In our
case, when we try to restart the thread by calling the TimerThread's `start()`
method, nothing happens. The `start()` method won't return an exception
condition, but the `run()` method also won't be called. The `isAlive()` method
also won't return `true`. In other words, never restart a thread. An instance of a
thread object should be used once and only once.

More Details for Restarting a Thread

What happens when you try to restart a thread? The answer is that it actually
depends on when you restart it. When the `stop()` method is called on a
thread (or the thread exits its `run()` method), it actually takes time for the
thread to stop. Hence, what happens when the `start()` method is called depends on a *race condition.* (Race conditions are discussed more fully in
Chapter 3.)

If the `start()` method is called before the stopping thread actually stops, an
error condition exists, and an exception will be thrown. The same is true if you
call `start()` on a thread object that has not been stopped.

If the `start()` method is called after the stopping thread has actually stopped,
nothing happens: the thread object is in a state where it cannot be restarted.

Can an already stopped thread be stopped? At first glance, this may seem an odd question. But the answer is yes, and the reason is that it avoids a race condition that
would occur otherwise. We know there are two ways a thread can be stopped, so
you could stop a thread that has already exited because its `run()` method terminated normally. If the Thread class did not allow the `stop()` method to be called
on a stopped thread, this would require us to check if the thread was still running
before we stopped it, and we'd have to avoid a race condition in which the `run()`
method could terminate in between the time when we checked if the thread was
alive and when we called the `stop()` method. This would be a big burden on the

Java developer, so, instead, the stop() method can be called on a thread that has already stopped.

What happens when we call the join() method for a thread that was stopped a long time ago? In the examples so far, we assumed the usage of the join() method was to wait for a thread to complete or to stop. But this assumption is not necessary; if the thread is already stopped, it will return immediately. This may seem obvious, but it should be noted that a race condition would have resulted if the join() method had required that the thread be alive when the method was first called.

The Stopping Thread and the Garbage Collector

The thread object, like any other object, is a candidate for garbage collection when it gets dereferenced. As developers, we should just note that the garbage collector behaves correctly with the threading system and not worry about the exact details. However, for those of us who are detail-oriented, here is how the garbage collector behaves with the threading system.

In all the examples so far, the garbage collector cannot collect the thread object even when the thread has completed or stopped. This is because we still have a reference to the TimerThread object after we signal it to stop. To be complete, we should manually dereference the thread object. However, this is necessary only to free the memory that stores the thread object. The threading system automatically releases any thread-specific resources (including those tied to the operating system) after the thread has completed or stopped whether or not we dereference the object.

Dereferencing a thread object for a running thread is also not a problem. The threading system keeps references to all threads that are running in the system. This is needed in order to support the currentThread() and enumerate() methods of the Thread class. The garbage collector will not be able to collect the thread object until the threading system also dereferences the object, which won't happen until the thread is no longer alive.

What would be the best way to join() with more than one thread? Let's look at the following code:

```
import java.applet.Applet;

public class MyJoinApplet extends Applet {
    Thread t[] = new Thread[30];
    public void start() {
        for (int i=0; i<30; i++) {
            t[i] = new CalcThread(i);
```

```
            t[i].start();
        }
    }

    public void stop() {
        for (int i=0; i<30; i++) {
            try {
                t[i].join();
            } catch (InterruptedException e) {}
        }
    }
}
```

In this example, we start 30 CalcThread objects. We have not actually defined the CalcThread class, but for this example, we assume it is a class that is used to calculate part of a large mathematical algorithm. In the applet's stop() method, we execute a loop waiting for all the started threads to be finished. Is this the best way to wait for more than one thread? Since it is possible to join() with an already stopped thread, it is perfectly okay to join() with a group of threads in a loop, even if the threads finish in an order different than the order in which they were started. No matter how we might have coded the join() loop, the time to complete the join() will be the time it takes for the last thread to finish.

Of course, there may be cases where a specific joining mechanism is desired, but this depends on details other than the threading system. There is no performance penalty to pay for joining in an order that is not the order of completion.

Summary

Here's a list of the methods of the Thread class that we introduced in this chapter:

Thread()
   Constructs a thread object using default values for all options.

Thread(Runnable target)
   Constructs a new thread object associated with the given Runnable object.

Thread(String name)
   Constructs a thread object with a name that is already assigned. This constructor is used when threading by inheritance.

Thread(Runnable target, String name)
   Constructs a thread object that is associated with the given Runnable object and is created with a name that is already assigned. This constructor is used when threading by interfaces.

void run()
   The method that the newly created thread will execute. Developers should override this method with the code they want the new thread to run; we'll

show the default implementation of the run() method a little further on, but it is essentially an empty method.

void start()

Creates a new thread and executes the run() method defined in this thread class.

void stop() (deprecated in Java 2)

Terminates an already running thread.

static void sleep (long milliseconds)

Puts the currently executing thread to sleep for the specified number of milliseconds. This method is static and may be accessed through the Thread class name.

static void sleep (long milliseconds, int nanoseconds)

Puts the currently executing thread to sleep for the specified number of milliseconds and nanoseconds. This method is static and may be accessed through the Thread class name.

boolean isAlive()

Determines if a thread is considered alive. By definition, a thread is considered alive from sometime before a thread is actually started to sometime after a thread is actually stopped.

void join()

Waits for the completion of the specified thread. By definition, join() returns as soon as the thread is considered "not alive." This includes the case in which the join() method is called on a thread that has not been started.

void join(long timeout)

Waits for the completion of the specified thread, but no longer than the timeout specified in milliseconds. This timeout value is subject to rounding based on the capabilities of the underlying platform.

void join(long timeout, int nanos)

Waits for the completion of the specified thread, but no longer than a timeout specified in milliseconds and nanoseconds. This timeout value is subject to rounding based on the capabilities of the underlying platform.

void setName(String name)

Assigns a name to the Thread instance.

String getName()

Gets the name of the Thread instance.

static Thread currentThread()

Gets the Thread object that represents the current thread of execution. The method is static and may be called through the Thread class name.

static int enumerate(Thread threadArray[])

> Gets all the thread objects of the program and stores the result into the thread array. The value returned is the number of thread objects stored into the array. The method is static and may be called through the Thread class name.

static int activeCount()

> Returns the number of threads in the program. The method is static and may be called through the Thread class name.

In this chapter, we have had our first taste of creating, starting, and stopping threads. This is achieved through the methods of the Thread class, which also contains methods that allow us to examine the status of threads, the names of threads, and the threads that our program is using. This provides us with the basics for writing simple, independent threads.

However, there are other issues that must be dealt with when it comes to threads: most notably, that communication between the individual threads must avoid the race conditions we outlined. This issue of communication, or synchronization, will be discussed in the next chapter.

3

Synchronization Techniques

In the previous chapter, we covered a lot of ground: we examined how to create and start threads, how to arrange for them to terminate, how to name them, how to monitor their life cycles, and so on. In the examples of that chapter, however, the threads that we examined were more or less independent: they did not need to share any data between them.

In this chapter, we look at the issue of sharing data between threads. Sharing data between threads is often hampered due to what is known as a *race condition* between the threads attempting to access the same data more or less simultaneously. In this chapter, we'll look at the concept of a race condition as well as examining a mechanism that solves race conditions. We will see how this mechanism can be used not only to coordinate access to data, but also for many problems in which synchronization is needed between threads. Before we start, let's introduce a few concepts.

A Banking Example

As an application designer for a major bank, we are assigned to the development team for the automated teller machine (ATM). As our first assignment, we are given the task of designing and implementing the routine that allows a user to withdraw cash from the ATM. A first and simple attempt at an algorithm may be as follows (see Figure 3-1 for the flow chart):

1. Check to make sure that the user has enough cash in the bank account to allow the withdrawal to occur. If the user does not, then go to step 4.

2. Subtract the amount withdrawn from the user's account.

3. Dispense the cash from the teller machine to the user.

4. Print a receipt for the user.

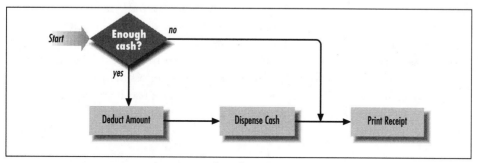

Figure 3-1. Algorithm flow chart for ATM withdrawal

Given this very simple algorithm, an implementation may be as follows:

```
public class AutomatedTellerMachine extends Teller {
    public void withdraw(float amount) {
        Account a = getAccount();
        if (a.deduct(amount))
            dispense(amount);
        printReceipt();
    }
}

public class Account {
    private float total;
    public boolean deduct(float t) {
        if (t <= total) {
            total -= t;
            return true;
        }
        return false;
    }
}
```

Of course, we are assuming that the Teller class and the getAccount(), dispense(), and printReceipt() methods have already been implemented. For our purposes, we are simply examining this algorithm at a high level, so these methods will not be implemented here.

During our testing, we run a few simple and short tests of the routine. These tests involve withdrawing some cash. In certain cases, we withdraw a small amount. In other cases, we withdraw a large amount. We withdraw with enough cash in the account to cover the transaction, and we withdraw without enough cash in the account to cover the transaction. In each case, the code works as desired. Being proud of our routine, we send it to a local branch for beta testing.

As it turns out, it is possible for two people to have access to the same account (e.g., a joint account). One day, a husband and wife both decide to empty the same account, and purely by chance, they empty the account at the same time. We now have a race condition: if the two users withdraw from the bank at the same time, causing the methods to be called at the same time, it is possible for the two ATMs to confirm that the account has enough cash and dispense it to both parties. In effect, the two users are causing two threads to access the account database at the same time.

Definition: Atomic

The term *atomic* is related to the atom, once considered the smallest possible unit of matter, unable to be broken into separate parts. When a routine is considered atomic, it cannot be interrupted during its execution. This can either be accomplished in hardware or simulated in software. In general, atomic instructions are provided in hardware that is used to implement atomic routines in software.

In our case, we define an atomic routine as one that can't be found in an intermediate state. In our banking example, if the acts of "checking on the account" and "changing the account status" were atomic, it would not be possible for another thread to check on the same account until the first thread had finished changing the account status.

There is a race condition because the action of checking the account and changing the account status is not *atomic*. Here we have the husband thread and the wife thread competing for the account:

1. The husband thread begins to execute the deduct() method.

2. The husband thread confirms that the amount to deduct is less than or equal to the total in the account.

3. The wife thread begins to execute the deduct() method.

4. The wife thread confirms that the amount to deduct is less than or equal to the total in the account.

5. The wife thread performs the subtraction statement to deduct the amount, returns `true`, and the ATM dispenses her cash.

6. The husband thread performs the subtraction statement to deduct the amount, returns `true`, and the ATM dispenses his cash.

The Java specification provides certain mechanisms that deal specifically with this problem. The Java language provides the `synchronized` keyword; in comparison with other threading systems, this keyword allows the programmer access to a resource that is very similar to a mutex lock. For our purposes, it simply prevents two or more threads from calling our `deduct()` method at the same time:

```java
public class Account {
    private float total;
    public synchronized boolean deduct(float t) {
        if (t <= total) {
            total -= t;
            return true;
        }
        return false;
    }
}
```

By declaring the method as synchronized, if two users decide to withdraw cash from the ATM at the same time, the first user executes the `deduct()` method while the second user waits until the first user completes the `deduct()` method. Since only one user may execute the `deduct()` method at a time, the race condition is eliminated.

Definition: Mutex Lock

A mutex lock is also known as a *mutually exclusive lock*. This type of lock is provided by many threading systems as a means of synchronization. Basically, it is only possible for one thread to grab a mutex at a time: if two threads try to grab a mutex, only one succeeds. The other thread has to wait until the first thread releases the lock; it can then grab the lock and continue operation.

With Java, there is a lock created in every object in the system. When a method is declared synchronized, the executing thread must grab the lock assigned to the object before it can continue. Upon completion of the method, the mechanism automatically releases the lock.

Under the covers, the concept of synchronization is simple: when a method is declared as synchronized, it must have a *token*, which we call a *lock*. Once the method has acquired this lock (we may also say the lock has been *checked out* or *grabbed*), it executes the method and releases (we may also say *returns*) the lock once the method is finished. No matter how the method returns—including via an exception—the lock is released. There is only one lock per object, so if two separate threads try to call synchronized methods of the same object, only one can execute the method immediately; the other thread has to wait until the first thread releases the lock before it can execute the method.

Reading Data Asynchronously

Let's look at a complete example. One of the primary uses for threads within a Java program is to read data asynchronously. In this section, we'll develop a class to read a network socket asynchronously.

Why is threading important for I/O? Whether you are reading from or writing to a file or network socket, a common problem exists, namely, that the action of reading or writing depends on other resources. These resources may be other programs; they may be hardware, like the disk or the network; they may be the operating system or browser. These resources may become temporarily unavailable for a variety of reasons: reading from a network socket may involve waiting until the data is available, writing large amounts of data to a file may take a long period of time to complete if the disk is busy with other requests, and so on. Unfortunately, the mechanism to check whether these resources are available does not exist in the Java API. This is particularly a problem for network sockets, where data is likely to take a long time to be transmitted over the network; it is possible for a read from a network socket to wait forever.

Why Asynchronous I/O?

The driving force behind asynchronous I/O is to allow the program to continue to do something useful while it is waiting for data to arrive. If I/O is not asynchronous and not running in a thread separate from the applet thread, we run into the problems we discussed in the previous chapter: mouse and keyboard events will be delayed, and the program will appear to be unresponsive to the user while the I/O completes.

The InputStream class does contain the `available()` method. However, not all input streams support that method, and on a slow network, writing data to a socket is also likely to take a long time. In general, checking for data via the `available()` method is much less efficient (and much harder to program) than creating a new thread to read the data.

The solution to this problem is to use another thread. Say that we use this new thread in an applet: since this new thread is independent of the applet thread, it can block without hanging the applet. Of course, this causes a new problem: when this thread finally is able to read the data, this data must be returned to the applet thread. Let's take a look at a possible implementation of a generic socket reader class that will read the socket from another thread:

```java
import java.io.*;
import java.net.*;

public class AsyncReadSocket extends Thread {
    private Socket s;
    private StringBuffer result;

    public AsyncReadSocket(Socket s) {
        this.s = s;
        result = new StringBuffer();
    }

    public void run() {
        DataInputStream is = null;
        try {
            is = new DataInputStream(s.getInputStream());
        } catch (Exception e) {}
        while (true) {
            try {
                char c = is.readChar();
                appendResult(c);
            } catch (Exception e) {}
        }
    }

    // Get the string already read from the socket so far.
    // This method is used by the Applet thread to obtain the data
    // in a synchronous manner.
    public synchronized String getResult() {
        String retval = result.toString();
        result = new StringBuffer();
        return retval;
    }

    // Put new data into the buffer to be returned
    // by the getResult method.
    public synchronized void appendResult(char c) {
        result.append(c);
    }
}
```

Here we have a Thread class, AsyncReadSocket, whose `run()` method reads characters from a socket. Whenever it gets any characters, it adds them to the StringBuffer `result`. If this thread hangs while reading the socket, it has no effect on any other threads in the program. An applet can call the `getResult()` method to get any data that has been received by this new thread; if no data is available, the `getResult()` method returns an empty string. And if the applet thread is off doing some other tasks, this socket thread simply accumulates the characters for the applet thread. In other words, the socket thread stores the data it receives at any time, while the applet thread can call the `getResult()` method at any time without the worry of blocking or losing data. An actual run of the two threads may look like the diagram in Figure 3-2.

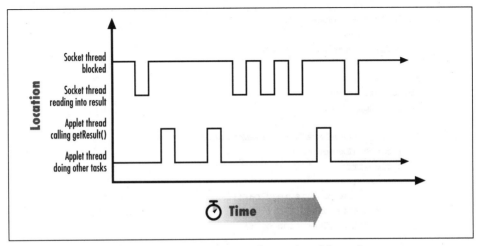

Figure 3-2. Possible time/location graph during a sample execution of the applet

One of the attractions of threaded programming is that it is simple to write many small, independent tasks, and that's just what we've done here. And since these small tasks are contained in one program, communication between the tasks (the threads) is as simple as communication between two methods in a single program. We just need a common reference somewhere that both threads can access. That "somewhere," in this case, is the `result` instance variable.

Note that we could not have written this class correctly without using the `synchronized` keyword to protect the socket thread and the applet thread from accessing the `result` buffer at the same time. Otherwise, we would have had a race condition. Specifically, if the `getResult()` and `appendResult()` methods were not synchronized, we could see this behavior:

1. The applet thread enters the `getResult()` method.

2. The applet thread assigns `retval` to a new string created from the `result` StringBuffer.

3. The socket thread returns from the readChar() method.

4. The socket thread calls the appendResult() method to append the character to the result StringBuffer.

5. The applet thread assigns result to a new (empty) StringBuffer.

The data that was appended to the StringBuffer in step 4 is now lost: it wasn't retrieved by the applet thread at step 2, and the applet thread discards the old StringBuffer in step 5. Note that there is another race condition here: if two separate threads call the getResult() method at the same time, they could both get copies of the same data from the StringBuffer, and that data would be processed twice.

When all actions on the result variable are atomic, our race condition problem is solved. We need only ensure that the result variable is accessed only in methods that are synchronized.

When Is a Race Condition a Problem?

A *race condition* occurs when the order of execution of two or more threads may affect some variable or outcome in the program. It may turn out that all the different possible thread orderings have the same final effect on the application: the effect caused by the race condition may be insignificant, and may not even be relevant. For example, a character lost in the AsyncReadSocket may not affect the final outcome of the program. Alternately, the timing of the threading system may be such that the race condition never manifests itself, despite the fact that it exists in the code.

A race condition is a problem that is waiting to happen. Simple changes in the algorithm can cause race conditions to manifest themselves in problematic ways. And, since different virtual machines will have different orderings of thread execution, the developer should never let a race condition exist even if it is currently not causing a problem on the development system.

At this point, we may have introduced more questions than answers. So before we continue, let's try to answer some of these questions.

How does synchronizing two different methods prevent the two threads calling those methods from stepping on each other? As stated earlier, synchronizing a method has the effect of serializing access to the method. This means that it is not possible to execute the same method in another thread while the method is already running. However, the implementation of this mechanism is done by a lock that is assigned to the object itself. The reason another thread cannot execute the same method at the same time is that the method requires the lock that is already held by the first thread. If two different synchronized methods of the same object are called, they also behave in the same fashion because they both require the lock of the same object, and it is not possible for both methods to grab the lock at the same time. In other words, even if two or more methods are involved, they will never be run in parallel in separate threads. This is illustrated in Figure 3-3: when thread 1 and thread 2 attempt to acquire the same lock (L1), thread 2 must wait until thread 1 releases the lock before it can continue to execute.

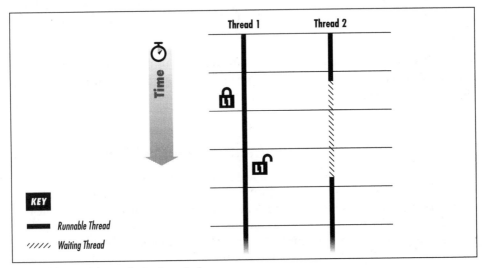

Figure 3-3. Acquiring and releasing a lock

The point to remember here is that the lock is based on a specific object and not on any particular method. Assume that we have two AsyncReadSocket objects called a and b that have been created in separate threads. One thread executes the a.getResult() method while the other thread executes the b.getResult() method. These two methods can execute in parallel because the call to a.get-Result() grabs the object lock associated with the instance variable a, and the call to b.getResult() grabs the object lock associated with the instance variable b. Since the two objects are different objects, two different locks are grabbed by the two threads: neither thread has to wait for the other.

Why do we need the appendResult() method? Couldn't we simply put that code into the run() method and synchronize the run() method? We could do that, but the result would be disastrous. Every lock has an associated scope; that is, the amount of code for which the lock is valid. Synchronizing the run() method creates a scope that is too large and prevents other methods from being run at all.

Definition: Scope of a Lock

The *scope of a lock* is defined as the period of time between when the lock is grabbed and released. In our examples so far, we have used only synchronized methods; this means that the scope of these locks is the period of time it takes to execute these methods. This is referred to as *method scope.*

Later in this chapter, we'll examine locks that apply to any block of code inside a method or that can be explicitly grabbed and released; these locks have a different scope. We'll examine this concept of scope as locks of various types are introduced.

The scope of the `run()` method is infinite, since the `run()` method executes an infinite loop. If both the `run()` method and `getResult()` method are synchronized, they cannot run in parallel in separate threads. Since the `run()` method has the task of opening the network socket and reading all the data from the socket until the connection is closed, it would need the object lock until the connection is closed. This means that while the connection is open, it would not be possible to execute the `getResult()` method. This is not the desired effect for a class that is supposed to read the data asynchronously.

How does a synchronized method behave in conjunction with a nonsynchronized method? Simply put, a synchronized method tries to grab the object lock, and a nonsynchronized method doesn't. This means it is possible for many nonsynchronized methods to run in parallel with a synchronized method. Only one synchronized method runs at a time.

Synchronizing a method just means the lock is grabbed when that method executes. It is the developer's responsibility to ensure that the correct methods are synchronized. Forgetting to synchronize a method can cause a race condition: if we had synchronized only the `getResult()` method of the AsyncReadSocket class and had forgotten to synchronize the `appendResult()` method, we would not have solved the race condition, since any thread could call the `appendResult()` method while the `getResult()` method was executing.

A Class to Perform Synchronization

Why do we need a new keyword to solve a race condition? Could we reengineer our algorithms so that race conditions do not exist? Let's see if we can reengineer the AsyncReadSocket class not to have a race condition by using trial and error (obviously not the best programming technique, but one that is useful for our purposes). We'll conclude that it is impossible to solve a race condition without direct support from the virtual machine, because everything that we might try requires two operations: testing and setting variable. Without some process in the virtual machine to ensure that nothing happens to the variable after it is tested and before it is set, a race condition can occur. But the investigation into a possible way to avoid the race condition will provide us with an important tool for our later use—the BusyFlag class.

At first glance, the easiest way to make sure that the two threads do not try to change the `result` variable, or any buffer at the same time, is to use the concept of a busy flag: if a thread needs to access the `result` variable, it must set the flag to busy. If the flag is already busy, the thread must wait until the flag is free, at which point it must set the flag to busy. The thread is then free to access the buffer without fear of it being accessed by the other thread. Once the task is completed, the thread must set the flag to not busy.

Why Have the BusyFlag Class at All?

Fixing race conditions using the BusyFlag class seems more like an academic exercise at this moment: why would you then want to use the BusyFlag class in place of the synchronization mechanism?

For all the cases encountered so far, we wouldn't. In other cases, one of the answers lies in the scope of the lock: the synchronization mechanism does not allow us to lock code at certain scopes. We will encounter cases where the scope of the lock cannot be solved by the synchronized mechanism. In addition, the concepts of the BusyFlag class will be useful to implement other mechanisms that we'll be exploring throughout the rest of this book.

Here's a possible implementation of the busy flag:

```
public class BusyFlag {
    protected Thread busyflag = null;

    public void getBusyFlag () {
        while (busyflag != Thread.currentThread()) {
            if (busyflag == null)
                busyflag = Thread.currentThread();
            try {
                Thread.sleep(100);
            } catch (Exception e) {}
        }
    }

    public void freeBusyFlag () {
```

```
        if (busyflag == Thread.currentThread()) {
            busyflag = null;
        }
    }
}
```

This BusyFlag class contains two methods. The method getBusyFlag() sits in a loop until it is able to set the busyflag to the current thread. As long as the busyflag is set to another thread, our thread waits for 100 milliseconds. As soon as the flag is set to null, our thread sets it to the current thread. The other method, freeBusyFlag(), frees the flag by setting it back to null. This implementation seems to solve the problem simply and elegantly. But it does not.

Why do we need to sleep for 100 milliseconds? Because there seems to be no way to detect changes in the flag without a polling loop. However, a polling loop that does not sleep() simply wastes CPU cycles that can be used by other threads. At the other extreme, it takes a minimum of 100 milliseconds to set the busy flag even if no thread is holding the flag in the first place. A possible enhancement that addresses this problem may be as simple as making the sleep time a variable, but no matter what we configure the time to be, we will be balancing whether we want to be able to set the flag in a decent amount of time versus the CPU cycles wasted in a polling loop.

Why do we sleep for 100 milliseconds even if the flag is not set? This is actually intentional. There is a race condition between the check to see if the flag is null and setting the flag. If two threads find that the flag is free, they can each set the flag and exit the loop. By calling the sleep() method, we allow the two threads to set busyflag before checking it again in the while loop. This way, only the second thread that sets the flag can exit the loop, and hence exit the getBusyFlag() method.

Of course, this is still a problem. As unlikely as it seems, it is still possible that this order of execution might occur:

1. Thread A detects that the busyflag is free.

2. Thread B detects that the busyflag is free.

3. Thread B sets the busyflag.

4. Thread B sleeps for 100 milliseconds.

5. Thread B wakes up, confirms that it has the busyflag, and exits the loop.

6. Thread A sets the busyflag, sleeps, wakes up, confirms it has the busyflag, and exits the loop.

This is an *extremely* unlikely occurrence, but possible nonetheless; hence, this code is not one that most programmers are willing to accept.

We could use the BusyFlag class to replace the synchronized method in our Account class like this:

```
public class Account {
    private float total;
    private flag = new BusyFlag();

    public boolean deduct(float t) {
        boolean succeed = false;
        flag.getBusyFlag();
        if (t <= total) {
            total -= t;
            succeed = true;
        }
        flag.freeBusyFlag();
        return succeed;
    }
}
```

The vast majority of the time, this BusyFlag class works. However, even if you ran a huge beta test across 100 bank ATMs for a period of one year without a single problem, would you be willing to bet your career on a AutomatedTeller class that uses our BusyFlag class?

What if multiple threads set the busyflag at the same moment? Is the act of setting the busy-flag variable atomic? The Java specification guarantees that setting any variable other than a double or a long is atomic, so in this example, it does not matter if multiple threads attempt to set the flag at the same moment. In the case where two threads are setting a long or a double, however, it is possible that the variable will be set incorrectly: part of the variable will contain the bits set by the first thread and the rest of the variable will contain the bits set by the second thread. However, atomicity does not insure thread communication; see the discussion of volatile in Appendix A.

Can we fix our BusyFlag class with the synchronization primitives? The problems that we encountered in the BusyFlag class are the same problems the BusyFlag class was meant to solve in the first place. This means that we can fix the problems in the BusyFlag class by using the synchronization primitives; we could use the BusyFlag class to solve other race conditions without worrying that it might break under certain conditions. The implementation (still not optimal) that solves this problem follows:

```
public class BusyFlag {
    protected Thread busyflag = null;
    public void getBusyFlag() {
        while (tryGetBusyFlag() == false) {
            try {
                Thread.sleep(100);
            } catch (Exception e) {}
        }
    }
}
```

```
public synchronized boolean tryGetBusyFlag() {
    if (busyflag == null) {
        busyflag = Thread.currentThread();
        return true;
    }
    return false;
}

public synchronized void freeBusyFlag() {
    if (busyflag == Thread.currentThread()) {
        busyflag = null;
    }
}
}
```

In this implementation of the BusyFlag class, we introduced a new method called tryGetBusyFlag(). It is essentially the same as the getBusyFlag() method except that it does not wait until the flag is free. If the flag is free, it sets the flag and returns true. Otherwise it returns false. You'll notice that this method is declared as synchronized. This means the system makes sure the thread that makes the call to the tryGetBusyFlag() method has grabbed the object lock during the execution of the method.

The freeBusyFlag() method is also declared as synchronized: the thread that made the method call must also grab the object lock before it can continue. Since there is only one object lock for each instance of the class, the lock that freeBusyFlag() will try to grab is the same lock tryGetBusyFlag() will grab. This means that there will be no race condition between threads trying to get the busyflag and the thread that frees the busyflag.

The Synchronized Block

Notice that the original getBusyFlag() method is not declared as synchronized. This is because it's not necessary: getBusyFlag() does not try to access the busyflag variable. Instead, it calls the tryGetBusyFlag() method, which accesses the busyflag and is, of course, synchronized. Let's take another look at the getBusyFlag() method, one that does not call the tryGetBusyFlag() method. Instead, this version gets the busyflag directly:

```
public synchronized void getBusyFlag() {
    while (true) {
        if (busyflag == null) {
            busyflag = Thread.currentThread();
            break;
        }
        try {
            Thread.sleep(100);
```

```
        } catch (Exception e) {}
    }
}
```

Let's assume that we do not want the inefficiency of an extra method call to the tryGetBusyFlag() method. In our new version of the getBusyFlag() method, we now access the busyflag directly. The getBusyFlag() method simply loops waiting for the flag to be freed, sets the flag, and returns. Since we are now accessing the busyflag directly, we must make the method synchronized or we will have a race condition.

Unfortunately, there is a problem when we declare this method to be synchronized. While declaring the method synchronized prevents other getBusyFlag() and tryGetBusyFlag() methods from being run at the same time (which prevents a race condition), it also prevents the freeBusyFlag() method from running. This means that if the flag is busy when getBusyFlag() is called, getBusyFlag() waits until the flag is freed. Unfortunately, since the freeBusyFlag() method will not run until the getBusyFlag() method frees the object lock, the busyflag will not be freed. This Catch-22 situation is termed *deadlock*. The deadlock in this case is a problem between a lock and a busyflag. More commonly, deadlock occurs between two or more locks, but the idea is the same.

An Example of Deadlock

We'll examine the concept of the deadlock in detail later in this chapter and again in Chapter 8. But before we continue, let's look at an example.

Let's assume that we are waiting in line at a bank. I am at the front of the line, waiting to withdraw some cash. Let's assume that the bank is out of cash, and I am actually willing to wait for some cash to be deposited. Let's also suppose that the bank has only one teller, and has a policy of not handling another transaction until the current transaction is finished. Since I am still waiting to receive my money, my transaction is not finished.

Suppose that you are behind me with a million dollars to deposit. Obviously, you cannot deposit the money until I am finished, and I will not be finished until you deposit the money. This is, of course, a very contrived situation, and simple common sense can resolve it. However, this is exactly what is happening in a less contrived way in our BusyFlag class example. Furthermore, because this is a subtle problem, we might not have noticed it during testing, much the same as the bank, with an ample amount of cash, wouldn't have noticed the potential deadlock when it tested its policy.

We have a problem in this implementation of getBusyFlag() because the scope in which we used the object lock was too large. All we need to do is hold the lock for the period during which we need to change the data (i.e., check and get the busyflag); it doesn't need to be held during the entire method. Fortunately, Java also provides us the ability to synchronize a block of code instead of synchronizing the entire method. Using this block synchronization mechanism on our getBusyFlag() method, we now obtain the following code:

```
public void getBusyFlag () {
    while (true) {
        synchronized (this) {
            if (busyflag == null) {
                busyflag = Thread.currentThread();
                break;
            }
        }
        try {
            Thread.sleep(100);
        } catch (Exception e) {}
    }
}
```

In this new implementation of the getBusyFlag() method, we only synchronized the period between checking the flag and setting it if it is not busy. This usage is very similar to the synchronized method usage, except that the scope during which the lock is held is much smaller.

Interestingly, this usage not only gives us more precise control over when the object lock is held, but it also allows us to select which object's lock to grab. In this case, since we want to grab the same object lock as in the tryGetBusyFlag() and freeBusyFlag() methods, we chose this as the object on which to obtain the lock. For synchronized methods, the lock that is obtained is the object lock of the class in which the method exists; in other words, the this object.

Nested Locks

Let's examine our BusyFlag class yet again. Suppose we add another method that finds out which thread owns the lock. This getBusyFlagOwner() method simply returns the busyflag, which just so happens to be the thread object that owns the lock. An implementation is as follows:

```
public synchronized Thread getBusyFlagOwner() {
    return busyflag;
}
```

Furthermore, let's make a modification to the freeBusyFlag() method to use this new getBusyFlagOwner() method:

```
public synchronized void freeBusyFlag () {
    if (getBusyFlagOwner() == Thread.currentThread()) {
```

Object or Reference?

With the introduction of the synchronized block, we can also choose the object to lock along with synchronizing at a block scope. Care must now be taken to distinguish between a physical object and an instance variable that refers to an object.

In our BusyFlag class, we could have used the synchronized block mechanism in the getBusyFlag(), tryGetBusyFlag(), and freeBusyFlag() methods. This allows us to pick any object as the lock object.

The busyflag variable would not be a good choice. This variable may change values during execution of the three methods, including taking the value of null. Locking on null is an exception condition, and locking on different objects defeats the purpose of synchronizing in the first place.

This might be obvious, but since picking inappropriate locks is a common mistake, let us reiterate it:

> Synchronization is based on actual objects, not references to objects. Multiple variables can refer to the same object, and a variable can change its reference to a different object. Hence, when picking an object to use as a lock, we must think in terms of physical objects and not references to objects.

As a rule of thumb, don't choose to synchronize a block on an instance variable that changes value during the scope of the lock.

```
        busyflag = null;
    }
}
```

In this version of the freeBusyFlag() method, we make a call to the getBusyFlagOwner() method to see if the current thread is the owner before freeing the busyflag. What is interesting here is that both the freeBusyFlag() and the getBusyFlagOwner() methods are synchronized. So what happens? Does the thread hang at the getBusyFlagOwner() method while waiting for the freeBusyFlag() method to free the object lock? If not, and the getBusyFlagOwner() method is allowed to run, what happens when that method completes? Does it free the object lock even though the freeBusyFlag() method still needs it? The answer to all these questions is that it all works the way you want it to.

A synchronized area (by which we mean a synchronized block or method) does not blindly grab the lock when it enters the code section and free the lock when it exits. If the current thread already owns the object lock, there is no reason to wait

---

Synchronized Method Versus Synchronized Block

It is actually possible to use only the synchronized block mechanism, even when we need to synchronize the whole method. For clarity in this book, we will synchronize the whole method with the *synchronized method* mechanism, and use the *synchronized block* mechanism otherwise. We leave it up to the personal preference of the programmer to decide when to synchronize on a block of code and when to synchronize the whole method.

Picking the whole method is the simplest technique, but as we have seen, it is possible to have deadlock because the scope is too large. It may also be inefficient to hold a lock for the section of code where it is actually not needed.

Using the synchronized block mechanism may also be a problem if too many locks are involved. As we shall see, it is possible to have a deadlock condition if we require too many locks to be grabbed. There is also an overhead in grabbing and releasing the lock, so it may be inefficient to free a lock just to grab it again a few lines of code later.

Theorists could probably insert a whole chapter on this issue. Our concern is mainly for the clarity of the code, and we decide which mechanism to use on a case-by-case basis. Any other reasons for choosing between the two mechanisms are beyond the scope of this book.

---

for the lock to be freed or even to grab the lock. Instead the code in the synchronized area merely executes. Furthermore, the system is smart enough not to free the lock if it did not initially grab it upon entering the synchronized area. This means that the `freeBusyFlag()` method can call the `getBusyFlagOwner()` method without any problems.

Unfortunately, our version of the locking mechanism, the BusyFlag class, is not so smart. It hangs waiting for the lock that it is currently holding to be freed. To solve this problem, we must reimplement the BusyFlag class with a counter. The object now checks to see if it already owns the lock and increases the count by one if it does. In the corresponding `freeBusyFlag()` method, it only frees the `busyflag` if the count is zero. This way a thread within the scope of a BusyFlag lock directly or indirectly (through method calls) enters other areas that are locked with the same BusyFlag instance.

Here's an implementation (still suboptimal) of the BusyFlag class with this modification:

```
public class BusyFlag {
    protected Thread busyflag = null;
    protected int busycount = 0;
```

```java
    public void getBusyFlag() {
        while (tryGetBusyFlag() == false) {
            try {
                Thread.sleep(100);
            } catch (Exception e) {}
        }
    }

    public synchronized boolean tryGetBusyFlag() {
        if (busyflag == null) {
            busyflag = Thread.currentThread();
            busycount = 1;
            return true;
        }
        if (busyflag == Thread.currentThread()) {
            busycount++;
            return true;
        }
        return false;
    }

    public synchronized void freeBusyFlag () {
        if (getBusyFlagOwner() == Thread.currentThread()) {
            busycount--;
            if (busycount == 0)
                busyflag = null;
        }
    }

    public synchronized Thread getBusyFlagOwner() {
        return busyflag;
    }
}
```

With this new implementation of the BusyFlag class, we can now lock any section
of code without worrying that we may already own the lock. We can also free the
lock without worrying. Both the synchronized mechanism and our BusyFlag class
can be used as nested locks. (The BusyFlag class is now beginning to resemble
another synchronization primitive known as a *semaphore.*)

Deadlock

While it is not too difficult to check if a thread already owns a lock before grabbing it, is it possible to prevent deadlock of any kind? Before we try to answer this
question, let's look further into just what deadlock is. Simplistically, deadlock is
when two or more threads are waiting for two or more locks to be freed and the
circumstances in the program are such that the locks will never be freed. We saw

this occur earlier, when we made the getBusyFlag() method synchronized. The fact that the freeBusyFlag() method was also synchronized made it impossible for the busyflag to be freed until the getBusyFlag() method returned. Since the getBusyFlag() method was waiting for the busyflag to be freed, it would wait forever.

That deadlock was caused by an object lock grabbed by the Java synchronization primitive and our own implementation of a lock mechanism, the BusyFlag class. Can this deadlock situation also be caused only with Java's synchronization primitives? The answer to this question is yes; furthermore, it may be difficult to predict deadlock or to detect deadlock when it occurs. Code that runs correctly every time during testing may contain potential deadlocks that occur only under certain conditions or on certain implementations of the Java virtual machine. To better illustrate this problem, let's examine some possible methods that may exist in any database system:

```
public void removeUseless(Folder file) {
    synchronized (file) {
        if (file.isUseless()) {
            Cabinet directory = file.getCabinet();
            synchronized (directory) {
                directory.remove(file);
            }
        }
    }
}
```

Suppose, in some database class, we have a method called removeUseless(). This method is called during the period when the program needs to clean up the database system. It is passed a folder object; this object represents some folder we have in our database system. There is some indication of uselessness that is calculated by the isUseless() method of the folder object. In order for us to act on the folder, we must make sure that we have the object lock of the folder. If we find that the folder is useless, we can simply remove the folder from the cabinet. The cabinet can be found by the getCabinet() method, and the folder can be deleted with the remove() method. Just as with the folder object, before we can act on the cabinet object, we must obtain its object lock. Now, let's also suppose that we have another method, called updateFolders():

```
public void updateFolders(Cabinet dir) {
    synchronized (dir) {
        for (Folder f = dir.first(); f != null; f = dir.next(f)) {
            synchronized (f) {
                f.update();
            }
        }
    }
}
```

This method is passed a cabinet object that represents a cabinet in our database system. In order for us to act on this cabinet, we must first obtain its object lock. Let's suppose that the act of updating the cabinet is done by cycling through all the folders in the cabinet and calling the update() method on the folders. Again, in order for us to update the folders, we must also grab the folder lock.

None of these methods is extraordinary; they could exist in one form or another in any database system. However, let's look at a possible run of this implementation as outlined in Figure 3-4. Assume the updateFolders() method is called from thread 1. The method locks the cabinet (L1). Now assume the removeUseless() method is called by thread 2. The removeUseless() method locks the folder (L2), determines that it is indeed useless, and proceeds to lock the cabinet (L1) in order to remove the folder. At this point, thread 2 blocks and waits until the cabinet object lock is freed.

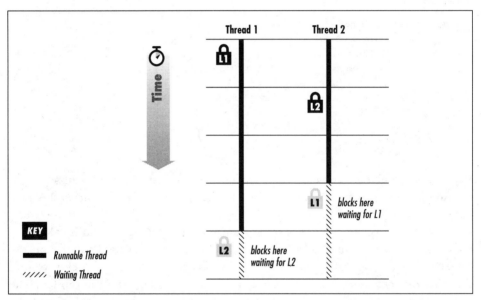

Figure 3-4. Deadlock in a database system

But what happens if the folder on which the removeUseless() method is working is now accessed by the updateFolders() method? When the updateFolders() method reaches this folder, it tries to grab the object lock for the folder (L2). At this point, the removeUseless() method has the folder lock and is waiting for the cabinet lock to be freed; the updateFolders() method holds the cabinet lock and is waiting for the folder lock to be freed. This is the classic deadlock situation, and it illustrates the problem that deadlock can be easy to program and hard to detect: both methods involved use a simple, straightforward algorithm, and there are no obvious signs in the code that deadlock can occur. Consider this problem in the light of a large system, where the code may have been developed by two engineers with no knowledge of each other's work; even the best program design would not guarantee deadlock prevention.

Can the system somehow resolve this deadlock, just as it was able to avoid the potential dead-lock when a thread tries to grab the same lock again? Unfortunately, this problem is different. Unlike the case of the nested locks, where a single thread is trying to grab a single lock twice, this case involves two separate threads trying to grab two different locks. Since a thread owns one of the locks involved, it may have made changes that make it impossible for it to free the lock. To be able to fix this problem, we can either redesign the program so that it doesn't run into this dead-lock condition, or provide a way for this deadlock to be avoided programmatically. In either case, it involves some sort of redesign. Given the complexity of the orig-inal design, this may involve a major overhaul of the database system.

How could you expect the Java system to resolve this deadlock automatically when even the developer may not be able to do so without overhauling the design? The answer is that you can't, and it doesn't. We will look at the design issues related to deadlock preven-tion in Chapter 8.

Return to the Banking Example

So, we just survived the ATM withdrawal problem. It turns out that this problem occurred so infrequently that the total cash involved with the problem transac-tions was only a few thousand dollars. Luckily, the bank kept records that were good enough to recover the cash. While our manager did not like the fact that we caused a major panic among the upper-level managers, she was somewhat impressed that we were able to track down the problem. While she still does not trust us completely, we still have a job and are able to design and enhance different parts of the ATM system.

The first thing we do is to look at our existing ATM code: we check and double check every piece of code for race conditions, using the synchronized mecha-nisms that we've learned so far to resolve the problems. Everything seems to be going well until one day the president of the bank receives a phone call from an irate customer. This customer did a balance inquiry at the ATM that showed a balance of $300. Immediately, he attempted to withdraw $290, but could not.

It turns out that in the very short period of time between when the customer checked his balance and attempted to withdraw the money, his wife withdrew $100 from another ATM. Even though the "correct" thing happened, it turned into a big political problem for the bank when the husband threatened to remove his $1 million business account from the bank if the bank "couldn't keep their records straight." So the bank established a new policy that only one ATM could operate on an account at the same time.

This means that we need a new lock scope for the account: the ATM class must be able to lock the account for the duration of a session with a user. This session could comprise transactions that span multiple methods in the ATM class, so the synchronized blocks and synchronized methods that we've learned about so far aren't sufficient to solve this problem: we need a lock that spans multiple methods.

Fortunately, we've already developed the BusyFlag class, so we're in position to solve this problem with little effort:

```java
public class AutomatedTellerMachine extends Teller {
    Account a;

    public boolean synchronized login(String name, String password) {
        if (a != null)
            throw new IllegalArgumentException("Already logged in");
        a = verifyAccount(name, password);
        if (a == null)
            return false;
        a.lock();
        return true;
    }

    public void withdraw(float amount) {
        if (a.deduct(amount))
            dispense(amount);
        printReceipt();
    }

    public void balanceInquiry() {
        printBalance(a.balance());
    }

    public void synchronized logoff() {
        a.unlock();
        a = null;
    }
}

class Account {
    private float total;
    private BusyFlag flag = new BusyFlag();

    public synchronized boolean deduct(float t) {
        if (t <= total) {
            total -= t;
            return true;
        }
        else return false;
    }
```

```
    public synchronized float balance() {
        return total;
    }

    public void lock() {
        flag.getBusyFlag();
    }

    public void unlock() {
        flag.freeBusyFlag();
    }
}
```

By using a BusyFlag lock, we're now able to lock at a "session" scope by grabbing the busyflag when the user logs into the ATM and releasing the busyflag when the user logs off the ATM. Locking at this scope cannot be directly achieved with the synchronization primitives within Java.

Being proud of the BusyFlag class, we now place the code into a class library, where it is accepted by the whole development team for the ATM project. Although it is a very simple class, it is also one of the most functional and is used in practically every part of the ATM system. However, we'll point out now that our current implementation of the BusyFlag class, while correct, is still suboptimal, but we can't solve that problem until we learn about the tools in the next chapter.

Synchronizing Static Methods

Throughout this chapter on synchronization, we kept referring to "obtaining the object lock." But what about static methods? When a synchronized static method is called, which object are we referring to? A static method does not have a concept of the this reference. It is not possible to obtain the object lock of an object that does not exist. So how does synchronization of static methods work? To answer this question, we will introduce the concept of a class lock. Just as there is an object lock that can be obtained for each instance of a class (object), there is a lock that can be obtained for each class. We will refer to this as the *class lock*. In terms of implementation, there is no such thing as a class lock, but it is a useful concept to help us understand how this all works.

When a static synchronized method is called, the program obtains the class lock before calling the method. This mechanism is identical to the case in which the method is not static; it is just a different lock. The same rule applies: if a synchronized static method calls another synchronized static method of the same class, the system is smart enough to support the nesting of class locks.

But how is the class lock related to the object lock? Apart from the functional relationship between the two locks, they are not operationally related at all. These are two distinct locks. The class lock can be grabbed and released independently of the object lock. If a nonstatic synchronized method calls a static synchronized method, it acquires both locks. Achieving deadlock between these two locks is a little difficult (but not impossible) to accomplish since a static method cannot call a nonstatic method without an object reference.

If a synchronized static method has access to an object reference, can it call synchronized methods of that object or use the object to lock a synchronized block? Yes: in this case the program first acquires the class lock when it calls the synchronized static method and then acquires the object lock of the particular object:

```
public class MyStatic {
    public synchronized static void staticMethod(MyStatic obj) {
        // Class lock acquired
        obj.nonStaticMethod();

        synchronized (obj) {
        // Class and object locks acquired
        }
    }
    public synchronized void nonStaticMethod() {
        // Object lock acquired
    }
}
```

Can a nonstatic method grab the static lock without calling a synchronized static method? In other words, can a synchronized block apply to the class lock? For example, something like this:

```
public class ClassExample {
    synchronized void process() {
        synchronized (the class lock) {
        // Code to access static variables of the class
        }
    }
}
```

The main reason for a nonstatic method to grab a class lock is to prevent a race condition for variables that apply to the class (i.e., static variables). This can be accomplished by calling a static synchronized method of the class. If for some reason this is not desired, we can also use the synchronized block mechanism on a common static object (using a static instance variable would probably be the best technique for storing such a common object). For example, we could use an object stored in a common location that can be accessed by all objects of a particular class type:

```
public class ClassExample {
    private static Object lockObject = new Object();
```

```
        synchronized void process() {
            synchronized (lockObject) {
                // Code to access static variables of the class
            }
        }
    }
```

The Class Lock and the Class Object

In this example, we are using the object lock of the Class object as a common lock for the class. We are using this object because there is a one-to-one correspondence of class objects and classes in the system. We have also mentioned that when a synchronized static method is called, the system will grab the class lock.

It turns out that there is actually no such thing as a class lock. When a synchronized static method is called, the system grabs the object lock of the class object that represents the class. This means the class lock is the object lock of the corresponding class object. Using both static synchronized methods and synchronized blocks that use the class object lock can cause confusion.

Finally, if creating a new object is not desired, you may also obtain the class object (that is, the instance of the `java.lang.Class` class) that represents the class itself. Objects of this class are used to represent classes in the system. For our purposes, we are using this class because there is a one-to-one ratio of classes and objects of the Class class that represents the classes. This class object can be obtained as follows:

```
    public class ClassExample {
        synchronized void process() {
            synchronized (Class.forName("ClassExample")) {
                // Code to access static variables of the class
            }
        }
    }
```

A call to the `forName()` method of the Class class returns this object. We can then use this class object as the locking object via the synchronized block mechanism.

Summary

In this chapter, we introduced the `synchronized` keyword of the Java language. This keyword allows us to synchronize methods and blocks of code.

We've also developed a synchronization primitive of our own: the BusyFlag, which allows us to lock objects across methods and to acquire and release the lock at will based on external events. These features are not available with Java's `synchronized` keyword, but they are useful in many situations.

This concludes our first look at synchronization. As you can tell, it is one of the most important aspects of threaded programming. Without these techniques, we would not be able to share data correctly between the threads that we create. While these techniques are good enough for many of the programs we will be creating, we introduce other techniques in the next chapter.

4

Wait and Notify

In the previous chapter, we took our first look into issues of synchronization. With the synchronization tools introduced, we now are able to have our own threads interoperate and safely share data with each other. It is possible for threads to share data without any race conditions. However, as we shall see, synchronization is more than avoiding race conditions: it includes a thread-based notification system that we'll examine in this chapter.

Back to Work (at the Bank)

Having just completed a sweep of all the code in the ATM system—synchronizing any potential problems using the techniques of Chapter 3—we have made the system much more robust. Many little hiccups that used to occur no longer show up. But most important, our BusyFlag class allows us to quickly make the modifications required by our president. The use of the BusyFlag class in this situation allows it to be adopted as a corporate standard and used throughout the whole ATM system.

As far as our manager is concerned, we're heroes—until another problem occurs: it turns out that a portion of the ATM system is facing performance problems. This portion of the system was developed by a coworker who made extensive use of the BusyFlag class. Since it is our class, we are given the task of trying to correct the problem. We start by revisiting the entire BusyFlag class:

```
public class BusyFlag {
    protected Thread busyflag = null;
    protected int busycount = 0;

    public void getBusyFlag() {
        while (tryGetBusyFlag() == false) {
```

```
        try {
            Thread.sleep(100);
        } catch (Exception e) {}
    }
}


public synchronized boolean tryGetBusyFlag() {
    if (busyflag == null) {
        busyflag = Thread.currentThread();
        busycount = 1;
        return true;
    }
    if (busyflag == Thread.currentThread()) {
        busycount++;
        return true;
    }
    return false;
}


public synchronized void freeBusyFlag () {
    if (getBusyFlagOwner() == Thread.currentThread()) {
        busycount--;
        if (busycount == 0)
            busyflag = null;
    }
}


public synchronized Thread getBusyFlagOwner() {
    return busyflag;
}
}
```

Upon revisiting the BusyFlag class, we notice the call to the sleep() method. We originally used this method to avoid eating up too many CPU cycles. At the time, we considered this an open issue. If the getBusyFlag() method sleeps for a long period of time, this might cause the method to wait too long and hence cause a performance problem. Conversely, if the method does not sleep enough, it might eat up too many CPU cycles and hence cause a performance problem. In either case, this has to be fixed: we have to find a way to wait only until the lock is freed. We need the getBusyFlag() method to grab the busyflag the moment the flag is freed and yet not eat any CPU cycles in a polling loop. We'll solve this problem in the next section.

Wait and Notify

Just as each object has a lock that can be obtained and released, each object also provides a mechanism that allows it to be a waiting area. And just like the lock mechanism, the main reason for this mechanism is to aid communication between threads.* The idea behind the mechanism is actually simple: one thread needs a certain condition to exist and assumes that another thread will create that condition. When this other thread creates the condition, it notifies the first thread that has been waiting for the condition. This is accomplished with the following methods:

void wait()

   Waits for a condition to occur. This is a method of the Object class and must be called from within a synchronized method or block.

void notify()

   Notifies a thread that is waiting for a condition that the condition has occurred. This is a method of the Object class and must be called from within a synchronized method or block.

---

wait(), notify(), and the Object Class

Interestingly enough, just like the synchronized method, the *wait and notify* mechanism is available from every object in the Java system. However, this mechanism is accomplished by method invocations, whereas the synchronized mechanism is done by adding a keyword.

The `wait()`/`notify()` mechanism works because these are methods of the Object class. Since every object in the Java system inherits directly or indirectly from the Object class, it is also an Object and hence has support for this mechanism.

What is the purpose of the wait and notify mechanism, and how does it work? The wait and notify mechanism is also a synchronization mechanism; however, it is more of a communication mechanism: it allows one thread to communicate to another thread that a particular condition has occurred. The wait and notify mechanism does not specify what the specific condition is.

Can wait and notify be used to replace the synchronized method? Actually, the answer is no. Wait and notify does not solve the race condition problem that the synchronized mechanism solves. As a matter of fact, wait and notify must be used in conjunction with the synchronized lock to prevent a race condition in the wait and notify mechanism itself.

---

* Under Solaris or POSIX threads, these are often referred to as *condition variables*; on Windows 95/NT, they are referred to as *event variables*.

Let's use this technique to solve the timing problem in the BusyFlag class. In our earlier version, the getBusyFlag() method would call tryGetBusyFlag() to obtain the busyflag. If it could not get the flag, it would try again 100 milliseconds later. But what we are really doing is waiting for a condition (a free busyflag) to occur. So we can apply this mechanism: if we don't have the condition (a free busyflag), we wait() for the condition. And when the flag is freed, we notify() a waiting thread that the condition now exists. This gives us the final, optimal implementation of the BusyFlag class:

```
public class BusyFlag {
    protected Thread busyflag = null;
    protected int busycount = 0;

    public synchronized void getBusyFlag() {
        while (tryGetBusyFlag() == false) {
            try {
                wait();
            } catch (Exception e) {}
        }
    }

    public synchronized boolean tryGetBusyFlag() {
        if (busyflag == null) {
            busyflag = Thread.currentThread();
            busycount = 1;
            return true;
        }
        if (busyflag == Thread.currentThread()) {
            busycount++;
            return true;
        }
        return false;
    }

    public synchronized void freeBusyFlag() {
        if (getBusyFlagOwner() == Thread.currentThread()) {
            busycount--;
            if (busycount == 0) {
                busyflag = null;
                notify();
            }
        }
    }

    public synchronized Thread getBusyFlagOwner() {
        return busyflag;
    }
}
```

In this new version of the getBusyFlag() method, the 100-millisecond sleep is removed and replaced with a call to the wait() method. This is the wait for the required condition to occur. The freeBusyFlag() method now contains a call to the notify() method. This is the notification that the required condition has occurred. This new implementation is much better than the old one. We now wait() until the busyflag is free—no more and no less—and we no longer waste CPU cycles by waking up every 100 milliseconds to test if the busyflag is free.

Wait and Notify and Synchronization

As noted, the wait and notify mechanism has a race condition that needs to be solved with the synchronization lock. Unfortunately, it is not possible to solve the race condition without integrating the lock into the wait and notify mechanism. This is why it is mandatory for the wait() and notify() methods to hold the locks for the objects for which they are waiting or notifying.

The wait() method releases the lock prior to waiting, and reacquires the lock prior to returning from the wait() method. This is done so that no race condition exists. If you recall, there is no concept of releasing and reacquiring a lock in the Java API. The wait() method is actually tightly integrated with the synchronization lock, using a feature not available directly from the synchronization mechanism. In other words, it is not possible for us to implement the wait() method purely in Java: it is a native method.

This integration of the wait and notify and the synchronized method is actually standard. In other systems, such as Solaris or POSIX threads, condition variables also require that a mutex lock be held for the mechanism to work.

There is another change: the getBusyFlag() method is now synchronized. The getBusyFlag() method was not synchronized in our earlier examples because the lock scope would have been too large. It would not have been possible for the freeBusyFlag() method to be called while the getBusyFlag() method held the lock. However, because of the way in which the wait() method works, there is no longer a danger of deadlock. The wait() method will release the lock, which will allow other threads to execute the freeBusyFlag() method. Before the wait() method returns, it will reacquire the lock, so that to the developer, it appears as if the lock has been held the entire time.

What happens when notify() is called and there is no thread waiting? This is a valid situation. Even with our BusyFlag class, it is perfectly valid to free the busyflag when there is no other thread waiting to get the busyflag. Since the wait and notify mechanism does not know the condition about which it is sending notification, it assumes that a notification for which there is no thread waiting is a notification

that goes unheard. In other words, if `notify()` is called without another thread
waiting, then `notify()` simply returns.

What are the details of the race condition that exists in wait and notify? In general, a
thread that uses the `wait()` method confirms that a condition does not exist (typically by checking a variable) and then calls the `wait()` method. When another
thread sets the condition (typically by setting that same variable), it then calls the
`notify()` method. A race condition occurs when:

1. The first thread tests the condition and confirms that it must wait.

2. The second thread sets the condition.

3. The second thread calls the `notify()` method; this goes unheard, since the
   first thread is not yet waiting.

4. The first thread calls the `wait()` method.

How does this potential race condition get resolved? This race condition is resolved by the
synchronization lock discussed earlier. In order to call `wait()` or `notify()`, we
must have obtained the lock for the object on which we're calling the `wait()` or
`notify()` method. This is mandatory: the methods will not work properly and will
generate an exception condition if the lock is not held. Furthermore, the `wait()`
method also releases the lock prior to waiting and reacquires the lock prior to
returning from the `wait()` method. The developer must use this lock to ensure
that checking the condition and setting the condition is atomic, which typically
means that the condition is held in an instance variable within the locked object.

*Is there a race condition during the period that the wait() method releases and reacquires the
lock?* The `wait()` method is tightly integrated with the lock mechanism. The
object lock is not actually freed until the waiting thread is already in a state in
which it can receive notifications. This would have been difficult, if not impossible, to accomplish if we had needed to implement the `wait()` and `notify()`
methods ourselves. For our purposes, this is an implementation detail. It works,
and works correctly. The system prevents any race conditions from occurring in
this mechanism.

*Why does the getBusyFlag() method loop to test if the tryGetBusyFlag() method returns false?
Isn't the flag going to be free when the wait() method returns?* No, the flag won't necessarily be free when the `wait()` method returns. The race condition that is solved
internally to the wait and notify mechanism only prevents the loss of notifications.
It does not solve the following case:

1. The first thread acquires the `busyflag`.

2. The second thread calls `tryGetBusyFlag()`, which returns `false`.

3. The second thread executes the `wait()` method, which frees the synchronization lock.

Wait and Notify and the Synchronized Block

In all the wait and notify examples so far, we have used synchronized methods. However, there is no reason we can't use the synchronized block syntax instead. The only requirement is that the object on which we are synchronizing must be the same object on which we call the wait() and notify() methods. An example could be as follows:

```
public class ExampleBlockLock {
    private StringBuffer sb = new StringBuffer();
    public void getLock() {
        doSomething(sb);
        synchronized (sb) {
            try {
                sb.wait();
            } catch (Exception e) {}
        }
    }
    public void freeLock() {
        doSomethingElse(sb);
        synchronized (sb) {
            sb.notify();
        }
    }
}
```

---

4. The first thread enters the freeBusyFlag() method, obtaining the synchronization lock.

5. The first thread calls the notify() method.

6. The third thread attempts to call getBusyFlag() and blocks waiting for the synchronization lock.

7. The first thread exits the freeBusyFlag() method, releasing the synchronization lock.

8. The third thread acquires the synchronization lock and enters the getBusyFlag() method. Because the busyflag is free, it obtains the busyflag and exits the getBusyFlag() method, releasing the synchronization lock.

9. The second thread, having received notification, returns from the wait() method, reacquiring the synchronization lock along the way.

10. The second thread calls the tryGetBusyFlag() method again, confirms that the flag is busy, and calls the wait() method.

If we had implemented the getBusyFlag() method without the loop:

```
public synchronized void getBusyFlag() {
    if (tryGetBusyFlag() == false) {
        try {
            wait();
            tryGetBusyFlag();
        } catch (Exception e) {}
    }
}
```

then in step 10 the second thread would have returned from the getBusyFlag() method even though the tryGetBusyFlag() method had not acquired the busyflag. All we know when the wait() method returns is that at some point in the past, the condition had been satisfied and another thread called the notify() method; we cannot assume that the condition is still satisfied without testing the condition again. Hence, we always need to put the call to the wait() method in a loop.

wait(), notify(), and notifyAll()

What happens when there is more than one thread waiting for the notification? Which thread actually gets the notification when notify() is called? The answer is that it depends: the Java specification doesn't define which thread gets notified. Which thread actually receives the notification varies based on several factors, including the implementation of the Java virtual machine and scheduling and timing issues during the execution of the program. There is no way to determine, even on a single platform, which of multiple threads receives the notification.

There is another method of the Object class that assists us when multiple threads are waiting for a condition:

void notifyAll()

> Notifies all the threads waiting on the object that the condition has occurred. This is a method of the Object class and must be called from within a synchronized method or block.

The Object class also provides the notifyAll() method, which helps us in those cases where the program cannot be designed to allow any arbitrary thread to receive the notification. This method is similar to the notify() method, except that all of the threads that are waiting on the object will be notified instead of a single arbitrary thread. Just like the notify() method, the notifyAll() method does not let us decide which threads get notification: they all get notified. By having all the threads receive notification, it is now possible for us to work out a mechanism for the threads to choose among themselves which thread should continue and which thread(s) should call the wait() method again.

Does notifyAll() Really Wake Up All the Threads?

Yes and no. All the waiting threads will wake up, but they still have to reacquire the object lock. So the threads will not run in parallel: they must each wait for the object lock to be freed. Thus only one thread can run at a time, and only after the thread that called the `notifyAll()` method releases its lock.

Why would you want to wake up all of the threads? There are a few possible reasons, one of which is if there is more than one condition to wait for. Since we cannot control which thread gets the notification, it is entirely possible that a notification wakes up a thread that is waiting for an entirely different condition. By waking up all the waiting threads, we can design the program so that the threads decide among themselves which should execute next.

Another reason is the case where the notification can satisfy multiple waiting threads. Let's examine a case where we need such control:

```
public class ResourceThrottle {
    private int resourcecount = 0;
    private int resourcemax = 1;

    public ResourceThrottle (int max) {
        resourcecount = 0;
        resourcemax = max;
    }

    public synchronized void getResource (int numberof) {
        while (true) {
            if ((resourcecount + numberof) <= resourcemax) {
                resourcecount += numberof;
                break;
            }
            try {
                wait();
            } catch (Exception e) {}
        }
    }

    public synchronized void freeResource (int numberof) {
        resourcecount -= numberof;
        notifyAll();
    }
}
```

We are defining a new class called the ResourceThrottle class. This class provides two methods, getResource() and freeResource(). Both of these methods take a single parameter that specifies how many resources to grab or release. The maximum number of resources available is defined by the constructor of the ResourceThrottle class. This class is similar to our BusyFlag class, in that our getResource() method would have to wait if the number of requested resources is not available. The freeResource() method also has to call the notify() method so that the waiting threads can get notification when more resources are available.

The difference in this case is that we are calling the notifyAll() method instead of the notify() method. There are two reasons for this:

- It is entirely possible for the system to wake up a thread that needs more resources than are available, even with the resources that have just been freed. If we had used the notify() method, another thread that could be satisfied with the current amount of resources would not get the chance to grab those resources because the system picked the wrong thread to wake up.

- It is possible to satisfy more than one thread with the number of resources we have just freed. As an example, if we free ten resources, we can then let four other threads grab three, four, one, and two resources, respectively. There is not a one-to-one ratio between the number of threads freeing resources and the number of threads grabbing resources.

By notifying all the threads, we solve these two problems with little work. However, all we have accomplished is to simulate a targeted notification scheme. We are not really controlling which threads wake up; instead, we are controlling which thread takes control after they all get notification. This can be very inefficient if there are many threads waiting to get notification, because many wake up only to see that the condition is still unsatisfied, and they must wait again.

If we really need to control which thread gets the notification, we could also implement an array of objects whose sole purpose is to act as a waiting point for threads and who are targets of notification of conditions. This means that each thread waits on a different object in the array. By having the thread that calls the notify() method decide which thread should receive notification, we remove the overhead of many threads waking up only to go back to a wait state moments later. The disadvantage of using an array of objects is, of course, that we will lock on different objects. This acquisition of many locks could lead to confusion or, even worse, deadlock. It is also more complicated to accomplish; we may even have to write a new class just to help with notification targeting:

```
public class TargetNotify {
    private Object Targets[] = null;

    public TargetNotify (int numberOfTargets) {
        Targets = new Object[numberOfTargets];
```

```
                for (int i = 0; i < numberOfTargets; i++) {
                    Targets[i] = new Object();
                }
            }

            public void wait (int targetNumber) {
                synchronized (Targets[targetNumber]) {
                    try {
                        Targets[targetNumber].wait();
                    } catch (Exception e) {}
                }
            }

            public void notify (int targetNumber) {
                synchronized (Targets[targetNumber]) {
                    Targets[targetNumber].notify();
                }
            }
        }
```

The concept is simple: in our TargetNotify class, we are using an array of objects for the sole purpose of using the wait and notify mechanism. Instead of having all the threads wait on the this object, we choose an object to wait on. (This is potentially confusing: we are not overriding the wait() method of the Object class here since we've provided a unique signature.) Later, when we decide which threads should wake up, we can target the notification since the threads are waiting on different objects.

Whether the efficiency of a targeted notification scheme outweighs the extra complexity is the decision of the program designer. In other words, both techniques have their drawbacks, and we leave it up to the implementors to decide which mechanism is best.

wait() and sleep()

The Object class also overloads the wait() method to allow it to take a timeout specified in milliseconds (though, as we mentioned in Chapter 2, the timeout resolution may not be as precise as one millisecond):

void wait(long timeout)

Waits for a condition to occur. However, if the notification has not occurred in timeout milliseconds, it returns anyway. This is a method of the Object class and must be called from a synchronized block or method.

void wait(long timeout, int nanos)

Waits for a condition to occur. However, if the notification has not occurred in timeout milliseconds and nanos nanoseconds, it returns anyway. This is a method of the Object class and must be called from a synchronized block or method.

These methods are provided to support external events. In cases where we are only concerned with a notification arriving, we normally do not use these methods. However, notifications can be dependent on external conditions, in which case we are also concerned with when a notification arrives. A timeout may be needed in case those conditions do not occur. As an example, we might write a program that connects to a stock feed server. The program may be willing to wait 30 seconds to connect to the server (that is, to satisfy the condition of being connected); if the connection does not occur within 30 seconds, the program may try to contact a backup server. We'd accomplish this by calling the wait(30000) method in our program.

We may still add a timeout when we know that a condition will eventually be satisfied so that we can accomplish other tasks. For example, let's assume that we needed to do other tasks in our getBusyFlag() method:

```
public synchronized void getBusyFlag() {
    while (tryGetBusyFlag() == false) {
        wait(100);
        doSomethingElse();
    }
}
```

In this version of getBusyFlag(), we wait() for the notification for up to 100 milliseconds. If this notification does not arrive within the requested time, we are awakened anyway. This is actually a very contrived example: we could have easily created another thread that does something else.

If we know that the notification will never arrive, what is the difference between wait(long) and sleep(long)? Let's say, for example, we do not use the notify() method on an object. Then, in theory, there is no reason to wait() on the object. However, the wait(long) method does have an extra benefit: it behaves like the sleep(long) method of the Thread class, except that it also releases and reacquires a lock. This means that if we are not using the wait and notify mechanism, we can still use the wait(long) method as a way of sleeping without holding the lock. For example, suppose we have the following class:

```
public class WaitExample {
    public synchronized void ProcessLoop() {
        processOne();
        try {
            wait(1000);
        } catch (Exception e) {}
        processTwo();
    }
}
```

The WaitExample class is a simple example of a method that needs to sleep for one second between two distinct operations, during which time it must give up the lock. If we had to code the same class without using the wait(long) method, it would add extra complexity:

```
public class WaitExample {
    public void ProcessLoop() {
        synchronized (this) {
            processOne();
        }
        try {
            Thread.sleep(1000);
        } catch (Exception e) {}
        synchronized (this) {
            processTwo();
        }
    }
}
```

As we said, this is a simple example: imagine if we had to code the following class without the use of the wait(long) method:

```
public class WaitExample {
    public synchronized void ProcessLoop() {
        processOne();
        for (int i=0; i<50; i++) {
            processTwo();
            try {
                wait(1000);
            } catch (Exception e) {}
        }
    }
}
```

Thread Interruption

The wait() method—like the sleep() and join() methods that we examined in Chapter 2—may under certain circumstances throw an InterruptedException. These methods all throw such an exception when the thread in which they are executing is interrupted, which occurs when another thread calls this method:

void interrupt() (Java 1.1 and above only)
Sends an interruption to the specified thread. If the thread is currently blocked in a thread-related method (i.e., the sleep(), join(), or wait() methods), the thread moves to an unblocked state; otherwise, a boolean flag is simply set to indicate that the thread has been interrupted.

Thread Interruption in Java 1.0

If you happen to have Java 1.0, you'll find that the various interrupt-related methods that we're describing in this section do not function: they all simply throw a NoSuchMethodError.

In Java 1.0.2—and browsers such as Netscape 3.0 and Internet Explorer 3.0 that are based on that release—these methods do not work properly. In particular, the `interrupt()` method is not able to interrupt a thread that is sleeping. While you can use the `isInterrupted()` method to determine if the `interrupt()` method has been called, the 1.0.2 implementation of these methods does not help you to deal with blocked threads.

Thread interruption works in Java 1.1 and later releases, but it does not work in many 1.1-based browsers. For now, we recommend that you use these methods only in Java applications or in applets run with the Java plug-in.

The effect of the `interrupt()` method depends on whether the target of the interruption is executing a method that might throw an exception based on that interruption. When the thread is executing the `sleep()`, `wait()`, and `join()` methods, those methods will throw an InterruptedException. Otherwise, a flag is set that the thread can examine to determine that the `interrupt()` method has been called.[*]

The `interrupt()` method is a method of the Thread class, and it is used by one thread to signal another thread: it is possible (although it doesn't really make sense) for a thread to interrupt itself. The target thread knows it has been interrupted if it is executing a method that will throw an InterruptedException. Otherwise, the target thread must use one of these methods to check if it has been interrupted:

static boolean interrupted() (Java 1.1 and above only)
> Returns a boolean that indicates whether the current thread has been interrupted. This is a static method of the Thread class and may be called through the class specifier. This method simply returns a flag that is set by the `interrupt()` method.

boolean isInterrupted() (Java 1.1 and above only)
> Returns a boolean that indicates whether the specified thread has been interrupted. This method simply returns a flag that is set by the `interrupt()` method.

---

* In some virtual machines, there's an additional possibility that we'll examine a little later.

The main difference between these two methods is that the interrupted()
method resets the value of the flag to false. The isInterrupted() method does
not change the value of the flag. Note that the interrupted() method is static
and operates on the current thread, whereas the isInterrupted() method is
dynamic and and must be executed on a thread object.

The point behind these methods is that the internal implementation of the
interrupt() method sets a value somewhere in the target thread object that indicates that the interrupt() method has been called; these methods simply return
that flag.

You can use the interrupt() method to signal a different outcome to a waiting
thread. One of the common uses of the wait and notify mechanism is in a
producer-consumer scenario: one or more threads are responsible for producing
data (for example, by reading it from some server), and one or more threads are
responsible for consuming data (for example, by parsing the data). When there is
no data to consume, consumer threads spend a great deal of time waiting:

```java
import java.util.*;

public class Consumer extends Thread {
    Vector data;
    public Consumer(Vector data) {
        this.data = data;
    }
    public void run() {
        Object o;
        while (true) {
            synchronized(data) {
                if (isInterrupted())
                    return;
                while (data.size() == 0) {
                    try {
                        data.wait();
                    } catch (InterruptedException ie) {
                        return;
                    }
                }
                o = data.elementAt(0);
                data.removeElementAt(0);
            }
            process(o);
        }
    }
}
```

Rather than stopping a consumer thread by setting a flag that its run() method
consults, we now rely on another thread to interrupt it. Note that there are two
possible outcomes here: if the interrupt arrives while the consumer is executing

the wait() method, an exception is thrown and the run() method returns. However, if the interrupt arrives while the consumer is executing the process() method, then the process() method will complete, and the consumer will exit the run() method when it next checks the interrupted flag. In order to prevent the interrupt from arriving at any other time, we must only send the interrupt from a thread that has synchronized on the data object that was passed into the constructor.

Be aware that the code internal to the Java virtual machine will not set the interrupted flag if the thread that is being interrupted is executing the sleep(), wait(), or join() methods. Consider the following code:

```
boolean done = false;
synchronized (lock) {
    while (!done) {
        try {
            lock.wait();
        } catch (InterruptedException ie) {
            done = isInterrupted();
        }
    }
}
```

In the catch clause, the variable done will be set to false and the loop will never exit.

In some circumstances, this may make the interrupt() method less useful in stopping a thread than directly setting a boolean flag in the target thread. However, because it will interrupt the sleep() and wait() methods, and because of some thread management techniques that we'll learn about in Chapter 10, the interrupt() method can be very useful in cases such as this.

Interrupted I/O

One area of confusion that surrounds the interrupt() method is in the area of I/O: can the interrupt() method affect a thread that is blocked while waiting for I/O? The answer for the time being is that it cannot, and you should not rely on its ability to do so. This may change in future releases of the virtual machine.

However, as it turns out, there are some implementations* of the virtual machine—most notably, the Solaris native-thread implementation—that cause the interrupt() method to interrupt any pending I/O. Hence, if a thread that is blocked on the read() method is the target of the interrupt() method, the read() method will throw an IOException. The particular IOException that is thrown varies: in Java 2, an InterruptedIOException is thrown; in 1.1, other excep-

---

* These various implementations of the virtual machine are discussed in Chapter 6.

tions (e.g., SocketException) are thrown. This may also change in future releases of the virtual machine: in the future, Solaris native-thread implementations may not allow I/O to be interrupted. In some green-thread versions of the virtual machine, some I/O methods will throw an InterruptedIOException, and some I/O methods will not. Interruptible I/O is not really possible on Windows, so Windows virtual machines do not support it.

So, what's a programmer to do? The safest answer is not to rely on the `interrupt()` method to unblock a thread that is waiting for I/O to complete: if you need to unblock such a thread, you should close the input or output stream on which the thread is blocked. If interruptible I/O is a generic feature added to Java virtual machines in the future, it will likely have a different interface. If you do rely on interruptible I/O, be aware that the I/O in question is not restartable: it's impossible to determine the state of the I/O and know at which point it should start again. The difficulty of dealing with the issue of restarting the I/O that has been interrupted is a prime reason why its implementation is inconsistent between virtual machines.

What if we want to use the interrupt() method more generically—that is, to get a thread to terminate, regardless of whether it's blocked on I/O or not? In our last example, we were able to take advantage of the fact that the `wait()` method had thrown an exception to know that there was no more data coming. If you want to do the same thing with I/O, you can do something like this:

```
import java.util.*;
import java.io.*;
import java.net.*;

class StockObservable extends Observable {
    String lastTick;

    void setTick(String s) {
        lastTick = s;
        setChanged();
        notifyObservers();
    }
}

public class StockHandler extends Thread {
    private BufferedReader br;
    private InputStream is;
    private Socket sock;
    private StockObservable stock;
    private volatile boolean done = false;
    private Object lock = new Object();

    class StockHandlerThread extends Thread {
        public void run() {
            String s;
```

```
            try {
                while ((s = br.readLine()) != null)
                    stock.setTick(s);
            } catch (IOException ioe) {}
            done = true;
            synchronized(lock) {
                lock.notify();
            }
        }
    }

    public StockHandler(StockObservable o, String host, int port)
                    throws IOException, UnknownHostException {
        sock = new Socket(host, port);
        is = sock.getInputStream();
        stock = o;
    }

    public void run() {
        br = new BufferedReader(new InputStreamReader(is));
        Thread t = new StockHandlerThread();
        t.start();
        synchronized(lock) {
            while (!done) {
                try {
                    lock.wait(Integer.MAX_VALUE);
                } catch (InterruptedException ie) {
                    done = true;
                    try {
                        t.interrupt();
                        is.close();
                        sock.close();
                    } catch (IOException ioe) {}
                }
            }
        }
    }
}
```

We've often mentioned that starting a separate thread to handle I/O is one of the more common uses of threads in Java; here's an example of that technique. This class sets up a socket to the stock server, reads data from that server, and publishes that data via the given observable object. The read() method in such a case would often block, and when it comes time to stop the thread, we have to have some way to get the read() method to terminate. This is accomplished by closing the socket from which the thread is reading.

However, what we've done in this example is to start two threads: one thread that is reading the data, and one thread that is waiting for an interrupt to occur (since the timeout is unlikely to occur). When the waiting thread is interrupted, it closes the input stream that the reading thread is blocked on, and both threads will then exit. This allows us to shut down the thread (and the socket associated with the thread) by interrupting the waiting thread:

```
Thread t = new StockHandler(...);
... Do other stuff until we need to shut down the handler ...
t.interrupt();
```

Now, clearly we could simply have exposed the socket and input stream instance variables so that any thread could have closed them directly. We'd rarely choose to do that, however, since it's better to encapsulate knowledge like that in the class to which it belongs. Similarly, we could have provided another method (e.g., a shutdown() method) that closes the socket and input stream. That sort of interface would have saved us a thread: the StockHandler class would read the data in its run() method and an external thread could execute its shutdown() method.

You can make an argument for and against including such a method in the interface for the StockHandler; we'll just mention again in passing that some of the thread management techniques that we'll look at in Chapter 10 make the interrupt() method a useful choice.

Finally, note that before we closed the input stream in order to get the stock handler thread t to unblock, we also called the interrupt() method on t. The primary reason for that is a bug: in Solaris 2.6 and earlier releases with a native-thread implementation of the virtual machine, the close() method in our example will block until the read() method that is being executed in the other thread also blocks. Although this bug is fixed in Solaris 2.7, it doesn't hurt to call the interrupt() method in any release so that our example will work on earlier Solaris releases, as well as on green-thread or Windows releases. More generally, the stock handler thread might be executing a wait() or sleep() method, in which case it would also be necessary to interrupt it.

Static Methods (Synchronization Details)

What about using wait() and notify() in a static method? The wait() and notify() methods are nonstatic methods of the Object class. Since static methods cannot call nonstatic methods without an object reference, static methods cannot call the wait() and notify() methods directly. But there is nothing preventing us from instantiating an object for the sole purpose of using it as a waiting point. This is just like the technique we used earlier when we tried to grab an object lock from a static method.

Using an actual object also allows the wait() and notify() methods from static and nonstatic methods to interoperate, much like using the synchronized block mechanism on a common object can allow static and nonstatic methods to inter-operate. The following versions of `staticWait()` and `staticNotify()` could be called from both static and nonstatic methods:

```
public class MyStaticClass {
    static private Object obj = new Object();

    public static void staticWait() {
        synchronized (obj) {
            try {
                obj.wait();
            } catch (Exception e) {}
        }
    }

    public static void staticNotify() {
        synchronized (obj) {
            obj.notify();
        }
    }
}
```

It's rare for threads that are executing static methods to interoperate with threads that are executing nonstatic methods in this manner. Nevertheless, by having a static version of the `wait()` and `notify()` methods, we allow interoperability to occur. These methods have different names because they have the same signatures as the `wait()` and `notify()` methods.

Summary

Here are the methods we introduced in this chapter:

void wait()

> Waits for a condition to occur. This is a method of the Object class and must be called from within a synchronized method or block.

void wait(long timeout)

> Waits for a condition to occur. However, if the notification has not occurred in `timeout` milliseconds, it returns anyway. This is a method of the Object class and must be called from a synchronized block or method.

void wait(long timeout, int nanos)

> Waits for a condition to occur. However, if the notification has not occurred in `timeout` milliseconds and `nanos` nanoseconds, it returns anyway. This is a method of the Object class and must be called from a synchronized block or method.

void notify()

> Notifies a thread that is waiting for a condition that the condition has occurred. This is a method of the Object class and must be called from within a synchronized method or block.

void notifyAll()

> Notifies all the threads waiting on the object that the condition has occurred. This is a method of the Object class and must be called from within a synchronized method or block.

void interrupt() (Java 1.1 and above only)

> Sends an interruption to the specified thread. If the thread is currently blocked in a thread-related method (i.e., the `sleep()`, `join()`, or `wait()` methods), the thread moves to an unblocked state; otherwise, a boolean flag is simply set to indicate that the thread has been interrupted.

static boolean interrupted() (Java 1.1 and above only)

> Returns a boolean that indicates whether the current thread has been interrupted. This is a static method of the Thread class and may be called through the class specifier. This method simply returns a flag that is set by the `interrupt()` method.

boolean isInterrupted() (Java 1.1 and above only)

> Returns a boolean that indicates whether the specified thread has been interrupted. This method simply returns a flag that is set by the `interrupt()` method.

With these methods, we are now able to interoperate between threads in an efficient manner. Instead of just providing protection against race conditions, we now have mechanisms that allow threads to inform each other about events or conditions without resorting to polling and timeouts. While the wait and notify mechanism is the most widely used of the mechanisms in this chapter, we also have the ability to interrupt a thread no matter what the thread is doing.

The two default techniques of synchronizing data and threads within Java—the synchronized keyword and the wait and notify methods—provide simple, robust ways for threads to communicate and cooperate. Although we will examine some advanced techniques for data synchronization in Chapter 8, these default techniques are good enough for most Java programs.

5

Useful Examples of Java Thread Programming

In the previous chapters, we examined some of the tools necessary to support the synchronization of data between threads. With these tools, we now are able to have our own threads interoperate with each other, with the system threads, or with the threads started by the standard Java libraries. This is possible because the tools allow for a thread to examine and modify shared data in a safe manner without race conditions. The ability to handle data safely provides us with the ability to exchange data, which, in turn, allows us to accomplish tasks in separate threads safely, which ultimately allows us to accomplish our goal.

In other words, we can now say that threading itself is just an implementation detail of our program. Ideally, true threading should feel like just another object that does something. And while threading itself is a powerful tool, in the end all you want to accomplish is to play the audio clip or read the data socket.

In this chapter, we examine some of the uses of threads. We will show how threads solve certain problems, and discuss the implementation details of these solutions, the threads themselves, and the mechanisms that are used to control and synchronize the threads. We will examine threads from the perspective of solving problems instead of examining features of the threading system.

Data Structures and Containers

Interestingly, our first set of examples does not require any threads to be created at all. Our first topic is the data types that can be used or passed between threads. When you create a data object, you do not always know how many threads will access that object: while these data objects may be accessed by many threads, they may also only be accessed by a single thread (in which case, synchronization of the object is not necessary). To begin, let's examine some operating system mechanisms used to pass data between processes.

In the Unix operating system, the first interprocess communications (IPC) techniques provided were message queues, semaphores, and shared memory. While Unix has added many mechanisms, these three are still popular and heavily used in many applications. The IPC mechanisms of Java—the synchronization lock and the wait and notify mechanism—are specifically for synchronization. Unlike the message queue and shared memory, no real data is actually passed between threads: the concern is synchronization, not communication.* The theory is that communication is easy if synchronization tools are available. For now, let's take a look at the message queue and shared memory and see if these communication mechanisms are useful for communicating between threads.

The Message Queue

We'll start with message queues:

```
import java.util.*;

public class MsgQueue {
    Vector queue = new Vector();
    public synchronized void send(Object obj) {
        queue.addElement(obj);
    }

    public synchronized Object recv() {
        if (queue.size() == 0) return null;

        Object obj = queue.firstElement();
        queue.removeElementAt(0);
        return obj;
    }
}
```

The implementation of the message queue is incredibly simple once we have the proper synchronization tools. In the multitasking paradigm, the operating system has to deliver the data that is sent into the queue from one application to another, as well as synchronizing the communication itself. Since threads share the same address space, data passing is accomplished by using a reference to a common data object. Once we are able to synchronize access to this data object, sending and receiving data using this message queue is simple. In our version of the

---

* This applies to most threading systems. In Solaris or POSIX threads, the main tools are the mutex lock, reader-writer locks, semaphores, and conditional variables, none of which actually passes any real data.

message queue, the queue is implemented using the Vector class that is implemented in the Java system. We simply need to make sure that we can safely add to and remove from this queue; this is accomplished by making sure that all accesses to this queue are synchronized. This implementation is so easy that we do not even need a MsgQueue class. Instead, we could have used the synchronized block mechanism on the Vector object directly, adding and removing the messages directly to and from the Vector. In other words, the message queue IPC is as simple to implement as any container class (that is, a class that holds collections of objects).

Shared Memory

A shared memory implementation may be as follows:

```
public class ShareMemory extends BusyFlag {
    byte memory[];
    public ShareMemory (int size) {
        memory = new byte[size];
    }

    public synchronized byte[] attach() {
        getBusyFlag();
        return memory;
    }

    public synchronized void detach() {
        freeBusyFlag();
    }
}
```

Just like the MsgQueue class, the ShareMemory class is also not difficult and may be unnecessary: we could just as easily have synchronized on the byte array object directly and we would not have needed to implement this class. The only advantage is that since we implemented the ShareMemory class as a subclass of the BusyFlag class, we can attach() and detach() from this shared memory at any scope, including a scope that is bigger than a single method.

The real point behind all this is that even though threads are somewhat analogous to processes, we have to learn to think about data differently than we would between two processes. To share data between processes requires specialized functions that are implemented in the operating system. But data in a Java program is always shared between threads. The fact that we don't have to do anything special to share this data means that we don't really need IPCs as we know them: instead, we have to constantly think threaded. Every time we develop a class, we should be concerned that it may be used by many threads simultaneously, whether our program actually contains many threads or not.

The Circular Linked List

So what about all the container classes we will develop? The linked list? The B-tree? The graph? Any other data structure we care to invent? When we implement one of these classes, should we implement it so that it can be accessed by multiple threads in parallel? The answer could be personal preference or corporate policy. It is, however, not difficult to make any container class safe for multiple threads. And it is arguably better to make it safe and not worry whether sometime in the future this container might be used across multiple threads. Let's take a look at a container class most of us have implemented at one time or another, the circularly linked list:

```
class CircularListNode {
    Object o;
    CircularListNode next;
    CircularListNode prev;
}
```

Just like any other linked list most of us have written, we will use a simple data structure node to store the object. We actually don't care what type of object we have in our list, so all we need is a reference to the Object class. This allows us to hold any type of object in our container (primitive types, of course, will need to be wrapped in their corresponding objects). We will also keep a reference to the previous node and to the next node in the circularly linked list. This is an implementation detail; we keep two references merely for efficiency in our search:

```
public class CircularList {
    private CircularListNode current;

    public synchronized void insert(Object o) {
        CircularListNode tn = new CircularListNode();
        tn.o = o;
        if (current == null) {
            tn.next = tn.prev = tn;
            current = tn;
        } else {                // Add before current node
            tn.next = current;
            tn.prev = current.prev;
            current.prev.next = tn;
            current.prev = tn;
        }
    }

    public synchronized void delete(Object o) {
        CircularListNode p = find(o);
        CircularListNode next = p.next;
        CircularListNode prev = p.prev;
        if (p == p.next) {      // Last object on the list
```

```
                current = null;
                return;
            }
        prev.next = next;
        next.prev = prev;
        if (current == p) current = next;
    }

    private CircularListNode find(Object o) {
        CircularListNode p = current;
        if (p == null)
            throw new IllegalArgumentException();
        do {
            if (p.o == o) return p;
            p = p.next;
        } while (p != current);
        throw new IllegalArgumentException();
    }

    public synchronized Object locate(Object o) {
        CircularListNode p = current;
        do {
            if (p.o.equals(o)) return p.o;
            p = p.next;
        } while (p != current);
        throw new IllegalArgumentException();
    }

    public synchronized Object getNext() {
        if (current == null)
            return null;
        current = current.next;
        return current.o;
    }
}
```

The implementation of our CircularList class is probably no different from any circularly linked list implementation we may have done before. We simply provide methods to insert() and delete() from the circularly linked list; once that list has the objects, we can pass this list to other methods that may process the list. This processing is done by simply cycling through the list with the getNext() method or by searching for a particular object using the locate() method.

How do we make this CircularList class safe for use by multiple threads? It's as simple as declaring all the methods as synchronized. By adding the synchronized keyword, we can now use this CircularList class safely across different threads simultaneously. In other words, by taking a few minutes to make the class safe, we can use this class as a form of interthread communication. With enough practice, we should use the synchronization tools without much effort.

Note that the find() method is not synchronized: as a private method that is called only by synchronized methods, there is no reason for it to be synchronized, though it wouldn't have hurt had we done so. Note also the subtle difference between the find() and locate() methods: as an internal method, the find() method returns objects of CircularListNode; the locate() method returns the actual object that was inserted into the list.

Synchronization and Efficiency

It can be argued that synchronizing a class just because it might be used by multiple threads is inefficient: it takes a certain amount of time to acquire the synchronization lock. This is a trade-off a developer must be aware of when designing a large program.

In this book, we've taken the view that it is easier to solve performance problems when they occur than to find bugs caused by a lack of data synchronization. For the most part, the Java API takes this view as well: classes such as the Hashtable and Vector class are all correctly synchronized and are safe to use in multithreaded programs.

In Java 2, however, there is a new set of container classes that are implemented with an eye toward efficiency rather than being thread safe. These classes are referred to as *collection classes*; they all extend either the java.util.Collection class or the java.util.Map class. For example, there is a HashMap class that provides the same semantics as the Hashtable class, except that the methods of the HashMap are not synchronized. Similarly, there is an ArrayList class that provides the same semantics as the Vector class, and so on.

Using these classes directly in your Java 2–based program may provide a small performance benefit. That's somewhat debatable, however, since the synchronization code of the reference virtual machine was completely overhauled in 1.1.6, with the result that the penalty for obtaining a synchronization lock was drastically reduced. So you'd need to make very heavy use of the methods in the classes that we're talking about to see any noticeable benefit for most programs. On the other hand, if you use the HashMap class without realizing that the same HashMap is being accessed by two threads and that a race condition causes an error in your program every 100 days, how much have you benefited from the faster code?

In Chapter 8, we'll show how we can safely use these and other thread-unsafe classes.

Simple Synchronization Examples

In this section, we'll look at two examples that use synchronization to perform complex synchronization tasks.

Barrier

Of all the different types of thread synchronization tools, the barrier is probably the easiest to understand and the least used. When we think of synchronization, our first thought is of a group of threads executing part of an overall task followed by a point at which they must synchronize their results. The barrier is simply a waiting point where all the threads can synch up either to merge results or to move on to the next part of the task. The synchronization techniques that we have discussed up to now were concerned with more complicated issues like preventing race conditions, handling data transfer and delivery, or signaling between threads.

Given its simplicity, why has the barrier not been mentioned up to this point? We have actually used this technique; however, we have used the Thread class itself to synch up the threads. By using the join() method, we have waited for all of the threads to terminate before we merged the results or started new threads for the next task.

There are a few problems with using the join() method. First, we must constantly create and terminate threads. This means that the threads may lose any state that they have stored in their previous operation. Second, if we must always create new threads, logical operations cannot be placed together: since new threads have to be created for each subtask, the code for each subtask must be placed in separate run() methods. It may be easier to code all of the logic as one method—particularly if the subtasks are very small:

```
public class Barrier {
    private int threads2Wait4;
    private InterruptedException iex;

    public Barrier (int nThreads) {
        threads2Wait4 = nThreads;
    }

    public synchronized int waitForRest()
        throws InterruptedException {
        int threadNum = --threads2Wait4;

        if (iex != null) throw iex;
        if (threads2Wait4 <= 0) {
            notifyAll();
            return threadNum;
        }
        while (threads2Wait4 > 0) {
            if (iex != null) throw iex;
            try {
                wait();
            } catch (InterruptedException ex) {
```

```
                iex = ex;
                notifyAll();
            }
        }
        return threadNum;
    }

    public synchronized void freeAll() {
        iex = new InterruptedException("Barrier Released by freeAll");
        notifyAll();
    }
}
```

Implementation of the Barrier class with the techniques of the previous chapters is straightforward. We simply have each thread that arrives at the barrier call the wait() method, while the last thread to arrive at the barrier has the task of notifying all of the waiting threads. If any of the threads receives an interruption, all of the threads will receive the same interruption. Another method, freeAll(), is also provided to generate an interruption on all of the threads. As an added benefit, a thread number is assigned to the threads to help distinguish the waiting threads. The last thread to reach the barrier is assigned the value of zero, and any threads that reach the barrier after it has been released are assigned a negative value. This indicates an error: if you send five threads through a barrier that is designed to synchronize four threads, the fifth thread will receive this negative value.

This implementation of the barrier is also a single-use implementation. Once the barrier reaches the thread limit as specified by the constructor, or an error is generated, the barrier will no longer block any threads. Given the simplicity of this implementation, having single-use instances of this class should not be a problem.

Here's an example of how we might use the Barrier class:

```
public class ProcessIt implements Runnable {
    String is[];
    Barrier bpStart, bp1, bp2, bpEnd;

    public ProcessIt (String sources[]) {
        is = sources;
        bpStart = new Barrier(sources.length);
        bp1 = new Barrier(sources.length);
        bp2 = new Barrier(sources.length);
        bpEnd = new Barrier(sources.length);

        for (int i=0; i < is.length; i++) {
            (new Thread(this)).start();
        }
    }
```

```java
public void run() {
    try {
        int i = bpStart.waitForRest();
        doPhaseOne(is[i]);
        bp1.waitForRest();
        doPhaseTwo(is[i]);
        bp2.waitForRest();
        doPhaseThree(is[i]);
        bpEnd.waitForRest();
    } catch (InterruptedException ex) {};
}

public void doPhaseOne(String ps) {
}

public void doPhaseTwo(String ps) {
}

public void doPhaseThree(String ps) {
}

static public void main(String args[]) {
    ProcessIt pi = new ProcessIt(args);
}
}
```

Using the Barrier class does not mean that we no longer need to create threads. In the ProcessIt class, we still need to create threads and implement the run() method; however, we only need to implement it once. All three phases of the process are done in the same run() method. The thread simply waits for the other threads before starting the next phase. We are also using a barrier to allow the threads to start at the same time and to assign them a thread number.

The flow of execution of this example is shown in Figure 5-1, which also shows how execution would proceed if we were using the join() method and creating new threads. There are some subtle differences between using a barrier and creating new threads. The first is that the barrier technique should not task the threading system as much since it does not destroy and create as many threads, which is sometimes an advantage. The second is that using the Barrier class means the application will never be single threaded because all the threads are always alive.* Using the Barrier class is a one-phase process, whereas using the Thread class is a two-phase process that requires that we first join() the threads—that is, become single threaded—and then create new threads.

---

* It can be argued that since all but one of the threads is waiting, the system is effectively single threaded.

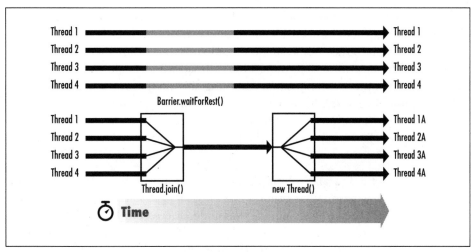

Figure 5-1. Comparison of the Barrier class with joining threads

The two-phase process, in which a single thread exists between the phases, allows tasks to be executed before the new threads are created. This is not possible when we use the Barrier class, since the only requirement for the threads to be released is a thread count. Complicated situations where setup and cleanup tasks need to be accomplished are a problem. A way to solve this problem is to modify the Barrier class to allow the barrier to execute setup code for the next phase. Unfortunately, this removes one of the advantages of the Barrier class—the ability to have code in a single location. Instead of having the implementation of the phases in separate run() methods, we will have the setup implementation for the different phases also protected by the Barrier class.

Here's how we code this solution without modifying the Barrier class:

```
public class ProcessIt implements Runnable {
    public void run() {
        try {
            int i = bpStart.waitForRest();
            doPhaseOne(is[i]);
            if (bp1.waitForRest() == 0)
                doPhaseTwoSetup();
            bp1b.waitForRest();
            doPhaseTwo(is[i]);
            if (bp2.waitForRest() == 0)
                doPhaseThreeSetup();
            bp2b.waitForRest();
            doPhaseThree(is[i]);
            bpEnd.waitForRest();
        } catch (InterruptedException ex) {};
    }
}
```

In this example, instead of having a single barrier between the phases, we now have two barriers. This is done to simulate the two-phase requirements of the cleanup and setup code. Effectively, since only one of the threads will execute the code, that portion of the code is single threaded. We are using the thread number returned by the barrier to determine which thread will execute code. In practice, there are many other techniques for choosing this thread, including making the determination once at the beginning or using a thread just to run the setup code. Furthermore, since we are now able to run cleanup and setup code, there is no need to declare all of the barriers at the beginning. Barrier definition and cleanup may be included in the setup code.

Barriers are useful for algorithms that have multiple passes. A compiler, for instance, often has passes that preprocess the code, parse the code, convert the code to intermediate format, optimize that code, and so on. Each of these passes may be implemented with several threads, each of which needs to wait between passes for all the other threads to complete their portions of the phase.

Condition Variables

Condition variables are a type of synchronization provided by POSIX threads. A condition variable is very similar to the Java environment's wait and notify mechanism—in fact, in most cases it is functionally identical. The four basic operations of a condition variable—wait(), timed_wait(), signal(), and broadcast()— map directly to the methods provided by the Java environment—wait(), wait(long), notify(), and notifyAll(). The implementations are also logically identical. The wait() operation of a condition variable requires that a mutex lock be held. It will release the lock while waiting and reacquire the lock prior to returning to the caller. The signal() function wakes up one thread, whereas the broadcast() function wakes up all waiting threads. These functions also require that the mutex lock be held during the call. The race conditions of a condition variable are solved in the same way as those of the Java environment's wait and notify mechanism.

There is a subtle difference. In the Java environment, the wait and notify mechanism is highly integrated with its associated lock. This makes the mechanism easier to use than its condition variable counterpart. Calling the wait() and notify() methods from synchronized sections of code is just a natural part of their use. Using condition variables, however, requires that you create a separate mutex lock, store that mutex, and eventually destroy the mutex when it is no longer necessary.

Unfortunately, Java's convenience comes with a small price. A condition variable and its associated mutex lock are separate synchronization entities. It is possible to use the same mutex with two different condition variables, to use two different mutexes with the same condition variable, or to use any combination of condition variables and mutexes. While the wait and notify mechanism is much easier to use and solves the problem for most cases of signal-based synchronization, it is not capable of assigning any synchronization lock to any notification object. When you need to signal two different notification objects while requiring the same synchronization lock to protect common data, a condition variable is more efficient.

Here is the implementation of the condition variable:

```
public class CondVar {
private BusyFlag SyncVar;

    public CondVar() {
        this(new BusyFlag());
    }

    public CondVar(BusyFlag sv) {
        SyncVar = sv;
    }

    public void cvWait() throws InterruptedException {
        cvTimedWait(SyncVar, 0);
    }

    public void cvWait(BusyFlag sv) throws InterruptedException {
        cvTimedWait(sv, 0);
    }

    public void cvTimedWait(int millis) throws InterruptedException {
        cvTimedWait(SyncVar, millis);
    }

    public void cvTimedWait(BusyFlag sv, int millis)
                                throws InterruptedException {
        int i = 0;
        InterruptedException errex = null;

        synchronized (this) {
            // You must own the lock in order to use this method.
            if (sv.getBusyFlagOwner() != Thread.currentThread()) {
                throw new IllegalMonitorStateException(
                            "current thread not owner");
            }

            // Release the lock (completely).
            while (sv.getBusyFlagOwner() == Thread.currentThread()) {
                i++;
                sv.freeBusyFlag();
            }
```

```
                    // Use wait() method.
                    try {
                        if (millis == 0) {
                            wait();
                        } else {
                            wait(millis);
                        }
                    } catch (InterruptedException iex) {
                        errex = iex;
                    }
                }

                // Obtain the lock (return to original state).
                for (; i>0; i--) {
                    sv.getBusyFlag();
                }

                if (errex != null) throw errex;
                return;
            }

            public void cvSignal() {
                cvSignal(SyncVar);
            }

            public synchronized void cvSignal(BusyFlag sv) {
                // You must own the lock in order to use this method.
                if (sv.getBusyFlagOwner() != Thread.currentThread()) {
                    throw new IllegalMonitorStateException(
                                    "current thread not owner");
                }
                notify();
            }

            public void cvBroadcast() {
                cvBroadcast(SyncVar);
            }

            public synchronized void cvBroadcast(BusyFlag sv) {
                // You must own the lock in order to use this method.
                if (sv.getBusyFlagOwner() != Thread.currentThread()) {
                    throw new IllegalMonitorStateException(
                                    "current thread not owner");
                }
                notifyAll();
            }
        }
    }
```

In this code, we simply reverse engineer the wait and notify mechanism, using the
BusyFlag class as the synchronization lock instead of the lock that is bound to the

object. Signaling between the threads is done with Java's wait and notify mechanism. And in order to solve the race condition that exists between the BusyFlag class and the CondVar class, we use the standard synchronization mechanism and the wait and notify mechanism.

The `cvWait()` mechanism is implemented in three sections. First, we must free the BusyFlag lock. This is done with the `freeBusyFlag()` method. Since the BusyFlag class is nestable, we must remove all the locks on the `busyflag`. In order to reacquire the lock at a later time, we have to keep track of the number of locks removed.

The second section simply calls the `wait()` method to map to Java's internal system. The final task is to reacquire the locks that were released earlier. The race condition that exists between the first two sections of the `cvWait()` method is solved by using a synchronized block around both sections. There is no need to extend this synchronization to the third section because the signal has already been received, and if we receive another signal at this point, that signal should just be ignored by this thread (this is analogous to what happens if the `wait()` method receives two simultaneous notifications).

The `cvSignal()` and `cvBroadcast()` methods simply map to the `notify()` and `notifyAll()` methods. These methods must also be synchronized in order to avoid a race condition with the `cvWait()` method.

Most of the time, when you use a condition variable instead of Java's wait and notify mechanism, you will want to set up two signaling channels (i.e., two variables) that are controlled by a single lock. In these cases, you will construct a single BusyFlag and construct all your condition variables using that BusyFlag. You will then use the methods of the CondVar class that do not require a BusyFlag parameter. For more complex cases, when you need to use different locks for the same variable, you will construct the CondVar without a BusyFlag and then pass a BusyFlag to the wait and signal methods.

One common use of the CondVar class is in buffer management. When threads are sending data to a buffer, they must stop when the buffer is full. Other threads that are reading data from the buffer must wait until data is available in the buffer. Here we have a single lock (associated with the buffer) but two conditions: empty and full. Condition variables allow a much cleaner implementation of this situation than does the simple wait and notify technique. We'll show an example of this later in this chapter.

A Network Server Class

In the socket networking model, the server side has to read from or write to many sockets that are connected to many clients. We already know that by reading data from a socket in a separate thread, we solve the problem of hanging while we're waiting for data. Threading on the server side has an additional benefit: by having a thread associated with each client, we no longer need to worry about other clients within any single thread. This simplifies our server-side programming: we can code our classes as if we were handling a single client at a time.

In this section, we'll develop such a server. But before we dive right in, let us review some networking basics.

Figure 5-2 shows the data connections between several clients and a server. The server-side socket setup is implemented in two steps. First, a socket is used for the purpose of listening on a port known to the client. The client connects to this port as a means to negotiate a private connection to the server.

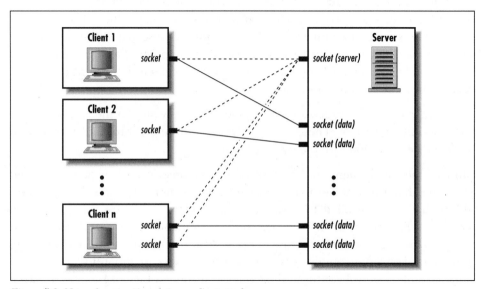

Figure 5-2. Network connections between clients and server

Once a data connection has been negotiated, the server and client then communicate through this private connection. In general, this process is generic: most programmers are concerned with the data sockets (the private connection). Furthermore, the data sockets on the server side are usually self-contained to a particular client. While it is possible to have different mechanisms that deal with many data sockets at the same time, generally the same code is used to deal with each of the data sockets independently of the other data sockets.

Since the setup is generic, we can place it into a generic TCPServer class and not have to implement the generic code again. Basically, this TCPServer class creates a ServerSocket and accepts connection requests from clients. This is done in a separate thread. Once a connection is made, the server clones (makes a copy of) itself so that it may handle the new client connection in a new thread:

```java
import java.net.*;
import java.io.*;

public class TCPServer implements Cloneable, Runnable {
    Thread runner = null;
    ServerSocket server = null;
    Socket data = null;
    volatile boolean shouldStop = false;

    public synchronized void startServer(int port) throws IOException {
        if (runner == null) {
            server = new ServerSocket(port);
            runner = new Thread(this);
            runner.start();
        }
    }

    public synchronized void stopServer() {
        if (server != null) {
            shouldStop = true;
            runner.interrupt();
            runner = null;
            try {
                server.close();
            } catch (IOException ioe) {}
            server = null;
        }
    }

    public void run() {
        if (server != null) {
            while (!shouldStop) {
                try {
                    Socket datasocket = server.accept();
                    TCPServer newSocket = (TCPServer) clone();

                    newSocket.server = null;
                    newSocket.data = datasocket;
                    newSocket.runner = new Thread(newSocket);
                    newSocket.runner.start();
                } catch (Exception e) {}
            }
        } else {
            run(data);
        }
    }
```

```
public void run(Socket data) {

    }
}
```

Considering the number of threads started by the TCPServer class, the implementation of the class is simple. First, the TCPServer class implements the Runnable
interface; we will be creating threads that this class will execute. Second, the class
is cloneable, so that a copy of this class can be created for each connection. And
since the copy of the class is also runnable, we can create another thread for each
client connection. Since the original TCPServer object must operate on the server
socket, and the clones must operate on the data sockets, the TCPServer class must
be written to service both the server and data sockets.

To begin, once a TCPServer object has been instantiated, the `startServer()`
method is called:

```
public synchronized void startServer(int port) throws IOException {
    if (runner == null) {
        server = new ServerSocket(port);
        runner = new Thread(this);
        runner.start();
    }
}
```

This method creates a ServerSocket object and a separate thread to handle the
ServerSocket object. By handling the ServerSocket in another thread, the
`startServer()` method can return immediately, and the same program can act
as multiple servers. We could have performed this initialization in the constructor
of the TCPServer class; there's no particular reason why we chose to do this in a
separate method.

The `stopServer()` method is the cleanup method for the TCPServer class:

```
public synchronized void stopServer() {
    if (server != null) {
        shouldStop = true;
        runner.interrupt();
        runner = null;
        try {
            server.close();
        } catch (IOException ioe) {}
        server = null;
    }
}
```

This method cleans up what was done in the `startServer()` method. In this
case, we need to terminate the thread we started; we do that by setting the flag that
will be checked in the `run()` method. In addition, we interrupt that thread, in

case the runner thread is hanging in the accept() method. Finally, we close() the socket that the thread was working on.

We also set the runner variable to null to allow the object to be reused: if the runner variable is null, the startServer() method can be called later to start another ServerSocket on the same port or on a different port.

Notice that the stopServer() method also checks to see if the server variable is null before trying to stop the server. The reason for this is that the TCPServer object will be cloned to handle the data sockets. Since this clone handles a data socket, we set the server variable to null in the clone. This extra check is done just in case the programmer decides to execute the stopServer() method from the clone instance that is handling a data socket.

The bulk of the logic comes in the run() method:

```
public void run() {
    if (server != null) {
        while (!shouldStop) {
            try {
                Socket datasocket = server.accept();
                TCPServer newSocket = (TCPServer) clone();

                newSocket.server = null;
                newSocket.data = datasocket;
                newSocket.runner = new Thread(newSocket);
                newSocket.runner.start();
            } catch (Exception e) {}
        }
    } else {
        run(data);
    }
}
```

What is interesting about this class is that the run() method contains some conditional code. Since the server instance variable is set in the startServer() method, the if statement in the run() method always succeeds. Later, we will be cloning this TCPServer object and starting more threads using the clone. The conditional code differentiates the clone from the original.

The handling of the ServerSocket is straightforward. We just need to accept() connections from the clients. All the details of binding to the socket and setting up the number of listeners are handled by the ServerSocket class itself. Once we have accepted a network connection from a client, we once again have a situation that benefits from threading.

However, in this case, instead of using a different Runnable class, we use the TCPServer class: more precisely, we clone our TCPServer object and configure it to run as a runnable object in a newly created thread. This is why the TCPServer's `run()` method checks to see if a ServerSocket object is available or not. The reason we cloned our TCPServer object was so we can have private data for each thread. By making a copy of the object, we make a copy of the instance variables that can then be set to the values needed by the newly created thread.

All code that handles the ServerSocket is in the `while` loop of the `run()` method. The rest of the `run()` method handles the client data socket:

```
public void run() {
    if (server != null) {
        ...
    } else {
        run(data);
    }
}


public void run(Socket data) {
}
```

The newly created thread running with the newly cloned runnable object first calls the `run()` method; for a data socket, the `run()` method just calls the overloaded `run(data)` method. As can be seen from the code, this `run(data)` method does absolutely nothing; using the TCPServer class by itself does nothing with the data sockets. To have a useful TCPServer, you must extend it:

```
import java.net.*;
import java.io.*;

public class ServerHandler extends TCPServer {
    public void run(Socket data) {
        try {
            InputStream is = data.getInputStream();
            OutputStream os = data.getOutputStream();

            // Process the data socket here.
        } catch (Exception e) {}
    }
}
```

All we need to do in our subclass is override the `run(data)` method; we only need to handle one data socket in the `run(data)` method. We do not have to worry about the ServerSocket or any of the other data sockets. When the `run(data)` method is called, it is running in its own thread with its own copy of the TCP-Server object. All the details of the ServerSocket and the other data sockets are hidden from this instance of the TCPServer class.

Once we have developed a specific version of the TCPServer class (in this case, the ServerHandler class), we create an instance of the class and start the server. An example usage of the ServerHandler class is as follows:

```
import java.net.*;
import java.io.*;

public class MyServer {
    public static void main(String args[]) throws Exception {
        TCPServer serv = new ServerHandler();

        serv.startServer(300);
    }
}
```

Using this ServerHandler class is simple. We just need to instantiate a TCPServer object and call its startServer() method. Since the ServerHandler object is also a TCPServer object, it behaves just like a TCPServer object; the only difference is that each data socket will have code that is specific to the ServerHandler class executed on its behalf.

The TCPServer Class and Applets

In our usage of the TCPServer class, we have implemented a standalone application whose purpose is to provide a service. This service is available to clients that are either applications or applets (or programs written in any language).

There are few cases imaginable where an applet should provide a network service. The purpose of an applet is to be downloaded to a browser and provide a service to the user. This service is on-demand and may be stopped at any time. There is no service that can be provided in this temporary environment that is useful to other clients on the network.

What other threading issues, most notably synchronization issues, are we concerned with in our TCPServer class? Basically, there are no issues we have not already seen. The startServer() and stopServer() methods are synchronized because they examine common instance variables that may change. The run() method does not have to be synchronized because the startServer() method is written to guarantee that the run() method is called only once.

Since all the calls to the run() method in each connection are done in a clone() of the TCPServer object, there is no reason to synchronize the data socket threads because they will be changing and examining different instances of the TCP-Server class. The separate threads that handle the data sockets are not sharing data and hence do not need to be synchronized. And if the ServerHandler class needed to share data, then the synchronization that would be done would be in the ServerHandler or one of its supporting classes.

In this example, we used the Runnable interface technique. Could we have derived from the Thread class directly instead of using the Runnable interface? Yes, we could have. However, using the Runnable interface makes it possible for the TCPServer class to start another thread with a clone of itself. Deriving from the Thread class requires a different implementation. This implementation probably requires that a new TCPServer class be instantiated instead of simply cloned.

We are not keeping a reference of the "data socket" thread objects anywhere; is this a problem? It is not a problem. As noted earlier, the threading system keeps an internal reference to every active thread in the system. As long as the stop() method has not been called on the thread or the run() method has not completed, the thread is considered active, and a reference is kept somewhere in the threading system. While removing all references to a thread object prevents the TCPServer from arranging for this data socket thread to terminate, the garbage collector cannot act on the thread object because the thread system still has a reference to it.

Have you noticed that it is difficult to tell that the ServerHandler class and the MyServer class are threaded? This is the goal that we have been trying to achieve. Threads are a tool, and the threading system is a service. In the end, the classes we create are designed to accomplish a task. This class, if designed correctly, does not need to show what tools it is using. Our ServerHandler class just needs to specify code that will handle one data socket, and the MyServer class just needs to start the ServerHandler service. All the threading stuff is just implementation detail. This concept shouldn't be that surprising: it's one of the benefits of object-oriented programming.

The AsyncInputStream Class

The AsyncReadSocket class we previously developed had a few problems:

- This class is specific to the network socket. We could also use an asynchronous I/O class for files, pipes, or any data stream. Ideally, we should have the ability to allow any data source to be asynchronous, not just network sockets.

  There is already a class structure for input from a stream. The top of this hierarchy is the InputStream class. Ideally, we should subclass the InputStream class. We can also benefit from the nested support of the FilterInputStream class and its subclasses.

- Unlike the TCPServer class, the AsyncReadSocket class does not do a good job at hiding the threading details.

Do we need to develop a new class for this? Doesn't the InputStream class have a method that supports asynchronous I/O? Although barely mentioned during the development of the AsyncReadSocket class, the InputStream class has the available() method that returns the number of bytes that can be read from the stream without blocking. Although this method sounds useful, it does not always suit our purposes because this method returns the number of bytes that have already been read and are available for processing. On some operating systems, this may include data that has been received at the machine and is being held by the operating system, but that's not universally true (though it is true on most common operating systems, including those from Microsoft, Apple, Sun, and other Unix vendors).

Hence, just because the `available()` method returns 0 does not indicate that a call to the `read()` method will block. Since avoiding calls that block is our primary purpose in developing this class, the `available()` method may not be suitable for our purpose.

In addition, we can usually benefit somewhat by buffering data within our program rather than relying on the data being buffered by the operating system. If we read this data from the operating system into our program while the program is otherwise unoccupied (when the user is thinking, for example), then the data will be available slightly faster to the program when it attempts to read the input stream, since the data has already been moved from the operating system into the program.

So what we need is an InputStream class whose `available()` method reports the correct number of bytes that can be actually read without blocking as well as buffering data within the program itself. This new class, the AsyncInputStream class, will be implemented just like our AsyncReadSocket class. It creates another thread that reads from the input stream. Since reading is done in another thread, the `read()` method is free to block if data is not available. Users of our AsyncInput-Stream class simply believe that we are an InputStream object. As shown in Figure 5-3, we are actually deriving from the FilterInputStream class, which is the base class for InputStream classes that contains InputStream instances.

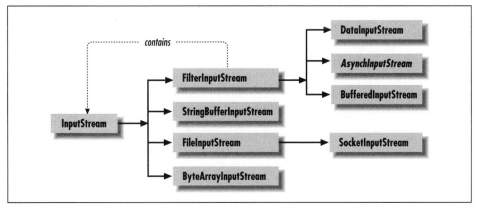

Figure 5-3. The Java InputStream class hierarchy

The fact that we start another thread to read the data is an implementation detail. Before we examine the policies and other details of our AsyncInputStream class, let's examine the AsyncInputStream class itself:

```java
import java.net.*;
import java.io.*;

public class AsyncInputStream extends FilterInputStream
                              implements Runnable {
    private Thread runner;              // Async reader thread
    private volatile byte result[];     // Buffer
    private volatile int reslen;        // Buffer length
    private volatile boolean EOF;       // End-of-file indicator
    private volatile IOException IOError; // I/O exceptions

    BusyFlag lock;                      // Data lock
    CondVar empty, full;                // Signal variables

    protected AsyncInputStream(InputStream in, int bufsize) {
        super(in);

        lock = new BusyFlag();          // Allocate sync variables.
        empty = new CondVar(lock);
        full = new CondVar(lock);

        result = new byte[bufsize];     // Allocate storage area
        reslen = 0;                     // and initialize variables.
        EOF = false;
        IOError = null;
        runner = new Thread(this);      // Start reader thread.
        runner.start();
    }

    protected AsyncInputStream(InputStream in) {
        this(in, 1024);
    }

    public int read() throws IOException {
        try {
            lock.getBusyFlag();
            while (reslen == 0) {
                try {
                    if (EOF) return(-1);
                    if (IOError != null) throw IOError;
                    empty.cvWait();
                } catch (InterruptedException e) {}
            }
            return (int) getChar();
        } finally {
```

```
                lock.freeBusyFlag();
        }
}

public int read(byte b[]) throws IOException {
    return read(b, 0, b.length);
}

public int read(byte b[], int off, int len) throws IOException {
    try {
        lock.getBusyFlag();
        while (reslen == 0) {
            try {
                if (EOF) return(-1);
                if (IOError != null) throw IOError;
                empty.cvWait();
            } catch (InterruptedException e) {}
        }

        int sizeread = Math.min(reslen, len);
        byte c[] = getChars(sizeread);
        System.arraycopy(c, 0, b, off, sizeread);
        return(sizeread);
    } finally {
        lock.freeBusyFlag();
    }
}

public long skip(long n) throws IOException {
    try {
        lock.getBusyFlag();
        int sizeskip = Math.min(reslen, (int) n);
        if (sizeskip > 0) {
            byte c[] = getChars(sizeskip);
        }
        return((long)sizeskip);
    } finally {
        lock.freeBusyFlag();
    }
}

public int available() throws IOException {
    return reslen;
}

public void close() throws IOException {
    try {
        lock.getBusyFlag();
        reslen = 0;                          // Clear buffer.
```

```
              EOF = true;                    // Mark end of file.
              empty.cvBroadcast();           // Alert all threads.
              full.cvBroadcast();
          } finally {
              lock.freeBusyFlag();
          }
      }

  public void mark(int readlimit) {
  }

  public void reset() throws IOException {
  }

  public boolean markSupported() {
      return false;
  }

  public void run() {
      try {
          while (true) {
              int c = in.read();
              try {
                  lock.getBusyFlag();
                  if ((c == -1) || (EOF)) {
                      EOF = true;             // Mark end of file.
                      in.close();             // Close input source.
                      return;                 // End I/O thread.
                  } else {
                      putChar((byte)c);       // Store the byte read.
                  }
                  if (EOF) {
                      in.close();             // Close input source.
                      return;                 // End I/O thread.
                  }
              } finally {
                  lock.freeBusyFlag();
              }
          }

      } catch (IOException e) {
          IOError = e;                        // Store exception.
          return;
      } finally {
          try {
              lock.getBusyFlag();
              empty.cvBroadcast();            // Alert all threads.
          } finally {
              lock.freeBusyFlag();
```

```
            }
        }
    }

    private void putChar(byte c) {
        try {
            lock.getBusyFlag();
            while ((reslen == result.length) && (!EOF)) {
                try {
                    full.cvWait();
                } catch (InterruptedException ie) {}
            }
            if (!EOF) {
                result[reslen++] = c;
                empty.cvSignal();
            }
        } finally {
            lock.freeBusyFlag();
        }
    }

    private byte getChar() {
        try {
            lock.getBusyFlag();
            byte c = result[0];
            System.arraycopy(result, 1, result, 0, --reslen);
            full.cvSignal();
            return c;
        } finally {
            lock.freeBusyFlag();
        }
    }

    private byte[] getChars(int chars) {
        try {
            lock.getBusyFlag();
            byte c[] = new byte[chars];
            System.arraycopy(result, 0, c, 0, chars);
            reslen -= chars;
            System.arraycopy(result, chars, result, 0, reslen);
            full.cvSignal();
            return c;
        } finally {
            lock.freeBusyFlag();
        }
    }
}
```

For our purposes, we aren't interested in the details of threading the I/O itself; there is no threading code in this class that we have not already seen in the Async-ReadSocket class. The new thread simply does a blocking read on the Input-Stream, and methods are provided so that the original thread can get the data in a nonblocking manner. The InputStream aspect of this class is interesting, but learning the Java data input system is not within the scope of this book.

Why is the discussion of this class important? And how is this class different from the Async-ReadSocket class? Although this class accomplishes the asynchronous read in the same fashion as the AsyncReadSocket class, it is also a FilterInputStream, and it is the relationship between the threaded I/O and the InputStream class that we are concerned with here. Since this class must behave as an InputStream, we cannot design the behavior of the class as optimally as if all we had been concerned with was communicating with the I/O thread. This is the sort of real-world trade-off that must be made when implementing threaded classes.

In order for the class to function correctly, we need to use practically every synchronization technique that we know. Let's start with a look at the instance variables and constructors of the AsyncInputStream class:

```
public class AsyncInputStream extends FilterInputStream
                        implements Runnable {
    private Thread runner;                    // Async reader thread
    private volatile byte result[];           // Buffer
    private volatile int reslen;              // Buffer length
    private volatile boolean EOF;             // End-of-file indicator
    private volatile IOException IOError;     // I/O Exceptions

    BusyFlag lock;                    // Data lock
    CondVar empty, full;              // Signal variables

    protected AsyncInputStream(InputStream in, int bufsize) {
        super(in);

        lock = new BusyFlag();        // Allocate sync variables.
        empty = new CondVar(lock);
        full = new CondVar(lock);

        result = new byte[bufsize];   // Allocate storage area
        reslen = 0;                   // and initialize variables.
        EOF = false;
        IOError = null;
        runner = new Thread(this);    // Start reader thread.
        runner.start();
    }

    protected AsyncInputStream(InputStream in) {
        this(in, 1024);
    }
```

The first three instance variables, `runner`, `result`, and `reslen`, are the important data of the class. `runner` is the reference to the I/O thread that is started by this class, and `result` and `reslen` are the data storage and the length that is being passed back from the I/O thread. This is an important difference from the AsyncReadSocket class, which did not support the concept of data size: the `getResult()` method of the AsyncReadSocket class did not allow the caller to specify the amount to read. Since an InputStream class can read any amount of data, we must keep track of available data in the buffers.

The `EOF` and `IOError` instance variables are also used for communication. In order to behave as an InputStream class, we must report end-of-file (EOF) conditions and throw exceptions on I/O errors. These EOF conditions and I/O exceptions are generated from the InputStream object contained in the AsyncInputStream class. We must save the EOF condition and catch the I/O exception in the I/O thread, and later indicate the EOF condition or throw the exception in the calling thread. If the AsyncInputStream class did not have to behave like an InputStream class, we could have designed a simpler error reporting system.

Data in the `result` buffer is protected by the `lock` instance variable, and we have associated two condition variables with the lock: the `empty` and `full` condition variables. This is an instance of the buffer management that we discussed with the CondVar class: we can have threads waiting on a single lock for two different conditions.

The first constructor of the AsyncInputStream class is straightforward. First, we just allocate and initialize the buffer and variables we will use to communicate with the I/O thread. Second, we instantiate and `start()` the I/O thread. The other constructor has the same signature as the FilterInputStream class, from which we inherit, and uses a default buffer size. By providing this constructor, we are behaving like all FilterInputStreams.

Let's start to look into the details of how data is passed back to the user:

```java
public int read() throws IOException {
    try {
        lock.getBusyFlag();
        while (reslen == 0) {
            try {
                if (EOF) return(-1);
                if (IOError != null) throw IOError;
                empty.cvWait();
            } catch (InterruptedException e) {}
        }
        return (int) getChar();
    } finally {
        lock.freeBusyFlag();
    }
}
```

```
    }

    private byte getChar() {
        try {
            lock.getBusyFlag();
            byte c = result[0];
            System.arraycopy(result, 1, result, 0, --reslen);
            full.cvSignal();
            return c;
        } finally {
            lock.freeBusyFlag();
        }
    }
```

In the InputStream class, the read() method reads a single byte from the input data stream. If an EOF is detected or an IOException is caught by the I/O thread, it would be placed in the EOF or IOError instance variables, respectively. The read() method returns a −1 to report an EOF or throws the IOException on behalf of the I/O thread.

The InputStream and the End of File

Obviously, in the case of the FileInputStream, the end-of-file indicator is reported when a read past the EOF is detected. But what does this indicator mean for other data sources?

The EOF can be caused by a number of reasons, such as the StringBufferInputStream reporting the end of the string, the ByteArrayInputStream reporting the end of the array, or the SocketInputStream reporting the closure of the network connection.

In any case, we should just use the indicator as the termination of any more data from the source and act appropriately. We should not be concerned with what the actual data source is.

Also, we check for the EOF and the I/O exception only when there is no more data in the buffer. Since the I/O thread is reading ahead, we must delay the EOF indicator or throw the exception in the read() method until the user has drained the input from the buffer: the user should see the EOF or exception at the same point in the data it actually occurred. The I/O thread stops reading when it receives either an EOF or an IOException, so we can safely assume all data in the buffer occurred before either condition happened.

Finally, in order to protect the result data buffer and the reslen length indicator, we use the lock BusyFlag. The getChar() method, which returns the next character, also uses this BusyFlag. You might ask why we are only using a single lock to protect four different instance variables. This is a design issue; the `result` and `reslen` variables are related, and it is unlikely that we would be examining or changing one without the other. The `EOF` and `IOError` variables are accessed only once during the lifetime of the I/O thread. It is wasteful to create a new BusyFlag for this purpose when a suitable lock is already available.

What happens when we do not have data available when a read is requested? The `read()` method must behave correctly if the application calls the method when data is not available. This means that the `read()` method must block under such conditions. In other words, the `read()` method must do what it was designed to avoid in the first place:

```
public int read() throws IOException {
    try {
        lock.getBusyFlag();
        while (reslen == 0) {
            try {
                if (EOF) return(-1);
                if (IOError != null) throw IOError;
                empty.cvWait();
            } catch (InterruptedException e) {}
        }
        return (int) getChar();
    } finally {
        lock.freeBusyFlag();
    }
}

private void putChar(byte c) {
    try {
        lock.getBusyFlag();
        while ((reslen == result.length) && (!EOF)) {
            try {
                full.cvWait();
            } catch (InterruptedException ie) {}
        }
        if (!EOF) {
            result[reslen++] = c;
            empty.cvSignal();
        }
    } finally {
        lock.freeBusyFlag();
    }
}
```

Obviously, the `read()` method cannot block by reading from the InputStream; the InputStream is under the control of the I/O thread and should not be accessed directly by the `read()` method. In order to simulate this blocking, we use the empty condition variable. The read() method simply waits for more data to arrive. When data arrives in the I/O thread, a signal is generated when the data is placed in the buffer. This is done by calling the cvSignal() method in the putChar() method. As can be seen by examining the run() method, the putChar() method is called by the I/O thread to place the data it receives in the data buffer:

```
public void run() {
    try {
        while (true) {
            int c = in.read();
            try {
                lock.getBusyFlag();
                if ((c == -1) || (EOF)) {
                    EOF = true;              // Mark end of file.
                    in.close();              // Close input source.
                    return;                  // End I/O thread.
                } else {
                    putChar((byte)c);        // Store the byte read.
                }
                if (EOF) {
                    in.close();              // Close input source.
                    return;                  // End I/O thread.
                }
            } finally {
                lock.freeBusyFlag();
            }
        }
    } catch (IOException e) {
        IOError = e;                         // Store exception.
        return;
    } finally {
        try {
            lock.getBusyFlag();
            empty.cvBroadcast();             // Alert all threads.
        } finally {
            lock.freeBusyFlag();
        }
    }
}
```

The code for the I/O thread is similar to the code in our AsyncReadSocket class. We simply read from the InputStream, blocking if necessary. When we receive data, we place it in the buffer using the putChar() method. Additionally, if we receive an EOF indicator or catch an IOException, we place that information into the appropriate instance variables. To allow all of these actions to take place safely with the other threads, we grab the same lock that is used by the read thread: the lock BusyFlag.

What will happen to all the blocking read threads when an EOF or IOException condition occurs? As we mentioned, we are using a condition variable to cause the `read()` method to behave in a blocking manner. However, when an EOF or IOException condition occurs, there can be no more future notifications, since no more data will be arriving. To solve this, we must use the `cvBroadcast()` method when these conditions occur. The threads can just wake up in turn, taking the available data from the buffer:

```
public void run() {
    try {
        while (true) {
            int c = in.read();
            try {
                lock.getBusyFlag();
                if ((c == -1) || (EOF)) {
                    EOF = true;              // Mark end of file.
                    in.close();              // Close input source.
                    return;                  // End I/O thread.
                } else {
                    putChar((byte)c);        // Store the byte read.
                }
                if (EOF) {
                    in.close();              // Close input source.
                    return;                  // End I/O thread.
                }
            } finally {
                lock.freeBusyFlag();
            }
        }

    } catch (IOException e) {
        IOError = e;                         // Store exception.
        return;
    } finally {
        try {
            lock.getBusyFlag();
            empty.cvBroadcast();             // Alert all threads.
        } finally {
            lock.freeBusyFlag();
        }
    }
}

public void close() throws IOException {
    try {
        lock.getBusyFlag();
        reslen = 0;                          // Clear buffer.
        EOF = true;                          // Mark end of file.
        empty.cvBroadcast();                 // Alert all threads.
```

```
                    full.cvBroadcast();
            } finally {
                lock.freeBusyFlag();
            }
        }
```

When no more data is available from the buffer, the remaining threads reading the InputStream return the EOF or IOError condition from their read() methods. We also do not have to worry about future read() method calls; they simply return the EOF or IOError condition that occurred.

The implementation of the available() method that works as desired—the method that was the reason for our AsyncInputStream class—is actually anticlimactic:

```
public int available() throws IOException {
    return reslen;
}
```

We simply return the number of bytes we have available in the buffer. Since the I/O thread is actually reading the InputStream, blocking if necessary, we know that there are usually no more bytes sitting on the network that are unaccounted for. There is, however, a maximum amount of data that is held by the buffer (which is user configurable), so that it's possible that the buffer could be full and data could be held in the network buffers as well.

Finally, we made three additional design decisions during the development of the AsyncInputStream class. While these decisions are important to the AsyncInput-Stream class, they will not be examined here, because they don't pertain to our discussion of threading issues. But to be complete, here is a brief overview:

- The read(byte[]) method, just like the read() method, blocks if data is not available. However, if data is available, but not enough to fill the byte array, the read(byte[]) method simply reads less than requested, returning the number of bytes actually read. We have chosen this implementation due to the design of the AsyncInputStream class: it works asynchronously, and this implementation best fulfills that design spirit.

- The skip() method skips only the number of bytes possible without blocking. This means that if the skip() method is called to skip more bytes than are available, it simply skips what is available and returns the number of bytes actually skipped. Again, this implementation best fulfills the design spirit of the AsyncInputStream class.

- The mark and reset feature of the AsyncInputStream class is not supported, even if this feature is supported in the InputStream class that we contain. There's no real reason why an asynchronous stream would support this, and if users really require this feature, they can always instantiate a BufferedInput-Stream object containing our AsyncInputStream object.

The AsyncOutputStream Class?

One of the main reasons we never implemented an AsyncWriteSocket class is usability. With data being buffered at so many places between the two ends of a network connection, there is less reason to worry about blocking for a long time during a `write()` call. However, although it's a rare case, it is possible for a `write()` method to block.

In the case of an AsyncOutputStream class, there is another complication: I/O exceptions that are thrown by the `write()` method of the contained OutputStream cannot be delivered correctly. The call to the AsyncOutputStream's `write()` method would have long since returned. This could be handled by throwing the exception on a later call to the `write()` method or on a call to the `close()` method. That's not a perfect solution, but it's common in cases where data that is written is buffered.

Those developers who want truly robust programs that write data asynchronously may consider implementing their own AsyncOutputStream based on the AsyncInputStream we've shown here.

Why did we use two condition variables rather than the wait and notify mechanism? We did this for efficiency. Here is a case where we have a single data source (the `result` buffer) that can have two conditions: it can be empty, in which case threads attempting to read must wait for data, or it can be full, in which case threads attempting to store data into the buffer must wait for it to be partially emptied. If we had relied on the wait and notify mechanism, then whenever either condition occurred we would have had to call the `notifyAll()` method, which would have woken up too many threads. This would have worked, since all threads recheck the condition when they wake up, but it is not as efficient as using the condition variables.

Instances of the AsyncInputStream class behave like any InputStream object. They can be used in cases where an InputStream object is normally used with no changes. While the AsyncInputStream class is also a Runnable type, that is just an implementation detail. Users of the AsyncInputStream class should not even know that a new thread has been started on their behalf when an AsyncInputStream object is instantiated.

Using TCPServer with AsyncInputStreams

Let's modify our ServerHandler class to read requests from clients in an asynchronous manner:

```
import java.net.*;
import java.io.*;
```

```
public class ServerHandler extends TCPServer {
    public void run(Socket data) {
        try {
            InputStream is =
                new AsyncInputStream(data.getInputStream());
            OutputStream os = data.getOutputStream();

            // Process the data socket here.
        } catch (Exception e) {}
    }
}
```

With a single line change to our ServerHandler class, we are now reading from the client in an asynchronous manner. We also practically doubled the number of threads started to provide this service. But from examining the source code, there is no indication that even one thread is started, much less two threads per client connected (plus an additional thread to handle the accept() method).

Summary

In this chapter, we have taken a look at some real examples of threads in action along with the issues of their synchronization. As we started to do in the previous chapter, we are now using threads simply as an implementation tool. We have started new threads and communicated between these threads, but users of our classes are not concerned with and may not even know that these threads exist.

We have also examined synchronization issues in cases where we have not started any threads at all. A simple item like a container class must be designed with threading in mind. This is because, although we may not start any threads, we are already threaded in our program. We must think of threading as not only an implementation detail in our classes, but also in all other classes in the system. Threading issues like deadlock and race conditions should always be involved in our class designs, whether or not we actually use threads in our classes at all.

6

Java Thread Scheduling

At this point, we've covered the fundamental aspects of Java's threading system and are able to write quite complex programs that exploit Java's threads to complete their tasks. We're now going to move into some of the specialized areas of threaded systems. The programming issues and techniques that we'll explore in the next few chapters of this book are not issues you'll grapple with every day, but when the need arises to have some explicit control over the behavior of your threads, these issues become very important.

To begin, in this chapter we'll look into the topic of thread scheduling. In most Java programs, there are more threads than there are CPUs on the machine that is hosting the program. Since each CPU is capable of running only one thread at a time, not all threads in your program will be running at any given instant. Determining which of the many threads in your program is running at any one time is the topic of Java thread scheduling.

The key to understanding Java thread scheduling is to realize that a CPU is a scarce resource. When there are two or more threads that want to run on a single-processor machine, they end up competing for the CPU, and it's up to someone—either the programmer, the Java virtual machine, or the operating system—to make sure that the CPU is shared between these threads. The same is true whenever there are more threads in a program than there are CPUs on the machine hosting the program. So the essence of this chapter is how to share CPUs between threads that want to access them.

In the earlier examples, we didn't concern ourselves with this topic because, in those cases, the details of thread scheduling weren't important to us. This was because the threads we were concerned with didn't normally compete for a CPU: they had specific tasks to do, but the threads themselves were usually short-lived or only periodically needed a CPU in order to accomplish their task. Consider the thread that is created automatically for you when you call the getImage() method to load an image. Most of the time, this thread isn't using a CPU because it's waiting for data to arrive over the network. When a burst of data does arrive, this thread quickly processes the data and then goes back and waits for more data; since the thread doesn't need a CPU very often, there was never a need to concern ourselves with the Java virtual machine's scheduling mechanism.

The topic of thread scheduling is a difficult one to address because the Java specification does not require implementations of the Java virtual machine to schedule threads in a particular manner. There are guidelines in the specification that are based on a particular thread's priority, but the guidelines are not absolute, and different implementations of the Java virtual machine follow these guidelines differently. In addition, some of the methods of the Thread class that are used to affect thread scheduling, namely the suspend() and resume() methods, have been deprecated beginning in Java 2 (and should really be avoided in all releases of Java). As a result, we cannot absolutely guarantee the order of execution of threads across all Java virtual machines.

The amount of time that we will spend on this topic is out of proportion to its relevance. This is surprising to many people, especially those to whom thread programming is a new topic, but the fact is that there are only rare times when we need to use the techniques of this chapter to affect the scheduling of Java threads. For the most part, we need to worry about how Java threads are scheduled only when one or more of the threads is CPU intensive over a relatively long period of time. The image-loading threads we mentioned earlier, for example, are CPU intensive, but only for short periods of time, and so we are not concerned about how those threads are scheduled.

An Overview of Thread Scheduling

We'll start by looking at the basic principles of how threads are scheduled. Any particular virtual machine may not follow these principles exactly, but these principles will form the basis for our understanding of thread scheduling.

Let's start by looking at an example with some CPU-intensive threads. What is the output of the following program?

```
class TestThread extends Thread {
    String id;

    public TestThread(String s) {
        id = s;
```

Characterizing Programs

Computer programs—written in Java or otherwise—are typically categorized in one of three ways:

CPU intensive

> Programs that require many CPU cycles to complete their task. They use the CPU to perform mathematical or symbolic calculations (e.g., manipulation of strings or images) that require a significant amount of time, but need little or no input from the user or from an external data source.

I/O intensive

> Programs that spend the vast majority of their time waiting for I/O operations to complete: reading or writing files to disk, reading or writing data on a network socket, or communicating with another program.

Interactive

> Programs that perform operations in response to user input. When the user executes a particular action, the program enters a CPU-intensive or an I/O-intensive phase before returning to wait for the next command. The TCPServer we examined in Chapter 5 belongs to this category, though the interaction comes from other (client) programs rather than from user input.

A single program may go through phases that belong to all these categories.

```
    }

    public void doCalc(int i) {
        // Perform complex calculation based on i.
    }

    public void run() {
        int i;
        for (i = 0; i < 10; i++) {
            doCalc(i);
            System.out.println(id);
        }
    }
}

public class Test {
    public static void main(String args[]) {
        TestThread t1, t2, t3;
        t1 = new TestThread("Thread 1");
```

```
            t1.start();
            t2 = new TestThread("Thread 2");
            t2.start();
            t3 = new TestThread("Thread 3");
            t3.start();
        }
    }
```

Assume that the doCalc() method is computationally expensive, requiring three to five seconds per call, and that it makes no calls to any other methods. Clearly, after the program has completed, we'll have 10 lines of output that say "Thread 1," 10 lines that say "Thread 2," and 10 lines that say "Thread 3," but what will the order of those output lines be?

It's common to assume that these output lines will be in some random order, perhaps something like this:

```
        Thread 1
        Thread 2
        Thread 2
        Thread 3
        Thread 1
        Thread 2
        Thread 3
        Thread 3
```

and so on. But it turns out that Java doesn't specify how threads are scheduled—in specific, it doesn't require the kind of schedules that would produce random output. It's just as likely that we'll see 10 lines that say "Thread 1" followed by 10 lines that say "Thread 2" followed by 10 lines that say "Thread 3." The implication in that case is that our first thread (Thread 1) runs to completion before our second thread (Thread 2) ever starts, and that our second thread runs to completion before our third thread ever starts.

To understand what's going on here, we need to explore some of the internal aspects of the Java threading mechanism. At a conceptual level, every thread in the Java virtual machine can be in one of four states:

Initial

A thread object is in the initial state from the period when it is created (that is, when its constructor is called) until the start() method of the thread object is called.

Runnable

A thread is in the runnable state once its start() method has been called. There are various ways in which a thread leaves the runnable state, but the runnable state can be thought of as a default state: if a thread isn't in any other state, it's in the runnable state.

Blocked

> A thread that is blocked is one that cannot be run because it is waiting for some specific event to occur. A simple example is the case of a thread that has opened a socket to some remote data server and attempts to read data from that server when data is not available. Threads that are sleeping or waiting on an object lock are also considered blocked.

Exiting

> A thread is in the exiting state once its `run()` method returns or its `stop()` method has been called.

It's frequently the case that more than one thread in a Java program is in the runnable state. When that happens, one thread from the pool of runnable threads will be selected to become the *currently running thread*. All the other threads in the pool of runnable threads remain in the runnable state, even though they are actually waiting for a chance to run (that is, to become the currently running thread). So the key question is which of the threads from the pool of runnable threads will be selected to become the currently running thread.

It simplifies our discussion for the present to speak of one currently running thread. On a machine with multiple processors and certain implementations of the virtual machine, there may be more than one currently running thread—perhaps as many currently running threads as the machine has processors. The selection of each of those threads for a particular CPU still follows the same principles that we're discussing here.

Java implements what is known as a preemptive, priority-based scheduler among its various threads. This means that each thread in a Java program is assigned a certain priority, a positive integer that falls within a well-defined range. This priority can be changed only by the programmer. The Java virtual machine never changes the priority of a thread, even when a thread changes between any of the various states outlined earlier, or even after a thread has been running for a certain period of time. So a thread with a priority of 5 will maintain that priority from the time it is created through its various changes between the runnable and blocked states until the thread terminates and enters the exiting state.

This priority value is important, because the scheduling principle followed by the Java virtual machine is that the currently running thread will be the thread that has the highest priority among all the threads that are in the runnable state. That's what we mean when we say that Java implements a priority-based scheduler. The Java virtual machine implements this scheduling in a preemptive fashion, meaning that when a high-priority thread enters the runnable state, the Java virtual machine interrupts (preempts) whatever lower-priority thread is running at the time so that the higher-priority thread can become the currently running thread.

Scheduling Example: Threads of Different Priorities

An example should make this clearer. Let's look at the following (incomplete) code example:

```
public class SchedulingExample implements Runnable {
    public static void main(String args[]) {
        Thread calcThread = new Thread(this);
        calcThread.setPriority(4);
        calcThread.start();

        AsyncReadSocket reader;
        reader = new AsyncReadSocket(new Socket(host, port));
        reader.setPriority(6);
        reader.start();

        doDefault();
    }

    public void run() {
        doCalc();
    }
}
```

This Java program has three threads: first, there's the default thread executing the main() method, which, after creating the other threads, is going to execute the doDefault() method. Second, there's the calculation thread (calcThread) that is going to execute the doCalc() method. And third, there's the reader Async-ReadSocket thread (from Chapter 3) that's reading a socket.

In the following discussion, we assume the threads we created are the only threads in the Java virtual machine, but as we already know, there are many other threads that have been created on our behalf. For simplicity, we'll ignore those threads, since, for the most part, they'll remain in the blocked state and won't affect this discussion. Figure 6-1 shows the transition of the threads in our example between their various states.

We start at time T1 with our single default thread executing the main() method. The initial thread has a priority of 5 and is the only active thread in the Java virtual machine. So the default thread is in the runnable state and is also the currently running thread. At time T2, the default thread creates the calcThread, gives it a priority of 4, and calls its start() method. Now there are two threads in the runnable state, but the default thread is still the currently running thread because it has a higher priority than calcThread. calcThread is in the runnable state, but it is waiting for the CPU.

The default thread continues execution: it creates the reader thread, gives it a priority of 6, and then calls the thread's start() method. After the default thread

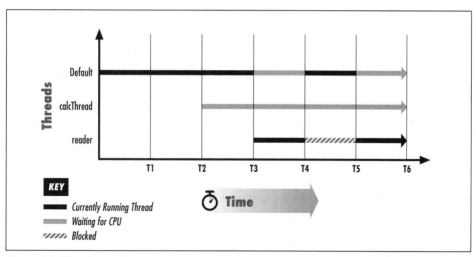

Figure 6-1. Thread state diagram

calls the reader thread's start() method, the reader thread enters the runnable state. Because reader has a higher priority than the default thread, reader becomes the currently running thread (at the expense of the default thread, which will no longer be running even though it's in the runnable state). These changes in the states of the threads are shown at time T3 in the diagram.

Now the reader thread executes the readChar() method on its socket. If no data is available, the reader thread enters the blocked state (shown at time T4). When this happens, the default thread begins execution from the point at which it was previously interrupted (in fact, the default thread will be completely unaware that it had been interrupted). The default thread continues to be the currently running thread until data becomes available to satisfy the readChar() method. When this data becomes available (at time T5), the Java virtual machine changes the state of the reader thread to the runnable state. When the Java virtual machine changes the state, it notices that this thread now has the highest priority of all the runnable threads, so it interrupts the default thread and makes the reader thread the currently running thread.

Meanwhile, calcThread has been patiently waiting for its chance to run, and it must continue to wait until both the default thread and the reader thread are blocked or have exited (or until some thread raises the priority of calcThread). calcThread is in danger of never becoming the currently running thread at all, a concept known as *CPU starvation*. In general, it is the responsibility of Java developers to ensure that none of the threads in their Java programs starve; the Java virtual machine never adjusts any thread's priority to compensate for that thread's lack of availability to the CPU (though some underlying operating systems may do so).

Scheduling Equal-Priority Threads

In most Java programs, we'll have multiple threads of the same priority; we need to expand our discussion to take this into account. What follows is a description of what happens at a conceptual level within the Java virtual machine. Once again, our intent here is to provide an illustration of how the thread scheduling within the Java virtual machine works, not to provide a blueprint of how any particular Java virtual machine is actually implemented.

We can conceive that the Java virtual machine keeps track of all the threads in a Java program by means of linked lists; every thread in the Java virtual machine is on a list that represents the state of that thread. A thread can have any one of eleven priorities, so we conceive of fourteen linked lists: one for all threads in the initial state, one for all threads in the blocked state, one for all threads in the exiting state, and one for each priority level. The list of threads at a given priority level represents only those threads that are currently in the runnable state: a thread in the runnable state at priority 7 will be on the priority 7 list, but when the thread blocks, it moves to the blocked linked list.

For simplicity, we conceive of these threads as being on an ordered list; in reality, they may be held in simple pools. Keeping the threads in a linked list implies that there is an order by which the threads will be selected to become the currently running thread, and while that is a useful way of thinking about the process, it is not necessarily the way an implementation may work.

Let's revisit our last example and this time change the priority of calcThread so that it is now the same as the default thread. If these two threads have the same priority, then our state diagram might look like Figure 6-2. Note that in the figure, we now start at time T2, since that's when things become interesting.

The difference now is that the default thread and calcThread have the same priority, so that when the reader thread blocks, the Java virtual machine does something different to select the currently running thread. In this example, we're concerned with only three of Java's internal lists: the list of priority 5 threads (the default thread and calcThread), the list of priority 6 threads (the reader thread), and the list of blocked threads. As the Java virtual machine enters time T2, when calcThread is started, those lists look like this:*

```
PRIORITY 5:  Default -> calcThread -> NULL
PRIORITY 6:  NULL
   BLOCKED:  NULL
```

---

* In these diagrams, the currently running thread is always the *last* thread on the highest priority, non-empty list: that thread was at the head of its list when it was selected to be the currently running thread, at which time it was also moved to the end of the list.

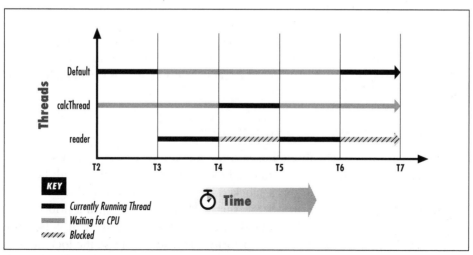

Figure 6-2. Thread state diagram for equal-priority threads

So the Java virtual machine selects the default thread to be the currently running thread since it is at the head of the non-empty list that has the highest priority. The Java virtual machine also alters the priority 5 list so that as it exits time T2; that list appears as:

```
PRIORITY 5:  calcThread -> Default -> NULL
```

At time T3, the default thread starts the reader thread, which will preempt the default thread. The Java virtual machine's internal lists now look like this:

```
PRIORITY 5:  calcThread -> Default -> NULL
PRIORITY 6:  reader -> NULL
  BLOCKED:   NULL
```

At T4 when the reader thread enters the blocked state, the Java virtual machine searches for a non-empty priority list and finds one at priority 5; the first thread in that list (calcThread) becomes the currently running thread and gets moved to the end of the list. So exiting time T4, the internal lists now look like this:

```
PRIORITY 5:  Default -> calcThread -> NULL
PRIORITY 6:  NULL
  BLOCKED:   reader -> NULL
```

And so we continue: every time the reader thread enters the blocked state, the default thread and calcThread change positions on the priority 5 list, and they alternate becoming the currently running thread.

In this example, we've posited the notion that when a thread is made the currently runnable thread, it is moved to the end of the list. As a result, every time the reader thread blocks, a different thread from the priority 5 list will become the currently running thread. While this is by far the most common implementation of the Java virtual machine, it is not a requirement: we know of one particular real-time operating system in which threads that are interrupted are not reordered as they are in this discussion. On that implementation (and any like it), the `calcThread` and `reader` thread would execute alternately and the default thread would starve.

Priority Inversion and Inheritance

In a typical priority-based threading system, something unusual occurs when a thread attempts to acquire a lock that is held by a lower-priority thread: because the higher-priority thread becomes blocked, it temporarily runs with an effective priority of the lower-priority thread. Say that we have a thread with a priority of 8 that wants to acquire a lock that is held by a thread with a priority of 2. Because the priority 8 thread is waiting for the priority 2 thread to release the lock, it ends up running with an effective priority of 2. This is known as *priority inversion.*

Priority inversion is often solved by *priority inheritance.* With priority inheritance, a thread that holds a lock that is wanted by a thread with a higher priority will have its priority temporarily and silently raised; its new priority becomes the same as the priority of the thread that it is causing to block. When the thread releases the lock, its priority is lowered to its original value.

Let's look at an example. Say that we have three threads: Thread2, Thread5, and Thread8, which have priorities, respectively, of 2, 5, and 8. We'll start at the point where Thread2 is the currently running thread, and the other threads are therefore blocked:

```
PRIORITY 2:   Thread2 -> NULL
PRIORITY 5:   NULL
PRIORITY 8:   NULL
   BLOCKED:   Thread5 -> Thread8 -> NULL
```

At this point in time, Thread2 has obtained a lock, but since no other thread wants the lock, its priority is not changed. Now, say that Thread5 unblocks; it will become the currently running thread:

```
PRIORITY 2:   Thread2 -> NULL
PRIORITY 5:   Thread5 -> NULL
PRIORITY 8:   NULL
   BLOCKED:   Thread8 -> NULL
```

Now, when Thread8 unblocks it will become the currently running thread. If it then attempts to acquire the lock held by Thread2, it will again block, but the priority of Thread2 will be adjusted to 8:

```
PRIORITY 2:   NULL
PRIORITY 5:   Thread5 -> NULL
```

```
PRIORITY 8:   Thread2 -> NULL
  BLOCKED:    Thread8 -> NULL
```

So Thread2 will be selected as the currently running thread, even though its programmed priority is lower than another runnable thread. When Thread2 releases its lock, its priority will be changed back to 2, and Thread8 will unblock (since the lock it was waiting for is no longer held):

```
PRIORITY 2:   Thread2 -> NULL
PRIORITY 5:   Thread5 -> NULL
PRIORITY 8:   Thread8-> NULL
  BLOCKED:    NULL
```

And, predictably, Thread8 will become the currently running thread.

The goal of priority inheritance is to allow the high-priority thread to run as soon as possible. If the inheritance did not occur in the above example, then Thread8 would have to wait until Thread5 blocked or exited before Thread2 could run and give up its lock. This would give Thread8 (temporarily) an equivalent priority of 2. Priority inheritance changes that scenario in favor of the higher-priority thread.

Priority inheritance is a common, but not mandatory, feature of Java virtual machines.

Round-Robin Scheduling

In our previous example, there was never a time when the calcThread and the default thread switched places on their priority queue without the reader thread intervening. Stated another way, the calcThread never preempts the default thread, and vice versa. This is confusing to many people, who assume that preemptive means that threads of the same priority will timeslice—that is, that they will periodically preempt each other.

The case in which threads of the same priority preempt each other is referred to as *round-robin scheduling* and is one of the more contentious aspects of Java thread scheduling. Nothing in the Java language specification requires a virtual machine to employ round-robin scheduling, but nothing prevents a virtual machine from implementing it either. Because of their ties to the operating system, many implementations of the virtual machine do employ round-robin scheduling, but many—especially on non-Windows platforms—do not.

This introduces a level of non-deterministic behavior into our discussion. On a platform that performs round-robin scheduling, threads of equal priority will periodically yield to each other. This process follows the same ideas we outlined above: the thread is selected to run and moves to the end of its priority queue. The presence of round-robin scheduling, however, means that periodically an internal timer will go off, which will interrupt the currently running thread and cause the next thread on the priority queue to become the currently running thread. But on a platform without round-robin scheduling, the currently running thread will continue to run until it blocks or until a higher-priority thread is able to run.

Threading Models

The absence or presence of priority inheritance or of round-robin scheduling among threads of equal priority is only one difference that exists between the scheduling of threads on different implementations of the Java virtual machine. These differences exist because the Java language specification has very little to say about thread scheduling, and different implementations have therefore leveraged the features of the host platform to provide support for Java threads.

In the very early days of Java, priority-based thread scheduling was thought to be absolute: the highest-priority runnable thread would always be the currently running thread. Many Java programming books (including the first release of this book) based their discussions of thread programming on that premise. The new version of the Java specification, however, says only this about thread scheduling: "Threads with higher priority are generally executed in preference to threads with lower priority. Such preference is not, however, a guarantee that the highest priority thread will always be running, and thread priorities cannot be used to reliably implement mutual exclusion."*

This clarification is an admission of how things work in the real world. Some operating systems cannot tell exactly when a blocked thread becomes runnable, and so there may be a small amount of time between when a high-priority blocked thread becomes runnable and when it actually becomes the currently running thread. In practice, that difference is rarely important, because you can't predict absolutely when a thread will become unblocked anyway. If there's a slight delay between when data arrives on a socket and when the thread reading the socket is unblocked, your program won't know; it will simply assume that the data was delayed slightly longer than it was. Java is not, after all, a real-time operating system.

More important, however, is that many implementations of the Java virtual machine now allow Java threads to be scheduled directly by the operating system rather than by the virtual machine itself. And while operating systems can generally follow the principle of priority-based scheduling that we've outlined here, they usually add some additional complexity to thread scheduling that affects the simple notion that we've outlined.

---

* *The Java Language Specification*, p. 415 (Addison-Wesley, 1996).

Hence, understanding how Java threads are ultimately scheduled requires an understanding of the particular virtual machine involved. There are two basic variations here:

The green-thread model

> In the green-thread model, the threads are scheduled by the virtual machine itself. That model—the original model for Java virtual machines—most closely follows the idealized priority-based scheduling that we've outlined here.

The native-thread model

> In this model, the threads are scheduled by the operating system that is hosting the virtual machine. Because of the variations in operating systems, this model leads to a number of subtle differences in the scheduling of Java threads, although they will all generally follow the model that we've discussed here.

Later in this chapter, we'll discuss the implementations of these thread models on several platforms and the subtle differences between these implementations with respect to thread scheduling.

When Scheduling Is Important

If the details of thread scheduling seem somewhat esoteric, here's the good news: most of the time, all the scheduling details in this chapter have no practical impact on your Java program. This is true, in general, of threaded programs under any operating system and with any threading library, but it's particularly true in the case of Java programs.

In a Java program, a thread is most often created because the programmer wants to call a method that may block—usually a `read()` method on a slow Input-Stream (such as a SocketInputStream), or the `Thread.sleep()` method to emulate a periodic timer, or the `wait()` method to wait for a particular event. As a result, threads in the Java virtual machine tend to oscillate between the blocked and runnable states quite often. And as long as every thread in the Java virtual machine blocks periodically, they will all get an opportunity to run: each thread becomes the currently running thread, blocks, exits the blocked state, is placed on the end of the list for its priority, and moves up through the list as other threads go through the same cycle.

Even in those cases where all the threads in the virtual machine do not periodically block, it's usually possible to ignore the issue of scheduling altogether. A Java program usually performs a specific task, and often the completion of that task is all that matters. A Java program that is charged with calculating and displaying four convolutions of a GIF image has to wait for all four convoluted images to be complete before it displays the final image. It's more convenient to program this so that each convolution is performed in a separate thread, but it will take the same amount of time to calculate all four convolutions whether each thread calculates its image sequentially or whether there's some sort of round-robin scheduling among the four threads. When the task of our Java program is divided into separate subtasks and each subtask is written as a separate thread, we can often ignore the scheduling of those separate threads because, in the end, all we care about is the completed task.

So when do we care about the scheduling mechanism of these threads? When all of these normal cases do not apply; specifically, when:

- There are one or more CPU-intensive threads in the program

and either

- Intermediate results of the calculations are interesting (e.g., if we wanted to see one of the four convolved GIF images as soon as possible)

or

- The threads are not performing a joint task; they're providing separate tasks that should, in fairness, either employ a round-robin scheduling paradigm (e. g., a server program that is acting on requests on behalf of several different users) or employ a sequential scheduling paradigm (e.g., a server that processes user requests on a first-come, first-served basis).

We'll look at these cases in more depth as we discuss the various mechanisms to achieve them.

Round-Robin Scheduling and "Fairness"

Many developers are surprised to learn that equal-priority Java threads are not automatically timesliced by a round-robin scheduler. Part of this surprise stems from the tendency to think of threads within a program as equivalent in theory to processes in an operating system: it has long been ingrained in our psyches that a timesliced scheduler is the fairest mechanism to deal with multiple processes. And, in an interactive user environment, that's usually the case.

There are, however, occasions when a round-robin scheduler is not the fairest scheduling algorithm available and the programmer is required to make sure that no timeslicing of threads occurs. Consider the case of a calculation server that accepts connections from multiple clients simultaneously and runs each client in a separate thread. This is an elegant server architecture, but the question of the best scheduling mechanism to employ with this architecture turns out to be a profound one.

Let's take the case of a CalcServer that performs some sort of complex, analytic calculation for each of the clients that connects to it; assume that the calculation requires some 5 seconds for each client. When five clients connect to the server at roughly the same time, the CalcServer starts five separate threads. If those threads are subject to timeslicing, it takes about 25 seconds for all threads to reach the end of their calculation, and because the CPU has been equitably shared, each thread reaches the end of its individual calculation at this 25-second mark. So each client receives an answer after 25 seconds.

If no round-robin scheduling is in effect in our CalcServer, however, then we have a different case: the clients still connect at the same time, but one client (somewhat arbitrarily) gets the opportunity to run its calculation to conclusion; the first client gets an answer in just 5 seconds instead of 25 seconds. Then the second client's calculation begins; the second client gets its answer after 10 seconds have passed, and so on. Only the fifth client has to wait the entire 25 seconds for an answer.

Which of these scheduling modes is the "fairest"? The answer to that depends on what happens during the 5 seconds the server calculates on behalf of the client. If the server provides just a single answer to the client, clearly the non-timesliced version is "fairest": on average, each client has to wait 15 seconds for an answer versus 25 seconds for the timesliced version. If, instead, the server provides five answers to the client—one for every second of calculation—then the timesliced version is "fairest": each client has one answer after 5 seconds, whereas in the non-timesliced version, the fifth client won't have its first answer until 21 seconds have passed.

In other words, this is once again the "intermediate results" requirement: if intermediate results are important to us, a round-robin scheduler provides the fairest results to all the threads. But if all we care about is the final answer, a round-robin scheduler on a single-CPU machine is not appropriate: in the best of cases, it doesn't provide any benefits, and in cases like our CalcServer calculator, it actually decreases throughput in the system.

This situation becomes more complicated on a system with multiple CPUs. If there are four CPUs available to run our five threads, then on a system that does not perform round-robin scheduling, the average client will receive an answer after 6 seconds: the first four will receive an answer after 5 seconds, and the last will receive one after 10 seconds. On the other hand, if round-robin scheduling is involved, the average answer will be received in 6.2 seconds. However, the distribution of those answers will all be very close to 6.2 seconds: in fact, we can essentially say that each client will get an answer in 6.2 seconds. So even though the average calculation time with round-robin scheduling is slightly greater, it may be perceived to be fairer. And in this case if all we care about is the final answer from all five threads, then round-robin scheduling will be faster: 6.2 seconds versus 10 seconds.

Scheduling with Thread Priorities

Let's delve into the programming that affects thread scheduling; we'll start by examining how to manipulate the priority level of Java threads. This is the most useful mechanism available to a Java programmer that affects scheduling behavior of threads; often, a few simple adjustments of thread priorities is all that's required to make a program behave as desired.

Priority-Related Calls in the Java API

In the Java Thread class, there are three static final variables that define the allowable range of thread priorities:

Thread.MIN_PRIORITY
> The minimum priority a thread can have

Thread.MAX_PRIORITY
> The maximum priority a thread can have

Thread.NORM_PRIORITY
> The default priority for threads in the Java interpreter

Every thread has a priority value that lies somewhere in the range between `MIN_PRIORITY` (which is 1) and `MAX_PRIORITY` (which is 10). However, not all threads can have a value anywhere within this range: each thread belongs to a thread group, and the thread group has a maximum priority (lower than or equal to `MAX_PRIORITY`) that its individual threads cannot exceed. We'll discuss this further in Chapter 10, but for now, you should be aware that the maximum thread priority for a thread within an applet is typically `NORM_PRIORITY` + 1. In addition, the virtual machine is allowed to create internal threads at a priority of 0, so that there are in effect 11 different priority levels for threads within the virtual machine.

The default priority of a thread is the priority of the thread that created it. This is often, but not always, `NORM_PRIORITY` (which is 5).

There are two methods in the Java Thread class that relate to the priority of a thread:

void setPriority(int priority)
> Sets the priority of the given thread. If `priority` is outside the allowed range of thread priorities, an exception is thrown. However, if the priority is within the allowed range of thread priorities but is greater than the maximum priority of the thread's thread group, then the priority is silently lowered to match that maximum priority.

Symbolic Thread Priority Values

The symbolic definition of priority constants is not necessarily useful. Typically, we like to think of constant values like these in terms of symbolic names, which allows us to believe that their actual values are irrelevant. Using symbolic names also allows us to change the variables and have that change reflected throughout our code.

Unfortunately, that logic doesn't always apply in the case of thread priorities: if we have to manipulate the individual priorities of the threads, we sometimes have to know what the range of those values actually is. If the range between the minimum and maximum priorities were 20, then we could have twenty different threads, each at a different priority. But if the range were only 5, our twenty threads would have to share priorities (on average, four threads at each priority level). So it's not enough to know that these constants exist; we often have to know that, in fact, the minimum Java thread priority is 1, the maximum is 10 (6 for applets), and the default is 5.

Virtual machines that use native threads complicate this matter even further, since the hosting operating system may not be able to support ten different thread priorities. That means that for all practical purposes, threads with different Java priorities may map to operating system threads with the same priority.

int getPriority()
>   Retrieves the priority of the given thread.

Using the Priority Calls

Let's look at an example of using these calls. Often, simply setting the priority of each of your threads is sufficient to achieve the required scheduling. If you have two threads in your program and one is usually blocked, all you need to do is set the priority of the thread that blocks above the priority of the other thread, and you'll prevent CPU starvation. We'll illustrate this example with a code fragment that is designed to calculate and display fractal images. The calculation of the fractal is very CPU intensive but has the advantage that it can be done in sections that can be displayed as each is computed. So we'll put the actual calculations into a separate, low-priority thread that calls the `repaint()` method after each section has been calculated. Meanwhile, our applet's initial thread spends most of its time blocked, waiting for an event from the user or for a repaint event.

Here's the skeleton code for our fractal applet:

```java
import java.applet.*;
import java.awt.*;

public class Fractal extends Applet implements Runnable {
    Thread calcThread;
    boolean sectionsToCalculate;
    static int nSections = 10;

    public void start() {
        Thread current = Thread.currentThread();
        calcThread = new Thread(this);
        calcThread.setPriority(current.getPriority() - 1);
        calcThread.start();
    }

    public void stop() {
        sectionsToCalculate = false;
    }

    void doCalc(int i) {
        // Calculate section i of the fractal.
    }

    public void run() {
        for (int i = 0; i < nSections && sectionsToCalculate; i++) {
            doCalc(i);
            repaint();
        }
    }

    public void paint(Graphics g) {
        // Paint the calculated sections.
    }
}
```

Consider what would happen in this example if we didn't lower the priority of the calculation thread. In that case, the applet would run through its init() and start() methods, and we'd be left with two threads at NORM_PRIORITY: the applet thread and the calculation thread. The applet thread blocks waiting for an event from the windowing system, so the calculation thread is the only runnable thread and hence becomes the currently running thread. The calculation thread calculates a section of the fractal and calls the repaint() method. This creates the necessary event to unblock the applet thread and move the applet thread into the runnable state.

However, the calculation thread is still in the runnable state, which means that the calculation thread remains the currently running thread. The applet thread is added to the end of the NORM_PRIORITY list, and if our Java virtual machine does not perform round-robin scheduling, the calculation thread will always remain the currently running thread. Thus, as long as there are sections of the fractal to calculate, the many calls to the repaint() method have no effect: the applet thread never gets the opportunity to become the currently running thread and repaint the screen.

If, however, we set the priority of the calculation thread lower than the priority of the applet thread, then when the calculation thread calls the repaint() method, the applet thread becomes the currently running thread since it is now the runnable thread with the highest priority. The applet thread executes the paint() method and moves again to the blocked state, allowing the calculation thread to become the currently running thread.

Note that this technique is also important if the user might interact with the applet while the fractal is calculating. If the calculation thread is at the same priority as the default applet thread, then the applet will not be able to respond to user input while the calculation thread is running.

When to Use Simple Priority-Based Calls

What are the circumstances in which this technique of setting the priority of certain threads is appropriate? You'll use this technique when both of the following are true:

- There is only one CPU-intensive thread (or one thread per CPU on the target machine).

- Intermediate results are interesting to the user.

That's clearly the case of the fractal calculation: there's one thread calculating the sections of the fractal, and each section is an interesting intermediate result. Mathematical models often benefit from the notion of successive refinement.

Image loading is another area where intermediate results are often important to the user: as parts of the image become available, they can be drawn on the screen so that the user sees them "scrolled" onto the screen. But remember: in the typical case, the Java program is loading the image over the network, which means that the thread reading the image will often block, so that there is no need to adjust any thread's priority. But if the Java program is calculating the image from some preloaded data set, lowering the priority of that thread is a good idea.

What if we had more than one CPU-intensive thread? In the case of the fractal, what if we'd set up a separate thread to calculate each section of the fractal? This is a programmatically elegant solution, but there's a danger here. When you have more than one CPU-intensive thread, you should lower the priority of each of the CPU-intensive threads. In that case, as long as each calculation thread is at a lower level than the applet thread, you get at least part of the behavior you want.

This may or may not give you the entire behavior that you want. On platforms that support round-robin scheduling among threads of equal priority, CPU-intensive threads will compete for the CPU, and the individual calculation of each section will take longer than if the calculation of an individual section is allowed to run to completion. This means that the user sees the sections of the fractal (that is, the intermediate feedback) more slowly than in the case where there is a single calculation thread.

On the other hand, if your program has as many CPU-intensive threads as the machine that it's running on has processors, then by using this technique you'll get the most out of the machine's resources and see the intermediate results as quickly as possible.

Popular Scheduling Implementations

We'll now look at how all of this plays out in the implementation of the Java virtual machine on several popular platforms. In many ways, this is a section that we'd rather not have needed to write: Java is a platform-independent language, and to have to provide platform-specific details of its implementations certainly violates that precept. But we stress that there are very few times when these details actually matter.

On the other hand, one of the hallmarks of Java in the real world is that vendors of Java virtual machines are allowed to compete over the implementation of those virtual machines: which one is faster, which one can run more threads, and so on. As long as the implementation of the virtual machine follows the Java language specification and conforms to the Java Compatibility Kit for testing, then it is a valid Java virtual machine. Because of the flexibility that the specification allows for thread scheduling, all of the implementations we'll discuss are certainly valid Java virtual machines (at least in the area of thread scheduling support).

Green Threads

The first model that we'll look at is the simplest. In this model, the operating system doesn't know anything about threads at all; it is up to the virtual machine to handle all the details of the threading API. From the perspective of the operating system, there is a single process and a single thread.

Each thread in this model is an abstraction within the virtual machine: the virtual machine must hold within the thread object all information related to that thread. This includes the thread's stack, a program counter that indicates which Java instruction the thread is executing, and other bookkeeping information about the thread. The virtual machine functions by loading this information into memory and operating on it: it will run the instruction pointed to by the program counter, get the next instruction and run that instruction, and so on.

When it is time for the virtual machine to run another thread, it will do so by saving all of the information regarding the state of the current thread and then replacing that information with the state of the target thread. The target thread's stack becomes the stack on which the virtual machine is operating, and the instruction that the virtual machine will next execute becomes the instruction pointed to by the program counter in the target thread.

Of course, this all happens at a logical level: the implementation of a particular virtual machine may be somewhat different. But the salient fact is that the operating system has no idea that the virtual machine has switched threads in this manner. As far as the operating system is concerned, the virtual machine is just executing arbitrary code; the fact that the code is emulating many different threads is unknown outside of the virtual machine.

This model is known in Java as the green-thread model. There is no particular significance to the term *green*—it does not mean that these threads are somehow unripe (that is, less robust or useful) than other thread models. In other circles, these threads are often called *user-level threads*, because they exist only within the user level of the application: no calls into the operating system are required to handle any of the thread details. In Solaris 1 (SunOS 4.1.3), this threading model was called *lwp*, but don't confuse that with the Solaris 2 LWP model, which we'll discuss later.

Because this model does not depend on the operating system to provide any thread-specific capabilities, green threads are fairly portable. In fact, the threading model itself is very portable, although it does require some code to be written in assembly language: for example, certain parts of the code must be able to execute an atomic test-and-set instruction on the CPU. Accessing this instruction is usually possible only in assembly code. But while the threading code itself is portable, use of green threads complicates other implementation details of the virtual machine: the virtual machine must handle all I/O in a nonblocking fashion, for example. This makes the virtual machine somewhat harder to write.

Still, the green-thread model remains the standard model for the reference implementation of Java, simply because it is more portable than the other models that we will discuss. And in fact, porting this model to most operating systems is not that daunting a task. It's often assumed that porting Java to Windows 3.1 is so difficult because of the lack of thread support in Windows 3.1. In fact, there are many user-level thread libraries available for Windows 3.1, and the green-thread library

---

User- and System-Level Threads

In most modern operating systems, the operating system is logically divided into two pieces: user level and system level. The operating system itself—that is, the operating system kernel—lies at system level. The kernel is responsible for handling system calls on behalf of programs that run at user level.

When a program running at user level wants to read a file, for example, it must call (or trap) into the operating system kernel, which will read the file and return the data to the program. This separation has many advantages, not the least of which is that it allows for a more robust system: if a program performs an illegal operation, it can be terminated without affecting other programs or the kernel itself. Only when the kernel executes an illegal operation will the entire machine crash.

Because of this separation, it is possible to have support for threads at the user level, the system level, or at both levels independently.

---

itself can easily run on that platform. Other problems, such as the lack of 32-bit support and porting the AWT, remain harder to overcome.

The green-thread model is common on most Unix platforms, although Unix platforms often also support a native-thread model. Java-enabled browsers on Unix platforms almost always use a green-thread model (although the Java plug-in may use either model).

Because threads in the green-thread model are unknown to the operating system, a Java virtual machine that is implemented with green threads can only run a single thread at a time, even on a machine that has many CPUs.

Scheduling of green threads

For the most part, green threads are scheduled exactly as we discussed earlier. In most implementations of green threads, there is no notion of round-robin scheduling, so green threads will not automatically timeslice. Scheduling is entirely the responsibility of the virtual machine, and the virtual machine usually changes the currently running thread only when another thread of higher priority becomes runnable (or when the currently running thread blocks). However, this is not a requirement of the Java specification, and a green-thread implementation could conceivably include a timer to do round-robin scheduling.

The reference implementation of the green-thread model uses priority inheritance, so that the priority of a thread will be temporarily raised if it is holding a lock on which a higher-priority thread is waiting.

Depending on the operating system, however, green threads may not exhibit a precise scheduling behavior: there may be a very small period of time during which a lower-priority thread is running even though a higher-priority thread may want to run.

As an example, consider what happens when a Java thread reads data from a socket that has no data. The expectation is that the thread will block—but the virtual machine itself cannot afford to block. Hence, the virtual machine must have some way of being notified when data is ready on the socket, and only then can it allow the thread to read the data on the socket. In most operating systems, that's possible using asynchronous I/O: when data is available on the socket, the virtual machine will receive a signal that will interrupt what it is presently doing. In response to the signal, the virtual machine can run the thread that wants to read the data.

In some operating systems, however, there is no facility for asynchronous I/O. In those cases the virtual machine must periodically poll the socket to see if data is available. This polling usually happens periodically, perhaps every few milliseconds. When data is available, then the virtual machine may schedule the thread that wants to read the data.

Now, say that a high-priority thread is waiting for data from the socket, and meanwhile, a lower-priority thread is performing some other calculation. If the virtual machine is dependent on polling the socket to see when data is ready, then there will be a very small window of time after data arrives on the socket and before the virtual machine next polls the socket. During this time, the lower-priority thread will still be executing, even though the higher-priority thread should be the one that is executing.

Situations like this almost never affect an actual program—the delay is very slight, and there are many other factors that may have influenced the program anyway: what if the pending data had been delayed even longer in coming across the network? What if another process on the machine prevented the Java application from running for a few microseconds? Java is not a real-time platform, so the scheduling anomaly that we've just described is unlikely to have any impact on a Java program.

However, be aware that this is one reason why even if one thread in the Java virtual machine causes another thread to become unblocked there may be a delay before the higher-priority thread actually runs. Say that we run the following code fragment in a low-priority thread:

```
public class LockTest {
    Object someObject = new Object();
    class ThreadA extends Thread {
```

```
        ThreadA() {
            setPriority(Thread.MAX_PRIORITY);
        }
        public void run() {
            synchronized(someObject) {
                someObject.wait();
            }
            someObject.methodA();
        }
    }
    class ThreadB extends Thread {
        ThreadB() {
            setPriority(Thread.NORM_PRIORITY);
        }
        public void run() {
            synchronized(someObject) {
                someObject.notify();
            }
            someObject.methodB();
        }
    }
    static void main(String args[]) {
        new ThreadA().start();
        new ThreadB().start();
    }
}
```

In this example, we're starting two threads: ThreadA, which has a priority of 10, and ThreadB, which has a priority of 5. Since we start ThreadA first, the expectation is that it will begin its run() method and block on the wait() method. Then ThreadB will start and notify ThreadA. In a strict priority model, ThreadA will wake up, preempt ThreadB, and execute the methodA() method. Then ThreadB will execute the methodB() method. However, we cannot assume that the priority scheduler of the green-thread model is strict enough to ensure that the methodA() method will be called before the methodB() method is called, even though that will happen in the vast majority of cases.

Windows Native Threads

In the native-threading model used on Windows 95 and Windows NT (more generally, on any 32-bit Windows operating system), the operating system is fully cognizant of the multiple threads that the virtual machine uses, and there is a one-to-one mapping between Java threads and operating system threads. Therefore, the scheduling of Java threads is subject to the underlying scheduling of threads by the operating system.

This model is usually simple to understand because every thread can be thought of as a process. The operating system scheduler makes no real distinction in this case between a process and a thread: it treats each thread like a process. Of course, there are still other differences in the operating system between a thread and a process, but not as far as the scheduler is concerned.

Since there are no popular green-thread implementations of Java virtual machines on Windows operating systems, virtually all virtual machines on the Windows platform will use the native Windows thread model. Java-enabled browsers typically use this model as well. However, there are many vendors of Java virtual machines for Windows, and the specifics of each one may vary.

Because the operating system knows about threads, Windows native threads tend to be somewhat heavyweight. This can limit the number of concurrent threads that can run on the platform, since with too many threads, the operating system becomes unresponsive. We'll show a pooling technique in the next chapter that helps us work around that problem.

But this implementation does allow multiple threads to run simultaneously on a machine with multiple CPUs. Each CPU—whether one or many—will select a currently running thread according to the guidelines that follow.

Scheduling of Windows native threads

In the Windows native threads model, the operating system takes an important role in thread scheduling. In particular, the operating system schedules threads just like it schedules processes. That means that threads are scheduled on a preemptive, priority-based mechanism, just as we'd hope, but there are a few complications added to the generic model we described earlier.

To begin, only seven priorities are recognized by the Windows operating system; these seven priorities must map onto the eleven Java thread priorities. Since one of these priorities is typically reserved for the internal 0-level Java thread priority, the end result is that the ten programmable Java thread priorities must map onto six Windows platform priorities. Different virtual machines will do this differently, but one common implementation performs the mapping listed in Table 6-1.

Table 6-1. Mapping of Java Thread Priorities on Win32 Platforms

Java Priority	Windows 95/NT Priority
0	THREAD_PRIORITY_IDLE
1 (Thread.MIN_PRIORITY)	THREAD_PRIORITY_LOWEST
2	THREAD_PRIORITY_LOWEST
3	THREAD_PRIORITY_BELOW_NORMAL

Table 6-1. Mapping of Java Thread Priorities on Win32 Platforms (continued)

Java Priority	Windows 95/NT Priority
4	THREAD_PRIORITY_BELOW_NORMAL
5 (Thread.NORM_PRIORITY)	THREAD_PRIORITY_NORMAL
6	THREAD_PRIORITY_ABOVE_NORMAL
7	THREAD_PRIORITY_ABOVE_NORMAL
8	THREAD_PRIORITY_HIGHEST
9	THREAD_PRIORITY_HIGHEST
10 (Thread.MAX_PRIORITY)	THREAD_PRIORITY_TIME_CRITICAL

On this implementation, having a thread of priority 3 and a thread of priority 4 will be the same as having two threads with a priority of 4.

In addition to seven priority levels, the Windows operating system also has five scheduling classes, and a thread in Windows is actually scheduled as a combination of its priority and its scheduling class. However, scheduling classes for threads are not easy to change, so they do not factor into a system where priorities can be changed dynamically by the programmer.

A second complication arises on this platform because the priority that a programmer can assign to a thread (that is, one of the seven platform-specific priorities) is only one piece of the information that the operating system uses to determine the absolute priority of a thread. There are other things that can affect the priority of a thread:

- Windows native threads are subject to priority inheritance.

- The actual priority of the thread is based on its programmed (or inverted) priority minus a value that indicates how recently the thread has actually run. This value is subject to continual adjustment: the more time passes, the closer to zero the value becomes. This primarily distinguishes between threads of the same priority, and it leads to round-robin scheduling between threads of the same priority. Hence, on Windows platforms, equal-priority threads will timeslice: all things being equal, each thread of the same priority will receive approximately the same amount of CPU time.

- On another level, a thread that has not run for a very long time is given a temporary priority boost. The value of this boost decays over time as the thread has a chance to run. This prevents threads from absolute starvation, while still giving preference to higher-priority threads over lower-priority threads. The effect of this priority boost depends on the original priority of the thread: when competing against a thread of priority 5, a thread of priority 3 will run more often than a thread of priority 1.

The upshot of all this is that it is very difficult to guarantee explicit ordering of thread execution on Windows platforms. However, because the operating system ensures that threads do not starve and that equal-priority threads timeslice, this is not usually a problem.

Solaris Native Threads

The last threading model that we'll look at is the most complex. At an operating system level, Solaris native threads provide a very flexible threading model, but much of that flexibility is lost to the Java programmer, since there is no interface in the Java API to exploit it. A Java programmer can use native methods to call the underlying thread libraries to get at features that aren't exposed by the Java API; while that's something that we generally discourage, we'll have no choice but to follow that path under certain circumstances.

Solaris native threads utilize a two-level model of programming: there are user-level threads, which are unknown to the operating system and are scheduled in the same manner as threads in the green-thread model that we looked at a little earlier. In addition, there are system-level threads (known as *lightweight processes*, or LWPs), which are known to the operating system and are scheduled in a manner very similar to the Windows thread model that we just discussed. The interplay between these two levels gives Solaris native threads their great flexibility (as well as their complexity).

The Solaris native-thread model is used by Sun's production version of its virtual machine; beginning with Java 2, it is available in Sun's reference version of the virtual machine as well. As of this writing, Netscape and Internet Explorer for Solaris (versions 4.0 and earlier) use the green-thread model; it is unknown if those browsers will use the native-thread version of the virtual machine in their Java 2-compatible releases. The HotJava browser can run with either thread model.

Because the operating system knows about these threads, Java programs using Solaris native threads can run multiple threads simultaneously on machines with multiple CPUs.

Scheduling of Solaris native threads

Scheduling of Solaris native threads is a little complex, but it follows the same principles that we've already seen. From the perspective of any particular LWP, the scheduling follows the green-thread model. At any point in time, an LWP will run the highest priority thread available. An LWP will not perform any timeslicing among the eligible threads: just as in the green-thread model, once an LWP selects a thread to run, it will continue to run that thread until a higher-priority thread becomes available. There is a difference, however, in how an LWP handles a thread that blocks; we'll look into that a little further on. There is a one-to-one mapping between the threads that an LWP can run and threads in a Java program; hence, in a Java virtual machine that has a single LWP, scheduling is very much like the green-thread model.

However, programs written with Solaris native threads typically have multiple LWPs, each of which is scheduled by the operating system. Although LWPs themselves have a priority, this priority is unknown to the Java programmer and is unaffected by the priority of the thread that the LWP has selected to run. Hence, all LWPs in the virtual machine have essentially the same priority, and—just like on a Windows platform—this priority is subject to periodic adjustment based on how recently the LWP has run. Thus, LWPs will timeslice among themselves.

Therefore, when an LWP runs, it runs the thread with the highest priority. The LWP eventually loses its timeslice, and another LWP runs. This second LWP chooses the remaining thread with the highest priority and runs that thread. This process continues throughout the lifetime of the virtual machine.

Consider the effects of this process in a virtual machine that has created two threads when given two LWPs by the operating system. Assume that both threads have a priority of 5. When the first LWP comes along, it picks (seemingly arbitrarily) one of the priority 5 threads and starts running it. Eventually, the LWP loses its timeslice; the second LWP comes along and picks the remaining priority 5 thread and begins running that thread. When it loses its timeslice and the first LWP starts running again, the first thread is run. And so it goes—the two threads are timesliced, because each LWP is being given a timeslice by the operating system.

Now, say that there are three threads of equal priority and only two LWPs. In this case, the first two threads will timeslice, and the third thread will not get to run at all (at least, not until one of the first two threads blocks or exits). Again, this is consistent with the scheduling model that we learned about earlier: a thread is subject to starvation unless other threads of the same or higher priority will all eventually block. An LWP, once it has selected a thread, will run that thread until the thread blocks or until a higher-priority thread becomes available.

So, suppose we have two threads and two LWPs, but this time, one thread has a priority of 5 and one has a priority of 4. Interestingly enough, these threads will still timeslice, which means that there will be times when the priority 4 thread is running even though the priority 5 thread is not blocked. When the first LWP comes along, it selects the priority 5 thread and runs that thread. When the second LWP begins to run, it must select a thread; as far as it is concerned, the only available thread is the priority 4 thread, since the priority 5 thread has already been assigned to an LWP. Hence, this second LWP begins running the priority 4 thread, even through the priority 5 thread is not blocked. The two threads timeslice in this example.

We do not mean to imply here that because the priority 5 thread has been running on a particular LWP, it is forever bound to that LWP. Such a situation (known as *bound threads*) is possible in a Solaris program, but most implementations of the Java virtual machine use unbound threads. The priority 5 thread may be displaced from its LWP when a higher-priority thread becomes runnable, at which point the priority 5 thread goes back into the pool of waiting threads. When the LWP running the priority 4 thread runs again, it will then displace the priority 4 thread in favor of the priority 5 thread because the priority 5 thread is not presently assigned to any LWP.

The rule of thumb, then, is that N number of LWPs in a Java virtual machine will be running (and timeslicing) the N threads with highest priority in the virtual machine (even if those threads have unequal priorities).

Finally, we note that Solaris native threads use priority inheritance.

LWPs in the virtual machine

How many LWPs *does the virtual machine have?* The answer varies according to the rules we will lay out here. To answer this question, we must delve into the details of the Solaris thread library a little more.

The Solaris thread model follows the Java threading API fairly well. In the thread library itself, there is the notion of thread priorities. This means that the actual scheduling of threads onto specific LWPs can be handled by the Solaris thread library itself, following the priority-based rules that the virtual machine expects. To the programmer, this scheduling is identical to when the virtual machine schedules using green threads.

The number of LWPs is controlled by the Solaris thread library according to the following guidelines:

- The virtual machine begins with one LWP. As the virtual machine creates threads, these threads all run on this single LWP, which schedules the individual threads on a priority basis—the highest thread will be the one that the LWP runs.

- When the thread makes a system call, it becomes (temporarily) bound to the LWP. A system call is any call that must use the kernel to perform work on its behalf. In the Java world, this includes reading or writing most streams (except for streams based on strings) and creating sockets. A thread that is bound to an LWP is not subject to preemption.

- If the system call returns immediately, then the LWP continues to execute the thread. But the thread at this point becomes unbound, meaning that if a higher-priority thread is created, the LWP will start running it instead.

- If the system call blocks, then the LWP to which it is bound also blocks. If all LWPs become blocked and there are threads that are waiting to run, then the operating system will automatically create a new LWP, which will select the highest priority thread in the pool of waiting threads and run that thread.

The virtual machine thus never creates new LWPs; that is handled by the operating system and the Solaris thread library. That means that the number of LWPs that exist in the Java virtual machine will be equal to the number of threads in the Java virtual machine that have ever been simultaneously blocked, plus one. In practice, this means that a typical Java application may start with five to seven LWPs, since during the initialization of the virtual machine, there may be four to six LWPs that are simultaneously blocked.

There are therefore usually at least two LWPs available to the Java program; the remaining LWPs tend to be blocked in the course of executing threads that are internal to the virtual machine itself. Hence, you can often rely on two threads of your program to be scheduled onto LWPs and to timeslice between them, even if they are not the same priority.

On a single-processor machine, this number of LWPs is usually sufficient. If it is insufficient—that is, if you create threads that block and tie up the existing LWPs—then new LWPs will be created on demand. If there are one or more unblocked threads in your Java program, there will always be at least one LWP to run those threads.

On a multiprocessor machine, however, this may not be a sufficient number of LWPs, especially if the threads in the Java program are CPU intensive and rarely block. If you have a machine with eight CPUs that's behaving as a calculation server and you only have two LWPs available, you will not see the scaling that you desire, no matter how many threads you create. In order to get the most benefit from this machine, you need at least eight available LWPs—one for each CPU—so that you can run eight CPU-intensive threads at the same time.

In this case, you must call the operating system–specific library in order to tell it that you want eight (or however many you desire) LWPs. We'll show an example of how to do that at the end of this section, but it involves using a native method to call the thr_setconcurrency() function of the Solaris thread library in order to create enough LWPs. Depending on your perspective, this can seem either very complicated or very cool.

This seems rather complicated. Do I really need to bother with it? Probably not. If you have a single-CPU machine, you definitely won't see a benefit from it—in fact, you'll slightly impede the performance of your machine, because you'll have too many LWPs competing for the CPU. If you have multiple CPUs, you'll only see a benefit if you have multiple threads that spend a significant amount of time executing code without blocking. If you write a chat server, then more LWPs isn't going to help you: while you might have a thread for each client attached to the server, those threads spend most of their time blocked, waiting for input from the clients. In that case, the thread library will create enough LWPs for you: it will create a number sufficient to hold all simultaneously blocked threads, and when a thread unblocks, it will already be on an LWP so that it can process its request.

So you really need to worry about the number of available LWPs only when you write something that has multiple CPU-intensive threads.

This seems pretty cool, but how do I know how many LWPs I need? This is a hard question to answer. Assuming that you have enough threads to demand it, the answer is that you need as many LWPs as you have threads that will be blocked simultaneously, plus one LWP for each thread that you want to run simultaneously. You'll see the best throughput when the number of running threads is equal to the number of CPUs on the machine. If there are any less, there will be idle CPUs that could be doing more work. If there are more, the LWPs will compete for CPU time.

Of course, there may be other things happening on the machine, which may lead you to want fewer LWPs than CPUs so that other programs can get a sufficient amount of CPU time. But there's never really an advantage to having more LWPs than there are CPUs—even if you have hundreds of threads that you want to timeslice, you can accomplish that better by introducing some scheduling techniques into your program rather than creating hundreds of LWPs. Despite their name, LWPs still require system resources, and they are much more resource-intensive than are threads. A Java virtual machine on Solaris can easily handle thousands of threads, but not necessarily thousands of LWPs.

Native Scheduling Support

The Java threading API that we've examined so far is somewhat incomplete for certain advanced scheduling uses. For example, there is no way to tell how many CPUs a machine has, or to set the number of LWPs that you want your Solaris virtual machine to have, or to set processor affinity masks so that certain threads run on certain processors. Unfortunately, the only way to overcome these limitations is to introduce native methods calls into your program.

We'll show just the basic outline of how to do that for certain calls in this section. We'll give a complete example, but the full details of Windows threads, Solaris or

POSIX threads, and the Java native interface (JNI) are beyond the scope of this book.

We'll start with a class that allows us to perform three operations: getting the number of CPUs on the machine and getting and setting the number of threads that we want the virtual machine to be able to run concurrently:

```
public class CPUSupport {
    static boolean loaded = false;
    static {
        try {
            System.loadLibrary("CPUSupportWin");
            loaded = true;
        } catch (Error e) {
            try {
            System.loadLibrary("CPUSupportSolaris");
                loaded = true;
            } catch (Error err) {
                System.err.println(
                        "Warning: No platform library for CPUSupport");
            }
        }
    }

    private static native int getConcurrencyN();
    private static native void setConcurrencyN(int i);
    private static native int getNumProcessorsN();

    public static int getConcurrency() {
        if (!loaded)
            // Assume green threads.
            return 1;
        return getConcurrencyN();
    }

    public static void setConcurrency(int n) {
        if (loaded)
            setConcurrencyN(n);
    }

    public static int getNumProcessors() {
        if (!loaded)
            // Assume green threads.
            return 1;
        return getNumProcessorsN();
    }
}
```

We've designed this class so that it will work on all platforms; if there is no plat-form-specific native library available, we'll assume the green-thread model. Of course, this can be easily adapted to include support for other operating systems if desired. Now all we need to do is to write the specific native library for the platforms that we want to support.

Implementing CPUSupport on Windows

Here's the code that implements the native library for Windows:

```
#include <jni.h>
#include <windows.h>

JNIEXPORT jint JNICALL Java_CPUSupport_getNumProcessorsN
                        (JNIEnv *env, jobject cls)
{
    static DWORD numCPU = 0;
    SYSTEM_INFO process_info;

    if (numCPU == 0) {
        GetSystemInfo(&process_info);
        numCPU = process_info.dwNumberOfProcessors;
    }
    return numCPU;
}

JNIEXPORT void JNICALL Java_CPUSupport_setConcurrencyN
                        (JNIEnv *env, jobject cls, jint kthreads)
{
    // For Windows the concurrency is always infinity.
    return;
}

JNIEXPORT jint JNICALL Java_CPUSupport_getConcurrencyN
                        (JNIEnv *env, jobject cls)
{
    // For Windows the concurrency is always infinity, but
    // we will return the number of processors instead.
    return Java_CPUSupport_getNumProcessorsN(env, cls);
}
```

To obtain the number of CPUs on Windows, we simply use the operating system's GetSystemInfo() function and extract the desired information. However, we're not able to affect the concurrency of threads on Windows: each Java thread is assigned to its own Windows thread. This leads to an effective concurrency of infinity (given an infinite amount of memory and CPU speed). So we return the number of processors instead, which gives us an idea of how many threads can run simultaneously.

To compile this code with the Microsoft C/C++ 5.0 compiler, execute this command:

```
cl -Ic:\java\include -Ic:\java\include\win32 -LD CPUSupportWin.c
```

You'll need to substitute the appropriate directory path for *c:\java* depending upon where your JDK is installed. The resulting DLL file (*CPUSupportWin.dll*) must be located in the PATH environment for the virtual machine to find it.

Implementing CPUSupport on Solaris

Here's the code required to support the CPUSupport class on Solaris:

```
#include <jni.h>
#include <thread.h>

JNIEXPORT jint JNICALL Java_CPUSupport_getConcurrencyN
        (JNIEnv * env, jobject class)
{
    return thr_getconcurrency();
}


JNIEXPORT void JNICALL Java_CPUSupport_setConcurrencyN
        (JNIEnv * env, jobject class, jint n)
{
    thr_setconcurrency(n);
}


JNIEXPORT jint JNICALL Java_CPUSupport_getNumProcessorsN
        (JNIEnv * env, jobject class)
{
    int num_threads;
    num_threads = sysconf(_SC_NPROCESSORS_ONLN);
    return num_threads;
}
```

Again, the implementation is predictably simple because it maps to operating system function calls. In this case, the getConcurrency() method will return the current number of LWPs, and the setConcurrency() method will set the current number of LWPs.

To compile this library with the Sun Workshop 4.2 C compiler, execute this command:

```
cc -I/usr/java/include -I/usr/java/include/solaris -mt -G -o \
libCPUSupportSolaris.so CPUSupportSolaris.c
```

If your JDK is installed in a place other than */usr/java*, change that pathname accordingly. Once the library is compiled, you must add it to your **LD_LIBRARY_PATH** environment in order for the virtual machine to find it.

Other Thread-Scheduling Methods

There are other methods in the Thread class that affect scheduling. As we'll see, these remaining methods are not always the most useful techniques with respect to Java scheduling because of the complications that arise in the various native-thread scheduling models and their use of timesliced scheduling. In addition, two of these methods have been deprecated in Java 2 and should not be used in any version of Java. But we'll complete our look at the API relating to thread scheduling in this section.

The suspend() and resume() Methods

There are two methods that can directly affect the state of a thread:

void suspend() (deprecated in Java 2)
    Prevents a thread from running for an indefinite amount of time.

void resume() (deprecated in Java 2)
    Allows a thread to run after being suspended.

The suspend() method moves a particular thread from the runnable state into the blocked state. In this case, the thread isn't blocked waiting for a particular resource, it's blocked waiting for some thread to resume it. The resume() method moves the thread from the blocked state to the runnable state.

In the section "An Overview of Thread Scheduling," earlier in this chapter, we posited the existence of four thread states. Actually, the suspended state is different from the blocked state, even though there is no real conceptual difference between them. Strictly speaking, the suspend() method moves a thread to the suspended state from whatever state the thread was previously in—including a blocked thread, which can be suspended just like any other thread. Similarly, the resume() method moves the thread from the suspended state to whatever state the thread was in before it was suspended—so a thread that has been resumed may still be blocked. But this is a subtle difference, and we'll persist in treating the blocked and suspended states as identical.

A common guideline is to use the suspend() and resume() methods to control the threads within an applet. This is a good idea: when the applet is not active, you don't want its threads to continue to run. Using this guideline, let's revise our fractal applet as follows:

```
import java.applet.Applet;
import java.awt.*;

public class Fractal extends Applet implements Runnable {
    Thread t;
```

```
        public void start() {
            if (t == null) {
                t = new Thread(this);
                t.setPriority(Thread.currentThread().getPriority() - 1);
                t.start();
            }
            else t.resume();
        }

        public void stop() {
            t.suspend();
        }

        public void run() {
            // Do calculations, occasionally calling repaint().
        }

        public void paint(Graphics g) {
            // Paint the completed sections of the fractal.
        }
    }
```

This example is better than our first fractal code: in the first case, when the user revisited the page with the fractal applet, the fractal calculation would have had to begin at its very beginning and redisplay all those results to the user as they were recalculated. Now, the applet can save the information of the fractal and simply pick up the calculation from the point at which the user interrupted it.

Alternatives to the suspend() and resume() methods

Despite the common use of the suspend() and resume() methods in this and other cases, there's a danger lurking in the code that has caused those methods to become deprecated. This danger exists in all releases of the Java virtual machine, however, so even though these methods are not deprecated in Java 1.0 or 1.1, you should not feel comfortable about using them in those earlier releases. In fact, the suspend() and resume() methods should never actually be used. The reasoning that we're about to outline applies to the stop() method as well, which has been deprecated beginning with Java 2 and should also be avoided in earlier releases.

The problem with using the suspend() method is that it can conceivably lead to cases of lock starvation—including cases where the starvation shuts down the entire virtual machine. If a thread is suspended while it is holding a lock, that lock remains held by the suspended thread. As long as that thread is suspended, no other thread can obtain the lock in question. Depending on the lock in question, all threads may eventually end up blocked, waiting for the lock.

You may think that with careful programming you can avoid this situation, by never suspending a thread that holds a lock. However, there are many locks internal to the Java API and the virtual machine itself that you don't know about, so you can never ensure that a thread that you want to suspend does not hold any locks. Worse yet, consider what happens if a thread is suspended while it is in the middle of allocating an object from the heap. The suspended thread may hold a lock that protects the heap itself, meaning that no other thread will be able to allocate any object. Clearly, this is a bad situation.

This is not an insurmountable problem; it would be possible to implement the virtual machine in such a way that a thread could not be suspended while it held a lock, or at least not while it held certain internal locks within the virtual machine. But Java virtual machines are not typically written like that, and the specification certainly does not require it. Hence, the suspend() method was deprecated instead. There is no danger in the resume() method itself, but since the resume() method is useful only with the suspend() method, it too has been deprecated.

A similar situation occurs with the stop() method. In this case, the danger is not that the lock will be held indefinitely—in fact, the lock will be released when the thread stops (details of this procedure are given in Appendix A). The danger here is that a complex data structure may be left in an unstable state: if the thread that is being stopped is in the midst of updating a linked list, for example, the links in the list will be left in an inconsistent state. The reason we needed to obtain a lock on the list in the first place was to ensure that the list would not be found by another thread in an inconsistent state; if we were able to interrupt a thread in the middle of this operation, we would lose the benefit of its obtaining the lock. So the stop() method has been deprecated as well.

The outcome of this is that no thread should suspend or stop another thread: a thread should only stop itself (by returning from its run() method) or suspend itself (by calling the wait() method). It may do this in response to a flag set by another thread, or by any other method that you may devise.

In earlier chapters, we showed what to do instead of calling the stop() method. Here's a similar technique that we can use to avoid calling the suspend() method:

```
import java.applet.Applet;
import java.awt.*;

public class Fractal extends Applet implements Runnable {
    Thread t;
    volatile boolean shouldRun = false;
    Object runLock = new Object();
    int nSections;
```

```
public void start() {
    if (t == null) {
        shouldRun = true;
        t = new Thread(this);
        t.setPriority(Thread.currentThread().getPriority() - 1);
        t.start();
    }
    else {
        synchronized(runLock) {
            shouldRun = true;
            runLock.notify();
        }
    }
}

public void stop() {
    shouldRun = false;
}

void doCalc(int i) {
    // Calculate the ith section of the fractal.
}

public void run() {
    for (int i = 0; i < nSections; i++) {
        doCalc(i);
        repaint();
        synchronized(runLock) {
            while (shouldRun == false)
                try {
                    runLock.wait();
                } catch (InterruptedException ie) {}
        }
    }
}

public void paint(Graphics g) {
    // Paint the completed sections of the fractal.
}
}
```

The start() method of the applet is still responsible for creating and starting the calculation thread; in addition, it now sets the shouldRun flag to true so that the calculation thread can test to see that it should calculate sections. When the run() method checks this flag and it is false, the run() method waits for the flag to be true. This waiting has the same effect as suspending the calculation thread. Similarly, the notification provided by the start() method has the same effect as resuming the calculation thread.

Suspending the thread is now a two-step process: the applet's stop() method sets a flag and the calculation thread's run() method tests that flag. Hence, there will be a period of time in this case when the applet is still calculating fractal sections even though the applet is no longer visible to the user. In general, there will always be a period of time using this technique between when you want the thread to stop or suspend and when the thread actually checks the flag telling it whether it should suspend itself. But this is a safer way than using the suspend() method (and, of course, there's no guarantee that the suspend() method will appear in future versions of the Java platform).

Why isn't access to the shouldRun flag synchronized in the applet's stop() method? Remember that setting or testing a boolean variable is already an atomic operation, so there is no need to synchronize the stop() method since it only needs to perform a single atomic operation. The other methods synchronize their sections because they are performing more than one operation on the shouldRun flag; in addition, they must hold a lock before they can call the wait() or notify() methods.

The yield() Method

A final method available for affecting which thread is the currently running thread is the yield() method, which is useful because it allows threads of the same priority to be run:

static void yield()

Yields the current thread, allowing another thread of the same priority to be run by the Java virtual machine.

There are a few points worth noting about the yield() method. First, notice that it is a static method, and as such, only affects the currently running thread, as in the following code fragment:

```
public class YieldApplet extends Applet implements Runnable {
    Thread t;
    public void init() {
        t = new Thread(this);
    }

    public void paint(Graphics g) {
        t.yield();
    }
}
```

When the applet thread executes the paint() method and calls the yield() method, it is the applet thread itself that yields, and not the calculation thread t, even though we used the object t to call the yield() method.

What actually happens when a thread yields? In terms of the state of the thread, nothing happens: the thread remains in the runnable state. But logically, the thread is moved to the end of its priority queue, so the Java virtual machine picks a new thread to be the currently running thread, using the same rules it always has. Clearly, there are no threads that are higher in priority than the thread that has just yielded, so the new currently running thread is selected among all the threads that have the same priority as the thread that has just yielded. If there are no other threads in that group, the `yield()` method has no effect: the yielding thread is immediately selected again as the currently running thread. In this respect, calling the `yield()` method is equivalent to calling `sleep(0)`.

If there are other threads with the same priority as the yielding thread, then one of those other threads becomes the currently running thread. Thus, yielding is an appropriate technique provided you know that there are multiple threads of the same priority. However, there is no guarantee which thread will be selected: the thread that yields may still be the next one selected by the scheduler, even if there are other threads available at the same priority.

Let's revisit our fractal example and see how it looks when we use the `yield()` method instead of priority calls:

```
import java.applet.Applet;
import java.awt.*;

public class Fractal extends Applet implements Runnable {
    Thread t;
    volatile boolean shouldRun = false;
    Object runLock = new Object();
    int nSections;

    public void start() {
        if (t == null) {
            shouldRun = true;
            t = new Thread(this);
            t.start();
        }
        else {
            synchronized(runLock) {
                shouldRun = true;
                runLock.notify();
            }
        }
    }

    public void stop() {
        shouldRun = false;
    }
```

```
    void doCalc(int i) {
        // Calculate the ith section of the fractal.
    }

    public void run() {
        for (int i = 0; i < nSections; i++) {
            doCalc(i);
            repaint();
            Thread.yield();
            synchronized(runLock) {
                while (shouldRun == false)
                    try {
                        runLock.wait();
                    } catch (InterruptedException ie) {}
            }
        }
    }

    public void paint(Graphics g) {
        // Paint the completed sections of the fractal.
    }
}
```

In this example, we are no longer setting the priority of the calculation thread to be lower than the other threads in the applet. Now when our calculation thread has results, it merely yields. The applet thread is in the runnable state; it was moved to that state when the calculation thread called the `repaint()` method. So the Java virtual machine chooses the applet thread to be the currently running thread, the applet repaints itself, the applet thread blocks, and the calculation thread again becomes the currently running thread and calculates the next section of the fractal.

This example suffers from a few problems. First, because the applet thread is at the same priority as the calculation thread, the user is unable to interact with the applet until the calculation thread yields. If, for example, the user selects a checkbox in the GUI, the program may not take appropriate action until the calculation thread yields. On platforms with native-thread scheduling, that usually will not happen, since the applet thread and the calculation thread will timeslice, but it can be a big problem on green-thread implementations.

Second, there is a race condition in this example—and in all examples that rely on the `yield()` method. This race condition only occurs if we're on a native-thread platform that timeslices between threads of the same priority, and like most race conditions, it occurs very rarely. In our previous code example, immediately after the calculation thread yields, it may be time for the operating system to schedule another thread (or LWP). This means that the calculation thread may be the next thread to run, even though it has just yielded. The good news in this case is that the program continues to execute, and the sections of the fractal get painted next time the calculation thread yields (or the next time the operating system schedules the applet thread).

In the worst case, then, a thread that yields may still be the next thread to run. However, that scenario can only apply when the operating system is scheduling the threads and the threads are timeslicing, in which case there was probably no need to use the `yield()` method at all. As long as a program treats the `yield()` method as a hint to the Java virtual machine that now might be a good time to change the currently running thread, a program that relies on the `yield()` method will run on green-thread implementations of the virtual machine (where the `yield()` method will always have the desired effect) as well as on native-thread implementations.

Yielding versus priority-based scheduling

When you need to have some control over thread scheduling, the question of which mechanism to use—calling the `yield()` method or adjusting individual thread priorities—tends to be somewhat subjective, since both methods have a similar effect on the threads. As is clear from the example we have used throughout this discussion, we prefer using the priority-based methods to control thread scheduling. These methods offer the most flexibility to the Java developer.

We rarely find the `yield()` method to be useful. This may come as a surprise to thread programmers on systems where the `yield()` method is the most direct one for affecting thread scheduling. But because of the indeterminate nature of scheduling among threads of the same priority on native-thread Java implementations, the effect of the `yield()` method cannot be guaranteed: a thread that yields may immediately be rescheduled when the operating system timeslices threads. On the other hand, if your threads yield often enough, this rare race condition won't matter in the long run, and using the `yield()` method can be an effective way to schedule your threads. The `yield()` method is also simpler to understand than the priority-based methods, which puts it in great favor with some developers.

Daemon Threads

The last thing that we'll address in conjunction with thread scheduling is the issue of daemon threads. There are two types of threads in the Java system: daemon threads and user threads. The implication of these names is that daemon threads are those threads created internally by the Java API and that user threads are those you create yourself, but this is not the case. Any thread can be a daemon thread or a user thread. All threads are created initially as user threads, so all the threads we've looked at so far have been user threads.

Some threads that are created by the virtual machine on your behalf are daemon threads. A daemon thread is identical to a user thread in almost every way: it has a priority, it has the same methods, and it goes through the same states. In terms of scheduling, daemon threads are handled just like user threads: neither type of thread is scheduled in favor of the other. During the execution of your program, a daemon thread behaves just like a user thread.

The only time the Java virtual machine checks to see if particular threads are daemon threads is after a user thread has exited. When a user thread exits, the Java virtual machine checks to see if there are any remaining user threads left. If there are user threads remaining, then the Java virtual machine, using the rules we've discussed, schedules the next thread (user or daemon). If, however, there are only daemon threads remaining, then the Java virtual machine will exit and the program will terminate. Daemon threads only live to serve user threads; if there are no more user threads, there is nothing to serve and no reason to continue.

The canonical daemon thread in the reference implementation of the Java virtual machine is the garbage collection thread (on other implementations, the garbage collector need not be a separate thread). The garbage collector runs from time to time and frees those Java objects that no longer have valid references, which is why the Java programmer doesn't need to worry about memory management. So the garbage collector is a useful thread. If we don't have any other threads running, however, there's nothing for the garbage collector to do: after all, garbage is not spontaneously created, at least not inside a Java program. So if the garbage collector is the only thread left running in the Java virtual machine, then clearly there's no more work for it to do, and the Java virtual machine can exit. Hence, the garbage collector is marked as a daemon thread.

There are two methods in the Thread class that deal with daemon threads:

void setDaemon(boolean on)

> Sets the thread to be a daemon thread (if on is `true`) or to be a user thread (if on is `false`).

boolean isDaemon()

> Returns `true` if the thread is a daemon thread and `false` if it is a user thread.

The `setDaemon()` method can be called only after the thread object has been created and before the thread has been started. While the thread is running, you cannot cause a user thread to become a daemon thread (or vice versa); attempting to do so will generate an exception. To be completely correct, an exception is generated any time the thread is alive and the `setDaemon()` method is called— even if `setDaemon(true)` is called on a thread that is already a daemon thread.

By default, a thread is a user thread if it was created by a user thread; it is a daemon thread if it was created by a daemon thread. The `setDaemon()` method is needed only if one thread creates another thread that should have a different daemon status.

Unfortunately, the line between a user thread and a daemon thread may not be that clear. While it is true that a daemon thread is used to service a user thread, the time it takes to accomplish the service may be longer than the lifespan of the user thread that made the request. Furthermore, there may be critical sections of code that should not be interrupted by the exiting of the virtual machine. For example, a thread whose purpose is to back up data does not have a use if there are no user threads that can process the data. However, during this backup of data to a database, the database may not be in a state that can allow the program to exit. Although this backup thread should still be a daemon thread, since it is of no use to the program without the threads that process the data, we may have to declare this thread as a user thread in order to protect the integrity of the database.

Ideally, the solution is to allow the thread to change its state between a user thread and daemon thread at any time. Since this is not allowed by the Java API, we can instead implement a lock that can be used to protect daemon threads. An implementation of the DaemonLock class is as follows:

```java
public class DaemonLock implements Runnable {
    private int lockCount = 0;

    public synchronized void acquire() {
        if (lockCount++ == 0) {
            Thread t = new Thread(this);
            t.setDaemon(false);
            t.start();
        }
    }

    public synchronized void release() {
        if (--lockCount == 0) {
            notify();
        }
    }

    public synchronized void run() {
        while (lockCount != 0) {
            try {
                wait();
            } catch (InterruptedException ex) {};
        }
    }
}
```

Implementation of the DaemonLock class is simple: we protect daemon threads by ensuring that a user thread exists. As long as there is a user thread, the virtual machine will not exit, which will allow the daemon threads to finish the critical section of code. Once the critical section is completed, the daemon thread can release the daemon lock, which will terminate the user thread. If there are no other user threads in the program at that time, the program will exit. The difference, however, is that it will exit outside of the critical section of code.

We'll see an example use of this class in Chapter 7.

Summary

Here are the methods of the Thread class that we introduced in this chapter:

void setPriority(int priority)

Sets the priority of the given thread. If `priority` is outside the allowed range of thread priorities, an exception is thrown. However, if the priority is within the allowed range of thread priorities but greater than the maximum priority of the thread's thread group, then the priority is silently lowered to match that maximum priority.

int getPriority()

Retrieves the priority of the given thread.

void suspend() (deprecated in Java 2)

Prevents a thread from running for an indefinite amount of time.

void resume() (deprecated in Java 2)

Allows a thread to run after being suspended.

static void yield()

Yields the current thread, allowing another thread of the same priority to be run by the Java virtual machine.

void setDaemon(boolean on)

Sets the thread to be a daemon thread (if on is true) or to be a user thread (if on is false).

boolean isDaemon()

Returns `true` if the thread is a daemon thread and `false` if it is a user thread.

We've spent a lot of time in this chapter discussing the priority and scheduling of threads. Scheduling is one of the gray areas of Java programming because actual scheduling models are not defined by the Java specification, which means that scheduling behavior may vary from platform to platform. The reason for this is Java's quest for simplicity: since the scheduling model of a program rarely affects the ultimate outcome or usefulness of that program, Java leaves the added complexity of explicit scheduling to the developer in those cases where the scheduling is important.

Accordingly, implementations of the Java virtual machine differ in the way they handle thread scheduling. The simplest model—the green-thread model—follows a rather strict priority-based scheduling algorithm; models that are implemented on top of operating-system-specific thread libraries follow the basic precepts of that algorithm, but they each take into account other factors when deciding which thread to run.

In the next chapter, we'll take a look at some scheduling techniques based on simple priority-based scheduling.

7

Java Thread Scheduling Examples

The thread methods that we looked at in the last chapter are great when you have a fixed number of well-known threads and can analyze the behavior of the threads in advance. The priority-based scheduling methods also were most useful when there were intermediate results in which the user might be interested. But there are times when you have independent threads that need a round-robin timesliced behavior regardless of the platform on which they're running. There are also times when it's convenient to create multiple threads, but you want to prevent the round-robin timesliced behavior you'd get on some platforms. And, because some platforms cannot handle large numbers of threads, there are cases when you want to limit the number of threads that your program uses.

We'll look at these issues in this chapter, and we'll provide four examples of how general-purpose scheduling can be achieved in a Java program. We start with the notion of a *thread pool*: a pool of a limited number of threads that can each run multiple objects in succession. A thread pool is useful for programs that may require more threads than can reasonably fit within a particular virtual machine.

Next, we move on to describe two round-robin-based schedulers: a very simple scheduler (most suitable for green-thread implementations) and a more generalized scheduler that is suitable for both ensuring and preventing round-robin scheduling. We present this scheduler for two reasons:

- There are limited times when such a scheduler is needed.

- The development of such a scheduler illustrates the issues you need to consider when programming with many arbitrary threads.

Finally, we will present a job scheduler. This scheduler is suitable for cases where it is important that a job is executed at a particular time.

Thread Pools

First, we'll look at a thread pool example. The idea behind the ThreadPool class is to set up a number of threads that can sit idle, waiting for work that they can perform. The rationale here is not, as you might expect, to pre-allocate the threads to save time: the overhead of starting a thread on many platforms is not really any less significant than the overhead of having a thread wait for work.

Instead, this class is designed to limit the number of threads that our program is using in an effort to utilize the resources of the machine more effectively. For example, the Java API uses this technique to limit the number of threads that are used to load images. If you set up a MediaTracker object, the Java API allocates four threads and retrieves images registered in the MediaTracker object four at a time. This limits the load that the program places on the server supplying the images as well as the bandwidth that the program will require in order to load the images.

This technique is often used in calculation servers. If your calculation server receives many simultaneous requests, you may consider it inefficient to set up a different thread for each request. If the server is running on a native-thread platform that's performing some round-robin scheduling, the requests have to compete for scarce CPU resources among themselves. It's often better in these cases to allow only as many simultaneous requests as there are processors on the machine (or even fewer if the machine is performing other work). On platforms that cannot handle large numbers of simultaneous threads, this technique is also useful to limit the number of threads that are active within a program.

Here's an implementation of a thread pool class:

```
import java.util.*;

public class ThreadPool {

    class ThreadPoolRequest {
        Runnable target;
        Object lock;

        ThreadPoolRequest(Runnable t, Object l) {
            target = t;
            lock = l;
        }
    }

    class ThreadPoolThread extends Thread {
        ThreadPool parent;
        volatile boolean shouldRun = true;
```

```
ThreadPoolThread(ThreadPool parent, int i) {
    super("ThreadPoolThread " + i);
    this.parent = parent;
}

public void run() {
    ThreadPoolRequest obj = null;
    while (shouldRun) {
        try {
            parent.cvFlag.getBusyFlag();
            while (obj == null && shouldRun) {
                try {
                    obj = (ThreadPoolRequest)
                            parent.objects.elementAt(0);
                    parent.objects.removeElementAt(0);
                } catch (ArrayIndexOutOfBoundsException aiobe) {
                    obj = null;
                } catch (ClassCastException cce) {
                    System.err.println("Unexpected data");
                    obj = null;
                }
                if (obj == null) {
                    try {
                        parent.cvAvailable.cvWait();
                    } catch (InterruptedException ie) {
                        return;
                    }
                }
            }
        } finally {
            parent.cvFlag.freeBusyFlag();
        }
        if (!shouldRun)
            return;
        obj.target.run();
        try {
            parent.cvFlag.getBusyFlag();
            nObjects--;
            if (nObjects == 0)
                parent.cvEmpty.cvSignal();
        } finally {
            parent.cvFlag.freeBusyFlag();
        }
        if (obj.lock != null) {
            synchronized(obj.lock) {
                obj.lock.notify();
            }
        }
        obj = null;
```

```
            }
        }
    }

    Vector objects;
    int nObjects = 0;
    CondVar cvAvailable, cvEmpty;
    BusyFlag cvFlag;
    ThreadPoolThread poolThreads[];
    boolean terminated = false;

    public ThreadPool(int n) {
        cvFlag = new BusyFlag();
        cvAvailable = new CondVar(cvFlag);
        cvEmpty = new CondVar(cvFlag);
        objects = new Vector();
        poolThreads = new ThreadPoolThread[n];
        for (int i = 0; i < n; i++) {
            poolThreads[i] = new ThreadPoolThread(this, i);
            poolThreads[i].start();
        }
    }

    private void add(Runnable target, Object lock) {
        try {
            cvFlag.getBusyFlag();
            if (terminated)
                throw new
                    IllegalStateException("Thread pool has shut down");
            objects.addElement(new ThreadPoolRequest(target, lock));
            nObjects++;
            cvAvailable.cvSignal();
        } finally {
            cvFlag.freeBusyFlag();
        }
    }

    public void addRequest(Runnable target) {
        add(target, null);
    }

    public void addRequestAndWait(Runnable target)
                        throws InterruptedException {
        Object lock = new Object();
        synchronized(lock) {
            add(target, lock);
            lock.wait();
        }
    }
```

```
        public void waitForAll(boolean terminate)
                                throws InterruptedException {
            try {
                cvFlag.getBusyFlag();
                while (nObjects != 0)
                    cvEmpty.cvWait();
                if (terminate) {
                    for (int i = 0; i < poolThreads.length; i++)
                        poolThreads[i].shouldRun = false;
                    cvAvailable.cvBroadcast();
                    terminated = true;
                }
            } finally {
                cvFlag.freeBusyFlag();
            }
        }

        public void waitForAll() throws InterruptedException {
            waitForAll(false);
        }
    }
```

The inner class in this example performs most of the work. Each thread waits for work; when it is signaled, it simply pulls the first object from the vector and executes that object. When execution of that object is finished, the thread must notify the lock associated with the object (if any) so that the addRequest-AndWait() method will know when to return; the thread must also notify the thread pool itself so that the waitForAll() method will check to see if it is time for it to return.

As a result, there are three waiting points in this code:

• Some request objects have an associated lock object (the Object created in the addRequestAndWait() method). The addRequestAndWait() method uses the standard wait and notify technique to wait on this object; it receives notification after the run() method has been executed by one of the Thread-PoolThread objects.

• A condition variable cvAvailable is associated with the cvBusyFlag. This condition is used to signal that work is available to be performed. Whenever the nObjects variable is incremented, work is available, so the add() method signals a thread that a new object is available. Similarly, when there are no objects in the vector to be processed, the ThreadPoolThreads wait on that condition variable.

• A condition variable cvEmpty is also associated with the cvBusyFlag. This condition is used to signal that all pending work has been completed—that is, that the nObjects variable has reached zero. The waitForAll() method waits for this condition, which is signaled by a ThreadPoolThread when it sets nObjects to zero.

We use condition variables for the last two cases because they share the same lock (the cvBusyFlag, which protects access to nObjects) even though they have different values for their condition. If we had used the standard wait and notify mechanism to signal threads that are interested in the value of nObjects, then we could not have controlled notification as well: whenever nObjects was set to zero, we'd have to notify all ThreadPoolThreads as well as notifying the thread that is executing the waitForAll() method.

Meanwhile, the ThreadPool class itself provides only a way to create the pool (which also sets the number of threads in the pool), to add objects to the pool, and to wait for all objects in the pool to finish. There's an unsurprising similarity here to the MediaTracker class; it's a simple extension to this class to add an ID to each object in the vector to mimic MediaTracker's interface more closely. In addition, the addRequestAndWait() method is similar to a technique that is used in the Java™ Foundation Classes (JFC) to allow arbitrary threads to operate with the JFC, even though those classes are not thread safe. We'll talk about that a little more in Chapter 8.

Note that objects that are to be run by the thread pool are expected to implement the Runnable interface. This is a potential source of confusion, since we usually use the Runnable interface to identify an object that is to be run within its own thread (and the Thread class itself implements the Runnable interface). It would be an error to create a thread object, add it to a thread pool with the addRequest() method, and then start the thread object explicitly—in this case, we expect the thread pool to run the object. But this interface seems to us to be cleaner than creating a new class or interface that would be used solely in this example. This interface also allows us to take existing code that uses threads and run those threads via a thread pool instead.

Interestingly enough, there is no way to shut down a thread pool automatically. If the thread pool object were to go out of scope, it would never be garbage collected: the thread pool thread objects (like all thread objects) are held in an internal data structure within the virtual machine, so they will not be garbage collected until they exit. And because they have a reference to the thread pool itself, the thread pool cannot be garbage collected until the thread pool threads are garbage collected. So we have to have some way of signaling the thread pool to exit: we do that by passing a true parameter to the waitForAll() method. Then, when the thread pool has run all of its jobs, the waitForAll() method arranges for the thread pool threads to terminate and marks the thread pool so that no more jobs can be added to it. The thread pool threads will then exit, and the thread pool can then be garbage collected.

Let's see an example of how to use the thread pool. Since we want to use the thread pool to limit the number of simultaneous threads, we'll use it in conjunction with the CPUSupport class that we developed in Chapter 6 so that the number of threads in the pool is equal to the number of CPUs on the machine. We'll use our TCPServer class as the basis for the entire example:

```java
import java.io.*;
import java.net.*;

public class TCPCalcServer extends TCPServer {
    class CalcObject implements Runnable {
        OutputStream os;
        InputStream is;

        CalcObject(InputStream is, OutputStream os) {
            this.os = os;
            this.is = is;
        }

        public void run() {
            // Perform calculation.
        }
    }

    ThreadPool pool;

    TCPCalcServer() {
        int numThreads = CPUSupport.getNumProcessors();
        CPUSupport.setConcurrency(numThreads + 5);
        pool = new ThreadPool(numThreads);
    }

    public static void main(String args[]) {
        try {
            new TCPCalcServer().startServer(3535);
        } catch (IOException ioe) {
            // Error processing omitted.
        }
    }

    public void run(Socket data) {
        try {
            pool.addRequest(new CalcObject(data.getInputStream(),
                                data.getOutputStream()));
        } catch (IOException ioe) {
            // Error processing omitted.
        }
    }
}
```

Remember that the real work of the TCPServer class is done in the run(data) method. In this case, we simply set up a new calculation object and add that object to the pool. We've shown a sample implementation of the skeleton of the calculation object as well, although we've left out the actual calculation. Once again, though, note that the CalcObject class implements the Runnable interface without being related to any specific thread.

Isn't the run(data) method already being run in a separate thread? Doesn't that conflict with our original goal of limiting the number of threads in the program? Our original goal was to limit the number of simultaneous threads that are active in the program. As this server is written, the thread that is created to call the run(data) method is very short-lived. So even though we still create a new thread for each client connection, the number of threads at any point in time is still fairly small. If you wanted to, you could rewrite the TCPServer class (rather than subclassing it), but this example should scale well.

Since this server is a calculation server, we need to set the number of LWPs for a Solaris system to ensure that we're taking advantage of all the CPUs available. We do that by setting the concurrency equal to the number of CPUs (adding 5 to account for I/O-bound threads in the virtual machine). And on all platforms, we set the number of threads in the pool to be the same as the number of CPUs so that we get the most effective use of the machine.

Round-Robin Scheduling

Our next examples show two ways of performing round-robin scheduling. These techniques are mostly useful for programs that will execute on a green-thread implementation of the Java virtual machine, since native-thread implementations all perform some sort of round-robin scheduling already. If you don't know which implementation your program will eventually run on, you may want to use one of these techniques to ensure round-robin scheduling, even if the underlying implementation is performing it for you: these techniques are not in conflict with native-thread implementations, though they do not necessarily provide a benefit on those platforms.

Remember that at issue here is the behavior of a Java program that contains one or more CPU-intensive threads. A Java program could have hundreds of threads that may only periodically need access to the CPU and otherwise spend most of their life in the blocked state: in that case, there isn't likely to be much competition for the CPU, and each thread gets an opportunity to run whenever it has work to do. We only face the problem of CPU starvation when there is at least one CPU-intensive thread that may potentially prevent all other threads from running.

If we have only a single CPU-intensive thread, there is no need for a complicated scheduling mechanism: all we need to do is lower the priority of the CPU-intensive thread below the priority of the other threads in our Java program. This allows the other threads to run whenever they have work to do, while the CPU-intensive thread continues to execute whenever the remaining threads are blocked. We'll build on this principle in our scheduler class: our CPU-intensive threads will all have a lower priority than threads that are mostly blocked.

We'll look at two schedulers in this section. The basic principle behind each scheduler is that each thread under its control is given a fixed amount of time during which it runs. When the specified time period elapses, another thread runs; this process proceeds indefinitely.

A Simple Round-Robin Scheduler

How do we go about creating a round-robin scheduler? Clearly, we need to begin with some sort of periodic timer; every time the timer goes off, we can make a different thread become the currently running thread. What do we need to do to make this happen?

The simplistic answer to this question is: nothing. That is, our simple scheduler is simply a high-priority timer that periodically wakes up only to go back to sleep immediately. This creates, in effect, a timer-based scheduling event: each time the timer thread wakes up, it becomes the currently running thread, which also adjusts the list of threads at the priority of the previously running thread:

```
public class SimpleScheduler extends Thread {
    int timeslice;

    public SimpleScheduler(int t) {
        timeslice = t;
        setPriority(Thread.MAX_PRIORITY);
        setDaemon(true);
    }

    public void run() {
        while (true)
            try {
                sleep(timeslice);
            } catch (Exception e) {}
    }
}
```

We'll use this class in the example from the beginning of Chapter 6 so that we can illustrate its behavior:

```
class TestThread extends Thread {
    String id;
```

```
    public TestThread(String s) {
        id = s;
    }

    public void doCalc(int i) {
    }
    public void run() {
        int i;
        for (i = 0; i < 10; i++) {
            doCalc(i);
            System.out.println(id);
        }
    }
}

public class Test {
    public static void main(String args[]) {
        new SimpleScheduler(100).start();
        TestThread t1, t2, t3;
        t1 = new TestThread("Thread 1");
        t1.start();
        t2 = new TestThread("Thread 2");
        t2.start();
        t3 = new TestThread("Thread 3");
        t3.start();
    }
}
```

In this program there are three threads (t1, t2, and t3) at the Java default
priority of NORM_PRIORITY, and the SimpleScheduler thread that runs at a priority
of MAX_PRIORITY. The SimpleScheduler thread is normally blocked, so the list of
threads starts out in this state:

```
PRIORITY 5:  t2 -> t3 -> t1 -> NULL
  BLOCKED:  SimpleScheduler -> NULL
```

At this point, t1 is the currently running thread, and we'll start to see output lines
that say "Thread 1." When SimpleScheduler wakes up, it moves to the runnable
state and, because it is the highest priority thread in the Java virtual machine, it
becomes the currently running thread:

```
PRIORITY 5:   t2 -> t3 -> t1 -> NULL
PRIORITY 10:  SimpleScheduler -> NULL
```

SimpleScheduler immediately executes the sleep() method, moving it back to
the blocked state; the Java virtual machine then selects the next thread in the list
(t2) as the currently running thread and moves it to the end of the list:

```
PRIORITY 5:  t3 -> t1 -> t2 -> NULL
  BLOCKED:  SimpleScheduler -> NULL
```

As this continues, each thread in the list of threads at priority 5 becomes the currently running thread in turn.

This scheduler requires that the virtual machine reorder the threads on a priority list whenever one of them is selected to run. As we mentioned in the last chapter, this is almost universally the case, but it is not a requirement of the Java specification, and we know of one real-time operating system on which this scheduling mechanism does not work.

Note that this mechanism still works for native-thread implementations. On a Windows implementation, the effect is that the currently running thread changes more often than specified by the sleep value within the SimpleScheduler, since the operating system will sometimes change the currently running thread while the scheduler is sleeping. On a Solaris implementation, the reordering of the threads will be dependent on the number of LWPs, but the interruption is sufficient to cause a single LWP to schedule another thread, which achieves the desired effect.

A More Complete Scheduler

Now we'll look into building a more complete scheduler that will schedule our threads in a round-robin fashion. We can also use it to limit round-robin scheduling on native-thread platforms that timeslice as their default behavior; this limiting is achieved simply by using a very large value as the timeslice that the scheduler gives to a particular thread. However, since there are circumstances on native-thread platforms where the highest priority thread is not necessarily the currently running thread, we cannot completely prevent some sort of round-robin scheduling on those platforms: the best we can do is to use this scheduler to bias the operating system to favor one particular thread.

The example we outline in this section assumes that there is a single CPU. If you need to use this technique on a machine with multiple CPUs, you will need to adjust the scheduler so that it creates N currently running threads rather than one currently running thread (where N is the number of processors on the machine). As written, this technique will work on machines with multiple processors—that is, it will prevent any CPU starvation—but it will have less of an effect on the overall scheduling of the threads.

We'll start building this scheduler by establishing threads at three priority levels:

Level 6

> The scheduler itself is a separate thread running at level 6. This allows it to run in favor of the default threads created by the Java virtual machine and APIs and in favor of any threads the scheduler is controlling. This thread spends most of its time sleeping (i.e., blocked), so it doesn't usually become the currently running thread.

Level 4

The scheduler selects one thread from all the threads it is controlling and assigns that thread a priority value of 4. Most of the time, this is the nonblocked thread with the highest priority in the Java virtual machine, so it is the thread favored to become the currently running thread.

Level 2

All remaining threads under control of our scheduler run at priority level 2. Since there is always a thread running at level 4, these threads usually do not run at this priority; they remain at this priority until they are selected by our scheduler to have a priority level of 4, at which time they become favored to be the currently running thread.

The idea behind the scheduler is that the programmer assigns certain threads to be under control of the scheduler. The scheduler selects one and only one of these threads and assigns it a priority of 4, while the rest of the threads have a priority of 2. The priority 4 thread is the currently running thread; from time to time, the scheduler itself wakes up and selects a different thread as the single priority 4 thread. On green-thread platforms, the priority 4 thread will always be selected as the currently running thread; on native-thread platforms, it will usually be selected as the currently running thread.

For all the threads in this scheduling system—the scheduler thread itself plus any threads the programmer designates to be controlled by our scheduler—it is clear that no CPU starvation will occur: the scheduler thread will always run when it needs to, and as long as that thread correctly adjusts the priorities of the remaining threads under its control, all other threads will get their opportunity to become the currently running thread.

In order to keep track of all the threads, we'll use the CircularList we developed in Chapter 5. This class gives us the queueing behavior we need to keep track of the threads under the control of our scheduler: we can add threads to the list with its insert() method, remove them with its delete() method, and, more important, go through the list by repeatedly calling its getNext() method.

Here's the first pass at our scheduler:

```
public class CPUScheduler extends Thread {
    private int timeslice;            // # of milliseconds thread should run
    private CircularList threads;     // All the threads we're scheduling

    public volatile boolean shouldRun = false; // Exit when this is set

    public CPUScheduler(int t) {
        threads = new CircularList();
        timeslice = t;
    }
```

```
public void addThread(Thread t) {
    threads.insert(t);
    t.setPriority(2);
}

public void removeThread(Thread t) {
    t.setPriority(5);
    threads.delete(t);
}

public void run() {
    Thread current;
    setPriority(6);
    while (shouldRun) {
        current = (Thread) threads.getNext();
        if (current == null)
            return;
        current.setPriority(4);
        try {
            Thread.sleep(timeslice);
        } catch (InterruptedException ie) {};
        current.setPriority(2);
    }
}
}
```

Although there are some necessary adjustments that we'll add to this scheduler throughout the rest of this chapter, this code is the essence of the scheduler. The refinements that we'll add are important in terms of making the class robust and thread safe, but they don't add to the basic functionality: we want to understand the functionality before we look at some of the subtle issues involved in this class.

The programmer uses two methods to interface with the scheduler: addThread(), which adds a thread to the list of thread objects under control of the scheduler, and removeThread(), which removes a thread object from that list.*

Given this interface, we can use the CPUScheduler class in the ThreadTest class we introduced at the beginning of this section:

```
class TestThread extends Thread {
    String id;

    public TestThread(String s) {
        id = s;
```

---

* There's a subtle error here, in that when the thread is removed from the scheduler, we assign it the default thread priority rather than the priority it had when it was added to the scheduler. The correct practice would be to save the thread's priority in the call to the addThread() method and then restore that priority in the removeThread() method; we'll leave that implementation to the reader.

```
        }

        public void doCalc(int i) {
        }

        public void run() {
            int i;
            for (i = 0; i < 10; i++) {
                doCalc(i);
                System.out.println(id);
            }
        }
    }

public class Test {
    public static void main(String args[]) {
        CPUScheduler c = new CPUScheduler(100);
        TestThread t1, t2, t3;
        t1 = new TestThread("Thread 1");
        t2 = new TestThread("Thread 2");
        t3 = new TestThread("Thread 3");
        c.addThread(t1);
        c.addThread(t2);
        c.addThread(t3);
        t1.start();
        t2.start();
        t3.start();
        c.start();
    }
}
```

When our program calls c.start(), the CPUScheduler's run() method gets called; it is this run() method that actually manipulates all the threads to create the timesliced, round-robin scheduling. At its base level, the logic for our scheduler is simple: it loops forever, going through all the threads in our circular list of threads and adjusting their priorities as it goes. In between, it sleeps for timeslice milliseconds. The current thread runs for that many milliseconds before the scheduler wakes up again and readjusts the thread's priority. When there are no threads left to schedule—which would happen if the programmer had called removeThread() on all the threads previously added—the CPUScheduler exits by returning from the run() method.

Let's examine how the four threads in our program—threads t1, t2, t3, and the CPUScheduler thread—will behave now. After we call the c.start() method, the threads in the program are in this state:

```
PRIORITY 2:  t1 -> t2 -> t3 -> NULL
PRIORITY 6:  CPUScheduler -> NULL
```

As the highest priority thread in the program, the CPUScheduler thread is the currently running thread. It starts executing the run() method, where the first thing it does is change the priority of thread t1 to 4:

```
PRIORITY 2:  t2 -> t3 -> NULL
PRIORITY 4:  t1 -> NULL
PRIORITY 6:  CPUScheduler -> NULL
```

The CPUScheduler, still the currently running thread, now sleeps, placing it into the blocked state. This causes t1 to become the currently running thread:

```
PRIORITY 2:  t2 -> t3 -> NULL
PRIORITY 4:  t1 -> NULL
   BLOCKED:  CPUScheduler -> NULL
```

When the CPUScheduler thread wakes up, it changes the priority of t1 back to 2 and the priority of t2 to 4:

```
PRIORITY 2:  t3 -> t1 -> NULL
PRIORITY 4:  t2 -> NULL
PRIORITY 6:  CPUScheduler -> NULL
```

And so the cycle continues.

Adjustment 1: Synchronizing data within the CPUScheduler

Now that we have the base logic of the CPUScheduler written correctly, we need to make sure the CPUScheduler class is itself thread safe and that we haven't introduced any race conditions into the scheduler by having incorrectly synchronized data. We'll go through this process in a series of stages because the example illustrates the necessary steps that you must take in designing any class to work with multiple threads.

At first glance, there don't appear to be any variables that need synchronization: the only instance variable that needs to be protected is the variable threads, and all changes to the threads variable occur via methods of the CircularList class that are already synchronized. But what would happen if you called the removeThread() method and removed the thread that the CPUScheduler has marked as the current thread? It would be an error for the CPUScheduler to change the priority of this thread once it has been removed from the threads list, so the removeThread() method must somehow inform the CPUScheduler that the current thread has been removed.

This means that the variable current must become an instance variable so that both the run() and removeThread() methods can access it. We can then synchronize access to that variable. Here's the new CPUScheduler class:

```
public class CPUScheduler extends Thread {
    ...
    private Thread current;
```

```
    public void removeThread(t) {
        t.setPriority(5);
        threads.delete(t);
        synchronized(this) {
            if (current == t)
                current = null;
        }
    }
    ...
    public void run() {
        ...
        try {
            Thread.sleep(timeslice);
        } catch (InterruptedException ie) {};
        synchronized(this) {
            if (current != null)
                current.setPriority(2);
        }
    }
}
```

Alternatively, we could make the `run()` and `removeThread()` methods themselves synchronized:

```
    public synchronized void run() {
        ...
    }

    public synchronized void removeThread(Thread t) {
        ...
    }
```

As we've seen, making the `run()` method synchronized is typically a bad idea, so we'll reject this idea for now, but we'll be revisiting this decision soon.

Adjustment 2: Making CPUScheduler thread safe

We've synchronized all the variables of our CPUScheduler, but we're still not protected from threads that exit while they are under our control.

In particular, the `run()` method changes the priority of a thread, which is a valid operation only if a thread is in the runnable state. What happens if the thread that we've assigned to level 4 exits its `run()` method while our CPUScheduler is sleeping? When the CPUScheduler wakes up, it tries to set the priority of that thread, which is now in the exiting state, to 2—an operation that generates an exception. Similarly, if the thread that is running decides to call the `stop()` method of one of the priority 2 threads in the CPUScheduler's list, then the next time the CPUScheduler selects that thread and sets its priority, we'll get an exception.

So we need to place all the calls to the `setPriority()` method inside a `try/catch` clause in order to be alerted to these types of situations. This means we must modify our code everywhere we call the `setPriority()` method:

```
public void removeThread(Thread t) {
    try {
        t.setPriority(5);
    } catch(Exception e) {}
    threads.delete(t);
    synchronized(this) {
        if (current == t)
            current = null;
    }
}

public void run() {
    while (shouldRun) {
        ...
        try {
            current.setPriority(4);
        } catch (Exception e) {
            removeThread(current);
        }
        ...
        synchronized(this) {
            if (current != null)
                try {
                    current.setPriority(2);
                } catch (Exception e) {
                    removeThread(current);
                }
        }
        ...
    }
}
```

Note that in in the `run()` method, when the exception is thrown we need to remove the thread from the list of threads we're interested in, which means that we must also use the `catch` clause in the `removeThread()` method.

Adjustment 3: More thread-safe modifications

We've made the methods of the CPUScheduler thread-safe, but what about the class itself? What if two threads try to create a CPUScheduler? This would be very confusing: we'd end up with two scheduling threads that would compete with each other to schedule other threads. So we need to allow only one instance of the class to be instantiated. We'll do this by creating a static variable in the class and testing it to make sure that an instance of the CPUScheduler class doesn't already exist. Because we can't make the constructor itself synchronized, we'll also need to introduce a synchronized method to access this static variable. Thus the constructor and related code for the class now look like this:

```
public class CPUScheduler extends Thread {
    private static boolean initialized = false;
    private synchronized static boolean isInitialized() {
        if (initialized)
            return true;
        initialized = true;
        return false;
    }

    public CPUScheduler(int t) {
        if (isInitialized())
            throw new SecurityException("Already initialized");
        threads = new CircularList();
        timeslice = t;
    }
}
```

Adjustment 4: Devising an exit mechanism

If all the threads under its control exit, the CPUScheduler itself exits. In a program where the tasks are well defined at the beginning of execution—like the TestThread class we've looked at so far—that might be fine. But what if we wanted to add the CPUScheduler to our TCPServer? As presently written, the CPUScheduler wouldn't work for that case: as soon as no clients were connected to the TCPServer, the CPUScheduler would exit, and any further clients that connected to the server would not be timesliced.

Instead, we need to make the CPUScheduler a daemon thread and adjust the logic of its run() method. This should make sense: the CPUScheduler is only useful when there are other threads in the program that it can schedule. In the TCP-Server case, there will always be at least one other thread in the program: the listener thread of the TCPServer. That listener thread creates other threads for the CPUScheduler to manipulate as clients connect to the server. The implementation of our timesliced TCPServer to perform calculations looks like this:

```
import java.net.*;
import java.io.*;

public class CalcServer {
    public static void main(String args[]) {
        CalcRequest r = new CalcRequest();
        try {
            r.startServer(3535);
```

```
        } catch (Exception e) {
            System.out.println("Unable to start server");
        }
    }
}

class CalcRequest extends TCPServer {
    CPUScheduler scheduler;
    CalcRequest() {
        scheduler = new CPUScheduler(100);
        scheduler.start();
    }

    void doCalc(Socket s) {
    }

    public void run(Socket s) {
        scheduler.addThread(Thread.currentThread());
        doCalc(s);
    }
}
```

Every time the run() method of the CalcRequest class is called, it is called in a new thread, so we need to add that thread to the CPUScheduler that was created in the constructor of the class. As long as the CPUScheduler doesn't exit when there are no threads to schedule (which now means simply that no client is currently connected), we'll have a timesliced calculation server. During an active session of our CalcServer, we'll have these threads:

One listener thread
    The thread that waits for connections and creates the client threads.

Zero or more client threads
    These threads execute the calculation on behalf of a connected client.

CPUScheduler thread
    The daemon thread performing the scheduling.

We can gracefully shut down the CalcServer by setting the shouldRun flag of the server to false; eventually the client threads complete their calculation and exit. When all the client threads have exited, only the daemon CPUScheduler thread remains in the program, and the program terminates.

We need to change the CPUScheduler so that instead of returning when there are no threads to be scheduled, it simply waits for more threads. Here's the entire code for the modified CPUScheduler class (we'll show the entire class here, since at this point, we have a complete implementation):

```
public class CPUScheduler extends Thread {
    private CircularList threads;
```

```java
private Thread current;
private int timeslice;
private static boolean initialized = false;
private boolean needThreads;

private static synchronized boolean isInitialized() {
    if (initialized)
        return true;
    initialized = true;
    return false;
}

public CPUScheduler(int t) {
    if (isInitialized())
        throw new SecurityException("Already initialized");
    threads = new CircularList();
    timeslice = t;
    setDaemon(true);
}

public synchronized void addThread(Thread t) {
    t.setPriority(2);
    threads.insert(t);
    if (needThreads) {
        needThreads = false;
        notify();
    }
}

public void removeThread(Thread t) {
    threads.delete(t);
    synchronized(this) {
        if (t == current)
            current = null;
    }
}

public synchronized void run() {
    setPriority(6);
    while (true) {
        current = (Thread) threads.getNext();
        while (current == null) {
            needThreads = true;
            try {
                wait();
            } catch (Exception e) {}
            current = (Thread) threads.getNext();
        }
        try {
            current.setPriority(4);
```

```
                } catch (Exception e) {
                    removeThread(current);
                    continue;
                }
                try {
                    wait(timeslice);
                } catch (InterruptedException ie) {};
                if (current != null) {
                    try {
                        current.setPriority(2);
                    } catch (Exception e) {
                        removeThread(current);
                    }
                }
            }
        }
    }
```

In the constructor, we've set the thread to be a daemon thread—the point of this adjustment. Note that we also changed the run() method so that when we try to retrieve a thread from the list, we loop until one is available. If no thread is in the list, we wait until one is available, which requires that we add a flag to the addThread() method to signify whether it should notify the CPUScheduler thread that a thread has been added.

In addition, note that we've changed the run() method itself to a synchronized method and replaced the call to the sleep() method with a call to the wait() method. This is one example of the exception to the general rule that the run() method should not be synchronized: since we actually spend more time waiting in this method than executing code, its quite okay to synchronize the run() method, since it will release the lock whenever it waits for something to happen.

Adjustment 5: Non-CPU-intensive threads

What happens in our scheduler if the currently running thread blocks? Let's see what would happen to our TestThread program if the currently running thread suddenly entered the blocked state. We'd start out with the threads in a state like this:

```
PRIORITY 2:   t3 -> t1 -> NULL
PRIORITY 4:   t2 -> NULL
  BLOCKED:    CPUScheduler -> NULL
```

Thread t2 is the currently running thread, executing its calculations while the CPUScheduler is sleeping. If t2 now enters the blocked state for some reason, we end up with threads in this state:

```
PRIORITY 2:   t3 -> t1 -> NULL
PRIORITY 4:   NULL
  BLOCKED:    t2 -> CPUScheduler -> NULL
```

This means that t3 becomes the currently running thread, even though it's at priority 2. When the CPUScheduler wakes up, it resets the priority of t2 to 2, sets the priority of t3 to 4, and goes back to sleep, leaving our threads in this state:

```
PRIORITY 2:   t1 -> NULL
PRIORITY 4:   t3 -> NULL
   BLOCKED:   t2 -> CPUScheduler -> NULL
```

Everything is okay again, but at some point it will be t2's turn to be priority 4. Since the CPUScheduler has no way of determining that t2 is blocked, it sets the priority of t2 to 4. The Java scheduler again selects one of the threads at priority 2 to be the currently running thread.

Our code was correct: the threads involved all got some timeslice in which to run. But there was a short period of time during which the CPUScheduler slept, the priority 4 thread blocked, and a priority 2 thread became the currently running thread. In effect, this priority 2 thread stole some CPU time; it could do this because there was a time gap between when the priority 4 thread blocked and the priority 6 thread woke up.

It's probably not a crisis that this happened, since once the CPUScheduler woke up, we got back to the thread state we wanted. We could have prevented this CPU stealing from happening if somehow we knew when the priority 4 thread had blocked. However, on a native-thread platform, we cannot prevent a lower-priority thread from running at some point anyway, which is really just a variation of the behavior that we're discussing here. So solving this problem is not something that we'll be able to do in an absolute sense.

It is conceivable that on a green-thread platform, we could create a new thread within the CPUScheduler class at priority 3. When the priority 4 thread blocks, this priority 3 thread would become the currently running thread; this priority 3 thread could inform the priority 6 thread that it should wake up and perform some scheduling. Note that on a native-thread platform this does not work: the priority 3 thread might still run even if the priority 4 thread has not blocked, and on a Windows platform, priority 3 and 4 share the same underlying operating system priority. Altering the priority levels of the threads to avoid this overlap—by, for example, running the scheduler at priority 8 and the target thread at priority 6—is a possibility, but we've seen that putting a CPU-intensive thread above the default priority level (especially the level at which the system GUI thread runs) is not always a good idea. And this does not prevent the priority 3 thread from running when the target thread is not blocked.

Even on a green-thread platform, this problem is impossible to solve in the general case. If all the threads to be scheduled were to block, then the priority 3 thread would continually run, consuming a lot of CPU resources but performing no real work. In the first edition of this book, we showed how to overcome that problem by suspending the priority 3 thread, but now the suspend() method has been deprecated, so that solution is no longer an option. And since the benefit provided by such a solution would be very marginal, we're not too worried that such a solution does not exist.

The moral of the story is what we've said all along: Java's scheduling mechanisms give you some control over how threads are scheduled, but that control is never absolute.

Job Scheduling

We'll conclude our examples with an examination of job scheduling. Unlike round-robin scheduling, job scheduling is not related to thread starvation prevention or fairness. The concept of job scheduling is more closely related to when a runnable object is executed than to how a runnable object is run.

There are many applications of job scheduling. We could have a word processor application that needs to save work every five minutes to prevent data loss. We could have a backup program that needs to do an incremental backup every day; this same program may also need to do a full backup once a week. In our Animate applet (see Chapter 2), we needed to generate a repaint request every second. At the time, we accomplished that by having the timer thread schedule itself by calling the sleep() method repeatedly. In that example, the scheduling of the repaint request was simple to implement, and we only had this single repeated job to schedule.

For more complex scheduling of jobs, or for programs that have countless jobs that need to be scheduled, having a dedicated job scheduler may be easier than implementing the scheduling of every job in the program. Furthermore, in the case of the timer thread, we needed to create a thread just to handle the job. If many jobs are required, a job scheduler may be preferred over having many threads that schedule themselves. This dedicated job scheduler can run all the jobs in its own thread, or it can assign the jobs to a thread pool to better use the thread resources of the underlying platform.

Here's an implementation of a job scheduler class:

```java
import java.util.*;

public class JobScheduler implements Runnable {
    final public static int ONCE = 1;
    final public static int FOREVER = -1;
    final public static long HOURLY = (long)60*60*1000;
    final public static long DAILY = 24*HOURLY;
    final public static long WEEKLY = 7*DAILY;
```

```java
final public static long MONTHLY = -1;
final public static long YEARLY = -2;

private class JobNode {
    public Runnable job;
    public Date executeAt;
    public long interval;
    public int count;
}
private ThreadPool tp;
private DaemonLock dlock = new DaemonLock();
private Vector jobs = new Vector(100);

public JobScheduler(int poolSize) {
    tp = (poolSize > 0) ? new ThreadPool(poolSize) : null;
    Thread js = new Thread(this);
    js.setDaemon(true);
    js.start();
}

private synchronized void addJob(JobNode job) {
    dlock.acquire();
    jobs.addElement(job);
    notify();
}

private synchronized void deleteJob(Runnable job) {
    for (int i=0; i < jobs.size(); i++) {
        if (((JobNode) jobs.elementAt(i)).job == job) {
            jobs.removeElementAt(i);
            dlock.release();
            break;
        }
    }
}

private JobNode updateJobNode(JobNode jn) {
    Calendar cal = Calendar.getInstance();
    cal.setTime(jn.executeAt);
    if (jn.interval == MONTHLY) {
        // There is a minor bug (see java.util.calendar).
        cal.add(Calendar.MONTH, 1);
        jn.executeAt = cal.getTime();
    } else if (jn.interval == YEARLY) {
        cal.add(Calendar.YEAR, 1);
        jn.executeAt = cal.getTime();
    } else {
        jn.executeAt =
            new Date(jn.executeAt.getTime() + jn.interval);
```

```
        }
        jn.count = (jn.count == FOREVER) ? FOREVER : jn.count - 1;
        return (jn.count != 0) ? jn : null;
    }

    private synchronized long runJobs() {
        long minDiff = Long.MAX_VALUE;
        long now = System.currentTimeMillis();

        for (int i=0; i < jobs.size();) {
            JobNode jn = (JobNode) jobs.elementAt(i);
            if (jn.executeAt.getTime() <= now) {
                if (tp != null) {
                    tp.addRequest(jn.job);
                } else {
                    Thread jt = new Thread(jn.job);
                    jt.setDaemon(false);
                    jt.start();
                }
                if (updateJobNode(jn) == null) {
                    jobs.removeElementAt(i);
                    dlock.release();
                }
            } else {
                long diff = jn.executeAt.getTime() - now;
                minDiff = Math.min(diff, minDiff);
                i++;
            }
        }
        return minDiff;
    }

    public synchronized void run() {
        while (true) {
            long waitTime = runJobs();
            try {
                wait(waitTime);
            } catch (Exception e) {};
        }
    }

    public void execute(Runnable job) {
        executeIn(job, (long)0);
    }

    public void executeIn(Runnable job, long millis) {
        executeInAndRepeat(job, millis, 1000, ONCE);

    }
```

```java
    public void executeInAndRepeat(Runnable job,
                                   long millis, long repeat) {
        executeInAndRepeat(job, millis, repeat, FOREVER);

    }
    public void executeInAndRepeat(Runnable job, long millis,
                                   long repeat, int count) {
        Date when = new Date(System.currentTimeMillis() + millis);
        executeAtAndRepeat(job, when, repeat, count);
    }

    public void executeAt(Runnable job, Date when) {
        executeAtAndRepeat(job, when, 1000, ONCE);
    }

    public void executeAtAndRepeat(Runnable job, Date when,
                                   long repeat) {
        executeAtAndRepeat(job, when, repeat, FOREVER);
    }

    public void executeAtAndRepeat(Runnable job, Date when,
                                   long repeat, int count) {
        JobNode jn = new JobNode();
        jn.job = job;
        jn.executeAt = when;
        jn.interval = repeat;
        jn.count = count;
        addJob(jn);
    }

    public void cancel(Runnable job) {
        deleteJob(job);
    }
}
```

Surprisingly, the implementation of a job scheduler is fairly simple: we just need to iterate over the requested jobs (the elements of the jobs vector) and either add the jobs that need to be executed to a thread pool for processing or start a new thread to execute the job. In addition, we need to find the time for the job that is due to run next, and wait for this time to occur. This entire process is then repeated.

For completeness, we've added a little complexity in our JobScheduler class. In addition to accepting a runnable object that can be executed and a time at which to perform the job, we also accept a count of the number of times the job is to be performed and the time to wait between executions of the job. Hence, after a job is executed, we need to calculate whether another execution is necessary and when to perform this execution.

In our JobScheduler class, this is all handled by a single thread that calls the `runJobs()` method. The task of deciding whether the job needs to be executed again is done by the `updateJobNode()` method; adding jobs to and deleting jobs from the requested jobs vector is accomplished by the `addJob()` and `deleteJob()` methods, respectively. Most of the logic for the JobScheduler class is actually the implementation of the many options and methods in the interface provided for the programmer.

There are eight methods provided to the programmer in our JobScheduler class:

public void execute(Runnable job)
> Used for jobs that are executed once; simply runs the job.

public void executeIn(Runnable job, long millis)
> Used for jobs that are executed once; runs the job after the specified number of milliseconds have elapsed.

public void executeAt(Runnable job, Date when)
> Used for jobs that are executed once; runs the job at the time specified.

public void executeInAndRepeat(Runnable job, long millis, long repeat)
public void executeInAndRepeat(Runnable job, long millis, long repeat, int count)
> Used for repeating jobs. These methods run the job after the number of milliseconds specified by the `millis` parameter has elapsed. Then they run the job again after the number of milliseconds specified by the `repeat` parameter has elapsed. This process is repeated as specified by the `count` parameter. If no count is specified, the job will be repeated forever.
>
> The constants HOURLY, DAILY, WEEKLY, MONTHLY, and YEARLY may also be passed as the `repeat` parameter. The HOURLY, DAILY, and WEEKLY parameters are provided for convenience. However, the MONTHLY and YEARLY parameters are processed differently by the job scheduler since the scheduler has to take into account the different number of days in the month and the leap year.

public void executeAtAndRepeat(Runnable job, Date when, long repeat)
public void executeAtAndRepeat(Runnable job, Date when, long repeat, int count)
> Used for repeating jobs. These methods run the job at the time specified, then run the job again after the specified number of milliseconds has elapsed. This process is repeated as specified by the `count` parameter. If no count is specified, the job will be repeated forever.
>
> These methods also support the HOURLY, DAILY, WEEKLY, MONTHLY, and YEARLY constants.

public void cancel(Runnable job)
> Cancels the specified job. No error is generated if the job is not in the requested jobs vector, since it is possible that the job has executed and been

removed from the vector before the `cancel()` method is called. If the same job is placed on the list more than once, this method will remove the first job that it finds on the list.

As rich as this set of methods is, it can be considered weak by those who have used job schedulers provided by some operating systems. In those systems, developers can specify criteria such as day of the week, day of the month, week of the year, and so on.

Criteria for jobs are often defined this way. We do not think of a backup as running on a particular day and time, but on a particular day of the week (e.g., every Sunday at 2:00 A.M.). Paychecks are issued on the 1st and 15th day of the month. Vacation time-shares are assigned by the week in the year. With design requirements that are modeled from the real world, the job scheduler may have to be modified to support these requirements.

The task of enhancing the job scheduler for these cases is left as an exercise for the reader. However, this is not very difficult to accomplish, given the availability of the Calendar class. For example, with this class, we can easily develop the enhancement for executing a job at a certain day of the week, starting from a particular day:

```
public void executeAtNextDOW(Runnable job, Date when, int DOW) {
    Calendar target = Calendar.getInstance();
    target.setTime(when);
    while (target.get(Calendar.DAY_OF_WEEK) != DOW)
        target.add(Calendar.DATE, 1);
    executeAt(job, target.getTime());
}
```

With this enhancement, we can now execute a job on Sunday like this:

```
executeAtNextDOW(job, new Date(), Calendar.SUNDAY);
```

Should the job scheduler be implemented by using a daemon thread? At first glance, this seems like a good choice. After all, if there are no user threads, then there are no jobs to be scheduled. The problem is that there may be jobs on the vector that are already scheduled and are waiting to be executed. Since these jobs do not schedule themselves, there are no threads assigned to them while they wait on the vector. It is therefore possible for all user threads to exit while there are still jobs to be scheduled. In this situation, if the job scheduler was configured as a daemon thread, it would exit with jobs still waiting to be executed.

By using the DaemonLock class that we developed in Chapter 6, we can do a little better: we can make the job scheduler a daemon thread, and we can ensure that it will exit only when there are no more jobs to schedule and there are no other user threads running. All we need to do is acquire the daemon lock when jobs are added to the scheduler, and release the daemon lock when jobs are removed from the scheduler. This only works when the job scheduler is constructed without a thread pool (that is, when each job will be run in a new thread), since the thread pool threads are not daemon threads.

Summary

We've shown four scheduling techniques in the chapter. The most useful of these is the notion of thread pools: a set of threads that sit idle until work is available for them. A thread pool is very useful in limiting the number of threads that are active within the virtual machine while making the best use of the host machine's CPU resources.

We've also shown two techniques that can be used to perform (or limit) round-robin scheduling. Neither of these techniques is completely satisfactory: the SimpleScheduler is not guaranteed to work on all platforms, even though it works on the vast majority of them, and the CPUScheduler may show some anomalous behavior when threads under its control block. Nonetheless, for CPU-intensive threads, these techniques are very useful when you need to influence the scheduling behavior that the Java virtual machine and its host operating system provide for you.

Finally, we've shown how to perform batch-oriented job scheduling without requiring multiple timer threads for each job. While this is a useful mechanism in its own right, it also shows how many of the other techniques that we've already developed can be applied to writing thread utilities.

8

Advanced Synchronization Topics

In this chapter, we will look into some of the more advanced issues related to data synchronization. When you write a Java program that makes use of several threads, issues related to data synchronization are those most likely to create difficulties in the design of the program, and errors in data synchronization are often the most difficult to detect, since they depend on events happening in a specific order. Often an error in data synchronization can be masked in the code by timing dependencies. You may notice some sort of data corruption in a normal run of your program, but when you run the program in a debugger or add some debugging statements to the code, the timing of the program is completely changed, and the data corruption no longer occurs.

Synchronization Terms

Programmers with a background in a particular threading system generally tend to use terms specific to that system to refer to some of the concepts we discuss in this chapter, and programmers without a background in certain threading systems will not necessarily understand the terms we choose to use. So here's a comparison of particular terms you may be familiar with and how they relate to the terms in this chapter:

Barrier

A barrier is a rendezvous point for multiple threads: all threads must arrive at the barrier before any of them are permitted to proceed past the barrier. Java has no barrier class, but we implemented one in Chapter 5.

Condition variable

A condition variable is not actually a lock: it is a variable associated with a lock. Condition variables are often used in the context of data synchronization.

Condition variables generally have an API that achieves the same functionality as Java's wait and notify mechanism; in that mechanism, the condition variable is actually the object the lock is protecting. We implemented a condition variable in Chapter 5.

Critical section

A critical section is the same as a synchronized method or block. Critical sections do not nest like synchronized methods or blocks.

Event variables

Event variables are the same as condition variables.

Lock

This term refers to the access granted to a particular thread that has entered a synchronized method or a synchronized block. We say that a thread that has entered such a method or block has acquired the lock. As we discussed in Chapter 3, this lock is associated with either a particular instance of an object or a particular class.

Monitor

A generic synchronization term used inconsistently between threading systems. In some systems, a monitor is simply a lock; in others, a monitor is similar to the wait and notify mechanism.

Mutex

Another term for a lock. Mutexes do not nest like synchronized methods or blocks and generally can be used across processes at the operating-system level.

Reader-writer locks

A lock that can be acquired by multiple threads simultaneously as long as the threads agree to only read from the shared data, or that can be acquired by a single thread that wants to write to the shared data. Java has no reader-writer locks, but we'll develop a reader-writer lock class later in this chapter.

Semaphores

Semaphores are used inconsistently in computer systems. Many developers use semaphores to lock objects in the same way Java locks are used; this usage makes them equivalent to mutexes. A more sophisticated use of semaphores is to take advantage of the counter associated with them to nest acquisition to the critical section of the code; Java locks are exactly equivalent to semaphores in this usage. Semaphores are also used to gain access to resources other than code; the example of acquiring resources that we showed in the ResourceThrottle class in Chapter 4 implements this type of semaphore behavior.

Preventing Deadlock

Deadlock between threads competing for the same set of locks is the hardest problem to solve in any threaded program. It's a hard enough problem, in fact, that we will not solve it—or even attempt to solve it. Instead, we'll try to offer a good understanding of deadlock and some guidelines on how to prevent it. Preventing deadlock is completely the responsibility of the Java developer—the Java virtual machine will not do deadlock prevention or deadlock detection on your behalf.

We'll look at deadlock in conjunction with the following code, which emulates how a kitchen might operate. When a cook wants to make cookies, she grabs the measuring cup to measure ingredients into the bowl; when a cook wants to make an omelette, he grabs a bowl, beats some eggs, and then measures out the eggs for each individual omelette. This is the order a typical cook uses to make these items, and as long as we have only one cook, everything is fine with these procedures. If we have two cooks, however, and one wants to make cookies while the other wants to make omelettes, we have a deadlock situation: the omelette maker needs the measuring cup to measure out the eggs that are in the mixing bowl; the cookie maker needs the bowl to put in the flour that is in the measuring cup:*

```
public class Kitchen {
    static MeasuringCup theCup;
    static Bowl theBowl;

    public void makeCookie() {
        synchronized(theCup) {
            theCup.measureOut(1, theFlour);
            synchronized(theBowl) {
                theBowl.putIngredients(theCup);
                theBowl.mix();
            }
        }
    }

    public void makeOmelette() {
        synchronized(theBowl) {
            Eggs e[] = getBrokenEggs();
            theBowl.putIngredients(e);
            theBowl.mix();
            synchronized(theCup) {
                theCup.measureOut(theBowl);
            }
```

---

* Obviously, the code examples in this section are not complete examples. In addition to lacking all the methods and classes to which we refer, we're missing some other useful methods as well. For example, our class does not include a recipe for soup, since a multithreaded recipe would spoil the broth.

```
        }
    }
}
```

Like previous examples of deadlock we've seen, this example is simple, but more complicated conditions of deadlock follow the same principles outlined here: they're harder to detect, but nothing more is involved than two or more threads attempting to acquire each other's locks.

Deadlock is difficult to detect because it can involve many classes that call each other's synchronized sections (that is, synchronized methods or synchronized blocks) in an order that isn't apparently obvious. Say we have 26 classes, A to Z, and that the synchronized methods of class A call those of class B, those of class B call class C, and so on, until those of class Z call those of class A. This leads us into the same sort of deadlock situation that we had between our makeCookie() and makeOmelette() methods, but it's unlikely that a programmer examining the source code would detect that deadlock.

Nonetheless, a close examination of the source code is the only option presently available to determine if deadlock is a possibility. Java virtual machines do not detect deadlock at runtime, and while it is possible to develop tools that examine the source code to detect potential deadlock situations, no such tools exist yet for Java.

The simplest way to avoid deadlock is to follow the rule that a synchronized method should never call a synchronized method. That's a good rule, often advocated, but it's not the ideal rule for two reasons:

- It's impractical: many useful Java methods are synchronized, and you'll want to call them from your synchronized method. As an example, we've called the addElement() method of Java's Vector class from several of our synchronized methods.

- It's overkill: if the synchronized method you're going to call does not in turn call another synchronized method, there's no way that deadlock can occur (which is why we always got away with calling the addElement() method from a synchronized method; the addElement() method makes no further synchronization calls). Generically, the synchronized method can call other synchronized methods in ways we'll explore later.

Nonetheless, if you can manage to obey this rule, there will be no deadlock in your program.

Another often-used technique to avoid deadlock is to lock some higher-order object that is related to the many lower-order objects we'll need to use: in our example, that means locking the kitchen instead of locking the individual utensils as we use them. This makes our methods synchronized as follows:

```
public class Kitchen {
    public synchronized void makeCookie() { ... }
    public synchronized void makeOmelette() { ... }
}
```

Of course, we don't need to lock everything. We could create a BusyFlag for the measuring cup and bowl combination and just acquire that lock whenever we needed one or the other utensil. We also could make it a programmatic rule that to use either the measuring cup or mixing bowl, you must acquire the lock only for the mixing bowl. All these variations of locking multiple objects suffer from the same lock granularity problem that we're about to discuss.

The problem with this technique is that it often leads to situations where the locking granularity is not ideal. By synchronizing the methods of the Kitchen class, we are essentially preventing more than one cook from using the kitchen at a time; the purpose of having multiple threads is to allow more than one cook to use the kitchen. If we've done our program design correctly, there was probably a reason why we attempted to acquire multiple locks rather than a single global lock. Solving deadlock issues by violating this design becomes somewhat counterproductive.

The most practical rule to avoid deadlock is to make sure that locks are always acquired in the same order. In the case of our deadlock example, this would mean making sure that the mixing bowl lock is always acquired before the measuring cup lock (or vice versa, as long as we're consistent). This implies the need for a lock hierarchy among classes. The lock hierarchy is unrelated to the Java class hierarchy: it is a hierarchy of objects rather than of classes. Furthermore, the hierarchy of the locks is unrelated to the hierarchy of the classes: the MeasuringCup and Bowl classes are probably sibling classes in the class hierarchy, but in the lock hierarchy, we must place one object above the other. The lock hierarchy is a queue rather than a tree: each object in the hierarchy must have one and only one parent object (as in the Java class hierarchy), but it must have one and only one descendant as well.

If you're developing a complex program in Java, it's a good idea to develop a lock hierarchy when you develop your class hierarchy; sample hierarchies are shown in Figure 8-1. But since there is no mechanism to enforce the lock hierarchy, it's up to your good programming practices to make sure that the lock hierarchy is followed.

We can use this rule to prevent deadlock in our kitchen by requiring that all methods acquire the bowl before the measuring cup even if they intend to use the measuring cup first. We'd rewrite the makeCookie() method like this:

```
public void makeCookie() {
    synchronized(theBowl) {
        synchronized(theCup) {
            theCup.measureOut(1, theFlour);
            theBowl.putIngredients(theCup);
            theBowl.mix();
        }
    }
}
```

Following this lock acquisition hierarchy is the best way to guarantee that deadlock will not occur in your Java program when you use the standard synchronization techniques of the Java language.

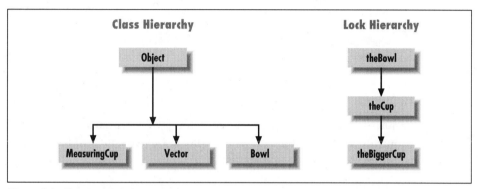

Figure 8-1. Class and lock hierarchies

What about the BusyFlag class that we've developed; could that be useful in preventing deadlock? The answer is yes, to a point. Using the BusyFlag class adds a certain complexity to a Java program, and it introduces the possibility of a new kind of deadlock that standard Java synchronization techniques don't allow. But the BusyFlag class also allows us to build more complicated deadlock recovery into our program, which may be useful in certain circumstances.

The feature in the BusyFlag class that helps us avoid deadlock is the `tryGet-BusyFlag()` method. In standard Java synchronization calls, there is no such concept as testing the acquisition of a lock: standard Java threads attempt to acquire the lock and block until the lock is acquired. The BusyFlag class allows us to see if we can acquire the lock and also attempts some sort of recovery if the flag is busy.

Let's rewrite our kitchen example to use the BusyFlag:

```
public class Kitchen {
    static MeasuringCup theCup;
    static Bowl theBowl;
    static BusyFlag theCupFlag, theBowlFlag;
```

```
    public void makeCookie() {
        theCupFlag.getBusyFlag();
        theCup.measureOut(1, theFlour);
        theBowlFlag.getBusyFlag();
        theBowl.putIngredients(theCup);
        theBowl.mix();
        theBowlFlag.freeBusyFlag();
        theCupFlag.freeBusyFlag();
    }

    public void makeOmelette() {
        theBowlFlag.getBusyFlag();
        Eggs e[] = getBrokenEggs();
        theBowl.putIngredients(e);
        theBowl.mix();
        theCupFlag.getBusyFlag();
        theCup.measureOut(theBowl);
        theCupFlag.freeBusyFlag();
        theBowlFlag.freeBusyFlag();
    }
}
```

So far we've just substituted the BusyFlag class for Java's standard synchronized blocks, with the effect that we can still have deadlock. But we could go further and rewrite the makeCookie() method like this:

```
    public void makeCookie() {
        theCupFlag.getBusyFlag();
        theCup.measureOut(1, theFlour);
        if (theBowlFlag.tryGetBusyFlag()) {
            theBowl.putIngredients(theCup);
            theBowl.mix();
            theBowlFlag.freeBusyFlag();
        }
        else {
            // ... Do something else ...
        }
        theCupFlag.freeBusyFlag();
    }
```

Here we've prevented deadlock by testing to see if the bowl's BusyFlag is free as we grab it. If the flag is free, we'll grab the lock and continue to make our cookies. Even if, at this point, another cook thread comes along to make an omelette, we won't have deadlock, because that thread blocks until we've released the locks for both the bowl and the cup.

Whether or not we've achieved anything by preventing deadlock depends on what logic we could put into the else clause of the makeCookie() method. Perhaps there is another bowl we could use in the else clause, but that doesn't do us any good: what if that bowl is being used by a cook thread executing the make-Trifle() method? The logic in the else statement must do one of two things: it must do either something that requires no utensils to be locked or something that allows the measuring cup's BusyFlag to be released. If we have a square of waxed paper available, we could put the flour onto the waxed paper and then wait for the bowl:

```
public void makeCookie() {
    theCupFlag.getBusyFlag();
    theCup.measureOut(1, theFlour);
    if (theBowlFlag.tryGetBusyFlag()) {
        theBowl.putIngredients(theCup);
        theBowl.mix();
        theBowlFlag.freeBusyFlag();
        theCupFlag.freeBusyFlag();
    }
    else {
        WaxedPaper thePaper = new WaxedPaper();
        thePaper.emptyOnto(theCup);
        theCupFlag.freeBusyFlag();
        theBowlFlag.getBusyFlag();
        theBowl.putIngredients(thePaper);
        theBowl.mix();
        theBowlFlag.freeBusyFlag();
    }
}
```

This type of logic would not have been possible with the synchronized keyword since we cannot release the lock at will. To use Java's synchronized keyword, we would always have had to use waxed paper:

```
public void makeCookie() {
    WaxedPaper thePaper = new WaxedPaper();
    synchronized(theCup) {
        theCup.measureOut(1, theFlour);
        thePaper.emptyOnto(theCup);
    }

    synchronized(theBowl) {
        theBowl.putIngredients(thePaper);
        theBowl.mix();
    }
}
```

The code using the synchronized keyword is certainly cleaner, easier to understand, and easier to maintain. But in a world where waxed paper is a rare commodity, the BusyFlag code has the advantage of not using scarce resources unless it is necessary to do so. In real-world programs, the scarce resource might be a slow but always available implementation of a particular algorithm, a very memory-intensive operation, or something similar.

Using the BusyFlag is also more complex than the technique of using the lock hierarchy. But here again, there is an advantage to the BusyFlag code: there is a larger degree of parallelism in the BusyFlag example than in the ordered lock acquisition example. In the BusyFlag example, one cook thread could be measuring the flour at the same time another cook thread is whisking the eggs for the omelette, whereas in the ordered lock acquisition example, the omelette maker must wait to whisk the eggs until the cookie maker has released both utensils.

You must decide whether these types of benefits outweigh the added complexity of the code when you design your Java program. If you start by creating a lock hierarchy, you'll have simpler code at the possible expense of the loss of some parallelism. We think that it's easier to write the simpler code first and then address the parallelism problems if they become a performance bottleneck.

Another Type of Deadlock

In our last example of the kitchen with the BusyFlag, we introduced the possibility of another type of deadlock that could not have occurred had we used only Java's synchronized keyword. At issue is what happens if a thread should die unexpectedly when it is holding a lock.

Let's simplify our example somewhat by changing the class so that it has only a single synchronized method. The class definition would look something like this:

```
public class Kitchen {
    public synchronized void makeCookie() { ... }
}
```

Now we have two cook threads, one that is executing the makeCookie() method and another that is blocked attempting to enter the makeCookie() method. Under normal circumstances, the first thread completes the makeCookie() method and exits the method, at which time the second thread has the opportunity to enter the makeCookie() method and make its own cookies.

What happens instead if the first thread encounters a runtime exception and terminates? Under many threading systems, this leads to a type of deadlock, because the thread that terminates does not automatically release the locks it held. Under those systems, the second thread would wait forever trying to make its batch of cookies because it can't acquire the lock. In Java, however, locks are always given up when the thread leaves the scope of the synchronized block, even if it leaves that scope due to an exception. So in Java, this type of deadlock never occurs.

But if we use the BusyFlag class instead of Java's synchronized keyword, we've introduced the possibility of this type of deadlock. In this case, our methods look like this:

```
public void makeCookie() {
    flag.getBusyFlag();
    // ... Do some work ...
    flag.freeBusyFlag();
}
```

If in the process of doing some work we encounter a runtime exception, the Busy-Flag will never be freed. This means that our second cook thread would never be able to make its batch of cookies. Note that this problem applies only to runtime exceptions, since Java requires you to catch all other types of exceptions. Often a runtime exception is a catastrophic error that you can't recover from anyway, so it may not matter if you didn't release the BusyFlag, but we wouldn't make that assumption.

There is a way around this: we can use Java's finally clause to make sure the BusyFlag is freed no matter what happens during the execution of our method. To use the BusyFlag so that it has the same lock semantics as the synchronized keyword, you need to do something like this:

```
public void makeCookie() {
    try {
        flag.getBusyFlag();
        // ... Do some work ...
    } finally {
        flag.freeBusyFlag();
    }
}
```

Now our BusyFlag behaves the same as if we'd used the synchronized keyword. Clearly, in the examples we've used in this chapter, we can always arrange our try/finally clauses so that the locks are released even when an exception is encountered. But in other examples we've seen, this is not always possible. One technique that is possible with the BusyFlag class is to release the lock in a method other than the one in which the lock was acquired. If you use that technique, you have to be aware that this new type of deadlock is still possible.

By the way, the fact that Java's synchronized keyword does not allow this type of deadlock is not necessarily a good thing. When a thread encounters a runtime exception while it is holding a lock, there's the possibility—indeed, the expecta-tion—that it will leave the data it was manipulating in an inconsistent state. If another thread is then able to acquire the lock, it may encounter this inconsistent data and proceed erroneously. In our example, if the first thread was in the middle of making chocolate-chip cookies when the runtime exception occurred, it would have left a bunch of ingredients in the bowl. Under normal circumstances, the makeCookie() method would have cleaned out the bowl, but when the exception occurred, that didn't happen. So now our second thread comes along attempting to make oatmeal-raisin cookies; the end result is chocolate-chip-oatmeal-raisin cookies.

We could put the logic that cleans the bowl into the finally clause in an attempt to prevent this problem, but what happens if that method throws an exception? Given Java's semantics, this problem is impossible to solve. In fact, it's exactly this problem that led to the deprecation of the stop() method: the stop() method works by throwing an exception, which has the potential to leave key resources in the Java virtual machine in an inconsistent state.

Hence, we cannot solve this problem completely. In many cases, it's better to use the BusyFlag and risk deadlock if a thread exits unexpectedly than to allow a second thread to use that inconsistent data. Consider a stock trading system in which a thread is in the process of updating the current price information when it encounters the runtime exception: if another thread accesses the incorrect current price and a trade is made on the wrong price, the exposure of the firm executing that trade could be in the millions of dollars. In cases like this, it's really better to use some sort of back-end database that has transactional integrity built into it so that you're protected against an unexpected thread termination. The logic to solve this problem is standard in every database package that implements a two-phase commit. You could write such logic into your Java program directly, but it's difficult to get right.

Lock Starvation

Whenever multiple threads compete for a scarce resource, there's a danger of starvation. Earlier we discussed this concept in the context of CPU starvation: with a bad choice of scheduling options, some threads never had the opportunity to become the currently running thread and suffered from CPU starvation.

A similar situation is theoretically possible when it comes to locks granted by the synchronized keyword. Lock starvation occurs when a particular thread attempts to acquire a lock and never succeeds because another thread is already holding the lock. Clearly, this can occur on a simple basis if one thread acquires the lock and never releases it: all other threads that attempt to acquire the lock will never succeed and will starve. But lock starvation can be more subtle than that: if there are six threads competing for the same lock, it's possible that each of five threads will hold the lock for only 20% of the time, thus starving out the sixth thread.

Like CPU starvation, lock starvation is not something most threaded Java programs need to consider. If our Java program is producing a result in a finite period of time, then eventually all threads in the program will acquire the lock, if only because all the other threads in the program have exited. But also like CPU starvation, lock starvation includes the question of fairness: there are certain times when we want to make sure that threads acquire locks in a reasonable order, so that one thread won't necessarily have to wait for all other threads to exit before it has its chance to acquire a lock.

Consider the case of two threads that are competing for a lock. Assume that thread A acquires the object lock on a fairly periodic basis, as shown in Figure 8-2.

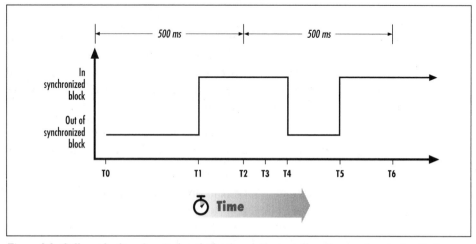

Figure 8-2. Call graph of synchronized methods; thread A repeatedly calls a synchronized method

Also assume that the two threads are operating under a timeslicing scheduler that selects a new thread every 500 milliseconds. Here's what happens at the various points on the graph:

T0

    At time T0, both thread A and thread B are in the runnable state, and thread A is the currently running thread.

T1

    Thread A is still the currently running thread, and it acquires the object lock when it enters the synchronized block.

T2

    A timeslice occurs; this causes thread B to become the currently running thread.

T3

    Very soon after becoming the currently running thread, thread B attempts to enter the synchronized block. This causes thread B to enter the blocked state, which in turn causes thread A to become the currently running thread. Thread A continues executing in the synchronized block.

T4

Thread A exits the synchronized block. This causes thread B to enter the runnable state but does not affect the timeslicing of the scheduler, so thread A continues to be the currently running thread.

T5

Thread A once again enters the synchronized block and acquires the lock. Thread B remains in the runnable state.

T6

Thread B once again becomes the currently running thread. It immediately tries to enter the synchronized block, but the lock for the synchronized block is once again held by thread A, so thread B immediately enters the blocked state. Thread A is left to become the currently running thread again, and we are now at the same state we were in at time T3.

It's possible for this cycle to continue forever, so that even though thread B is often in the runnable state, it can never acquire the lock and actually do useful work.

Clearly this example is a pathological case: the timeslicing must occur only during those time periods when thread A holds the lock for the synchronized block. With two threads, that's extremely unlikely and generally indicates that thread A is holding the lock almost continuously. With several threads, however, it's not out of the question that one thread may find that every time it is scheduled, another thread already holds the lock the first wants.

The common pitfall that creates lock starvation is to implement code similar to the following:

```
public class MyThread extends Thread {
    public void run() {
        while (true) {
            synchronized(someObject) {
                // ... Do some calculations ...
            }
        }
    }
}

public class Test {
    public static void main(String args[]) {
        MyThread t1, t2;
        t1 = new MyThread();
        t2 = new MyThread();
        t1.start();
```

```
            t2.start();
    }
}
```

At first glance, we might expect this code to work just fine, thinking that when thread t1 exits the synchronized block, thread t2 then immediately gets the lock on someObject and the two threads continue alternating the acquisition of the lock. But as we've seen, that is not the case: unless the timeslicing occurs during the short interval between the end of the synchronized block (when the lock is released) and the beginning of the next iteration of the loop (when the lock is reacquired), thread t2 will never acquire the someObject lock and will never become the currently running thread. Adding a call to the yield() method will solve this simple case, but it is not a general solution.

There are two points to take away from this:

Acquisition of locks does not queue

> When a thread attempts to acquire a lock, it does not check to see if another thread is already attempting to acquire the lock (or, more precisely, if another thread has tried to acquire the lock and blocked because it was already held). In pseudocode, the process looks like this:

```
while (lock is held)
    wait for a while
acquire lock
```

> For threads of equal priority, there's nothing in this process that prevents a lock from being granted to one thread even if another thread is waiting.

Releasing a lock does not affect thread scheduling

> When a lock is released, any threads that were blocked waiting for that lock are moved from the blocked state into the runnable state. However, no actual scheduling occurs, so none of the threads that have just moved into the runnable state becomes the currently running thread; the thread that has just released the lock remains the currently running thread (again, assuming that all threads had the same priority).

Nonetheless, lock starvation remains, as might be guessed from our example, something that occurs only in rare circumstances. In fact, each of the following circumstances must be present for lock starvation to occur:

Multiple threads are competing for the same lock

> This lock becomes the scarce resource for which some threads may starve.

> There must be a period of time during which there is not enough CPU time to accommodate all the threads. At least two threads must always be in the runnable state during this time period, or a thread that holds the lock must enter the blocked state while it still holds the lock (which is generally a bad thing).

If there is adequate CPU time to satisfy all threads, and no thread blocks while holding the lock, then a thread that wants to acquire the lock must at some point actually acquire the lock, if only because it's the only thread in the runnable state.

The results that occur during this period of contention must be interesting to us

If, for example, we're calculating a big matrix, there's probably a point in time at the beginning of our calculation during which multiple threads are competing for the same lock and the CPU. But since all we care about is the final result of this calculation, it doesn't matter to us that some threads are temporarily starved for the lock: we'll still get the final answer in the same amount of time.

As in the case of CPU starvation, we're only concerned about lock starvation if there's a period of time during which it matters that the lock be given out fairly.

These threads must all have the same priority

In the example we discussed earlier, if thread B has a higher priority than thread A, consider what would happen at time T4. When thread B moves from the blocked state to the runnable state because thread A has released the lock, thread B becomes the currently running thread by virtue of its priority.

Of course, if thread A has a higher priority than thread B, thread B would still never get the opportunity to become the currently running thread, but in that case, thread B would be subject to CPU starvation rather than lock starvation.

These threads must be under control of a round-robin scheduler

If the equal-priority threads are not under control of a round-robin scheduler, they are again subject to CPU starvation rather than lock starvation. Note also that this round-robin scheduler must not adjust the priorities of the threads, or the previous rule might be violated. Threads that are under control of the SimpleScheduler in Chapter 7 are subject to lock starvation, as are native threads.

All of the properties of lock starvation stem from the fact that a thread attempting to acquire a lock checks only to see if another thread already holds the lock, and not if another thread is already waiting for the lock. So if we're in one of those rare situations where lock starvation can occur, we need to develop a lock that has a queue associated with it so that the lock is given out fairly to every thread that wants to acquire the lock.

This is a simple class to write: we can use the Vector class to implement the queue, and then we need only write methods to allow classes to acquire and release the lock. The getBusyFlag() method places requests on the queue, and the freeBusyFlag() method notifies the next thread on the queue that the lock is now available.

Our QueuedBusyFlag class then looks like this:

```java
import java.util.Vector;

public class QueuedBusyFlag extends BusyFlag {
    protected Vector waiters;

    public QueuedBusyFlag() {
        waiters = new Vector();
    }

    public synchronized void getBusyFlag() {
        Thread me = Thread.currentThread();
        if (me == busyflag) {
            busycount++;
            return;
        }
        waiters.addElement(me);
        while ((Thread) waiters.elementAt(0) != me) {
            try {
                wait();
            } catch (Exception e) {}
        }
        busyflag = me;
        busycount = 0;
    }

    public synchronized void freeBusyflag() {
        if (Thread.currentThread() != busyflag)
            throw new IllegalArgumentException(
                            "QueuedBusyflag not held");
        if (busycount == 0) {
            waiters.removeElementAt(0);
            notifyAll();
            busyflag = null;
        }
        else busycount--;
    }

    public synchronized boolean tryGetBusyflag() {
        if (waiters.size() != 0 && busyflag != Thread.currentThread())
            return false;
        getBusyFlag();
        return true;
    }
}
```

Although QueuedBusyFlag shares the same interface as the BusyFlag class, we've had to reimplement a number of methods. When a thread attempts to acquire a lock, it enters the getBusyFlag() method and puts itself into the waiters vector. It then waits until it is the first element in the waiters vector. Similarly, when a thread releases the lock, it removes itself from the waiters vector and notifies the other threads waiting on the vector that they should check to see if they are now first in line.

This implementation is a little inefficient, in that it relies on the notifyAll() method to wake up the threads waiting to acquire the lock. If there are 30 threads waiting for the lock, all 30 threads will be wakened, even though only one thread will acquire the lock and the other 29 threads will just call the wait() method again. So you only want to use this technique in those special cases when you know that lock starvation will be a problem. We could develop a more efficient implementation by using the targeted notification technique we discussed in Chapter 4; we leave that as an exercise for the reader.

Since it is a BusyFlag, we can use this new class in a predictable fashion:

```
public class DBAccess {
    private QueuedBusyFlag lock;

    public DBAccess() {
        lock = new QueuedBusyFlag();
    }
    public Object read() {
        Object o;
        try {
            lock.getBusyFlag();
            o = someMethodThatReturnsData();
            return o;
        } finally {
            lock.freeBusyFlag();
        }
    }

    public void write(Object o) {
        try {
            lock.getBusyFlag();
            someMethodThatSendsData(o);
        } finally {
            lock.freeBusyFlag();
        }
    }
}
```

There are no surprises to this code: the only difference between running code like this and running code with a standard BusyFlag is that the requests to the database in this case will be granted sequentially, whereas if we used a standard BusyFlag, the requests would be granted in a somewhat random order (depending on the underlying platform).

Reader-Writer Locks

Sometimes you need to read information from an object in an operation that might take a fairly long period of time. You'll need to lock the object so that the information you read is consistent, but you don't necessarily need to prevent another thread from also reading data from the object at the same time: as long as all the threads are only reading the data, there's no reason why they shouldn't read the data in parallel, since this doesn't affect the data each thread is reading.

In fact, the only time we need data locking is when the data is being changed; that is, when the data is being written. The change to the data introduces the possibility that a thread reading the data sees the data in an inconsistent state. Until now, we've been content to have a lock that allowed only a single thread to access that data whether the thread is reading or writing the data, based on the theory that the lock is only held for a short period of time.

If the lock needs to be held for a long period of time, it makes sense to consider the possibility of allowing multiple threads to read the data simultaneously so that these threads don't need to compete against each other to acquire the lock. Of course, we must still allow only a single thread to write the data, and we must make sure that none of the threads that were reading the data are still active while our single writer thread is changing the internal state of the data.

Consider the case of a binary tree that contains some sort of information that is designed to be searched quite often by multiple threads. Depending on the amount of information contained in the binary tree, searching for a particular entry may require a long period of time. The interface for such a binary tree might look like this:

```
public class BTree {
    public synchronized boolean find(Object o) {
        // Perform time-consuming search, returning the object if
        // found or null if the object is not found
    }

    public synchronized void insert(Object o) {
        // Perform a time-consuming insert
    }
}
```

The problem here is that if two threads call the find() method at the same time, one of them blocks while it waits to acquire the lock; this thread remains blocked for a long time while the first thread continues to perform its search. If these two threads are operating in a timesliced environment, they won't be able to timeslice since they're competing for the same single lock; if they're running on a machine with multiple CPUs, they won't both be able to execute at the same time on separate CPUs. If this binary tree is part of a server that is to be accessed by multiple clients, we'd really like the threads calling the find() method to operate in parallel.

This is where the reader-writer lock comes in. If we have a lock that allows multiple threads to read a data structure simultaneously, we could use an interface that looks like this:

```
public class BTree {
    RWLock lock;
    public boolean find(Object o) {
        try {
            lock.lockRead();
            // Perform time-consuming search, returning the object
            // if found or null if the object is not found.
            return answer;
        } finally {
            lock.unlock();
        }
    }

    public void insert(Object o) {
        try {
            lock.lockWrite();
            // Perform a time-consuming insert.
        } finally {
            lock.unlock();
        }
    }
}
```

We now have the capability of allowing multiple threads to read the binary tree simultaneously, even though the binary tree still can be updated only by a single thread.

The bad news is that the Java API does not provide anything like reader-writer locks; the good news is that writing your own reader-writer lock is not difficult. We'll now look at a simple implementation of a reader-writer lock:

```
import java.util.*;

class RWNode {
    static final int READER = 0;
    static final int WRITER = 1;
    Thread t;
    int state;
    int nAcquires;
    RWNode(Thread t, int state) {
        this.t = t;
        this.state = state;
```

```
            nAcquires = 0;
        }
    }

    public class RWLock {
        private Vector waiters;

        private int firstWriter() {
            Enumeration e;
            int index;
            for (index = 0, e = waiters.elements();
                                    e.hasMoreElements(); index++) {
                RWNode node = (RWNode) e.nextElement();
                if (node.state == RWNode.WRITER)
                    return index;
            }
            return Integer.MAX_VALUE;
        }

        private int getIndex(Thread t) {
            Enumeration e;
            int index;
            for (index = 0, e = waiters.elements();
                                    e.hasMoreElements(); index++) {
                RWNode node = (RWNode) e.nextElement();
                if (node.t == t)
                    return index;
            }
            return -1;
        }

        public RWLock() {
            waiters = new Vector();
        }

        public synchronized void lockRead() {
            RWNode node;
            Thread me = Thread.currentThread();
            int index = getIndex(me);
            if (index == -1) {
                node = new RWNode(me, RWNode.READER);
                waiters.addElement(node);
            }
            else node = (RWNode) waiters.elementAt(index);
            while (getIndex(me) > firstWriter()) {
                try {
                    wait();
                } catch (Exception e) {}
            }
```

```java
            node.nAcquires++;
    }
    public synchronized void lockWrite() {
        RWNode node;
        Thread me = Thread.currentThread();
        int index = getIndex(me);
        if (index == -1) {
            node = new RWNode(me, RWNode.WRITER);
            waiters.addElement(node);
        }
        else {
            node = (RWNode) waiters.elementAt(index);
            if (node.state == RWNode.READER)
                throw new IllegalArgumentException("Upgrade lock");
            node.state = RWNode.WRITER;
        }
        while (getIndex(me) != 0) {
            try {
                wait();
            } catch (Exception e) {}
        }
        node.nAcquires++;
    }


    public synchronized void unlock() {
        RWNode node;
        Thread me = Thread.currentThread();
        int index;
        index = getIndex(me);
        if (index  > firstWriter())
            throw new IllegalArgumentException("Lock not held");
        node = (RWNode) waiters.elementAt(index);
        node.nAcquires--;
        if (node.nAcquires == 0) {
            waiters.removeElementAt(index);
            notifyAll();
        }
    }
}
```

The interface to the reader-writer lock is very simple: there's a method
lockRead() to acquire the read lock, a method lockWrite() to acquire the write
lock, and a method unlock() to release the lock (only a single unlock() method
is required, for reasons we'll explore in a moment). Just as in our QueuedBusy-
Flag class, threads attempting to acquire the lock are held in the waiters vector
until they are first in line for the lock, but the definition of first in line has
changed somewhat.

> # A Reader-Writer Lock Is a Single Lock
>
> You might be tempted to think of the reader-writer lock as two separate but re-
> lated locks: a lock to read and a lock to write. You might be led to think this
> because of our vocabulary: we consistently refer to a reader lock and a writer
> lock as if there were two separate locks involved in this process. On a logical
> level, that's true, and we'll continue to use that vocabulary, but we're actually
> implementing a single lock.

Because we need to keep track of how each thread wants to acquire the lock—
whether it wants to acquire the read lock or the write lock—we need to create a
class to encapsulate the information of the thread that made the request and the
type of request it made. This is the RWNode class; our `waiters` queue now holds
elements of type RWNode instead of the Thread elements that were present in the
QueuedBusyFlag class.

The acquisition of the read lock is the same as the logic of the QueuedBusyFlag
class except for the new definition of *first in line*. First in line for the read lock
means that no other node ahead of us in the `waiters` queue wants to acquire the
write lock. If the nodes that are ahead of us in the `waiters` queue want only to
acquire the read lock, then we can go ahead and acquire the lock. Otherwise, we
must wait until we are in position zero.

The acquisition of the write lock is stricter: we must be in position 0 for the lock in
order to acquire it, just as was required in our QueuedBusyFlag class.

The logic to keep track of the number of times a particular thread has acquired a
lock has undergone a slight change. In the QueuedBusyFlag class, we were able to
keep track of this number as a single instance variable. Since the read lock can be
acquired by multiple threads simultaneously, we can no longer use a simple
instance variable; we must associate the `nAcquires` count with each particular
thread. This explains the new logic in both acquisition methods that checks to see
if there is already a node associated with the calling thread.

Our reader-writer lock class does not have the notion of "upgrading" a lock; that
is, if you hold the reader lock, you cannot acquire the writer lock. You must explicitly release the reader lock before you attempt to acquire the writer lock, or you
will receive an IllegalArgumentException. If an upgrade feature were provided,
the class itself would also have to release the reader lock before acquiring the
writer lock. A true upgrade is not possible.

Finally, our reader-writer lock class contains some helper methods to search the
`waiters` queue for the first node in the queue that represents a thread attempting
to acquire the write lock (`firstWriter()`) and to find the index in the queue of

the node associated with the calling thread (getIndex()). We can't use the
Vector class indexOf() method for this purpose because we'd have to pass the
indexOf() method an object of type RWNode, but all we have is a thread.

Figure 8-3 shows the state of the waiters queue through several attempts at lock
acquisition. Threads that have acquired the lock have a white background,
whereas threads that are waiting to acquire the lock have a shaded background;
each box notes whether the thread in question is attempting to acquire the read
or the write lock.

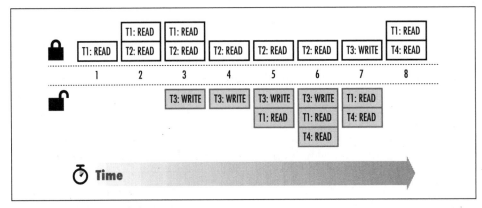

Figure 8-3. Reader-writer lock queue

At point 1, thread T1 has acquired the read lock. Since it is the only thread in the
waiters queue, the getIndex() method returns 0 while the firstWriter()
method returns MAX_VALUE. Since the index was less than the first writer, the lock
is granted. At point 2, thread T2 has requested (and been granted) the read lock
based on the same logic. Here's a point at which two threads simultaneously have
the read lock.

At point 3, thread T3 attempts to acquire the write lock. Because the index of T3
in the queue is 2, it cannot grab the lock and instead executes the wait() method
inside the lockWrite() method. Then at point 4, thread T1 releases the read
lock. The unlock() method calls notifyAll(), which wakes up T3, but because
T3's index in the queue is now 1, it again executes the wait() method.

At point 5, thread T1 again attempts to acquire the read lock, but this time,
because its index in the queue (2) is greater than the index of the first writer (1),
it does not immediately get the lock and instead executes the wait() method
inside the lockRead() method. We might be tempted at this point to allow T1 to
acquire the read lock since T2 already has the read lock and we generally allow
multiple simultaneous acquisitions of the read lock. But if we implement that
logic, we will starve the threads attempting to acquire the write lock: we could have

multiple threads acquiring the read lock, and even though they might individually give up the lock frequently, one of them could always prevent a thread from acquiring the write lock. That's the rationale for always putting the requesting thread into the `waiters` queue and then testing its index against other threads in the queue, as happens again at point 6.

At point 7, thread T2 releases the read lock, notifying all other threads that the lock is free. Because T3 is a writer lock with an index of 0, the `lockWrite()` method gives it the lock while the other threads in the `lockRead()` method execute `wait()`.

Finally, at point 8, thread T3 releases the lock. This time when the two remaining threads are notified that the lock is free, they are both able to acquire it, as their indices are less than `MAX_VALUE` (the integer returned when there are no threads attempting to acquire the write lock). Once again we have multiple threads that have simultaneous access to the read lock. This is also a case where the `notifyAll()` method makes it easy to wake up multiple threads at once.

Priority-Inverting Locks

The last example that we'll look at in this section is the starvation that is associated with priority inversion. On the virtual machines that we've looked at, priority inversion is solved by priority inheritance.

But what if we need to use the BusyFlag class to lock at a large scope in our program? How does priority inheritance affect our BusyFlag class? Not surprisingly, it does not have any affect on the behavior of this class, because we are only simulating a lock, and are using Java's synchronization locks only to protect against the race conditions that occur within this task. Once a BusyFlag is acquired and the `getBusyFlag()` method exits, the synchronization lock protecting the `getBusyFlag()` method is released. As far as the Java virtual machine is concerned, no synchronization locks are held at this point.

A low-priority thread that holds a BusyFlag will never have its priority adjusted by the virtual machine if a high-priority flag attempts to acquire the same BusyFlag: because they never attempt to execute the same synchronized method at the same time, the virtual machine is unaware that they are competing with each other at all.

We can easily implement a version of the BusyFlag class that has support for priority inheritance:

```
public class PriorityBusyFlag extends BusyFlag {
    protected int currentPriority;

    public synchronized void getBusyFlag() {
        while (tryGetBusyFlag() == false) {
```

```
            Thread prevOwner = getBusyFlagOwner();
            try {
                int curP = Thread.currentThread().getPriority();
                if (curP > prevOwner.getPriority()) {
                    prevOwner.setPriority(curP);
                }
                wait();
            } catch (Exception e) {}
        }
    }

    public synchronized boolean tryGetBusyFlag() {
        boolean succeed = super.tryGetBusyFlag();
        if (succeed)
            currentPriority = Thread.currentThread().getPriority();
        return succeed;
    }

    public synchronized void freeBusyFlag() {
        if (getBusyFlagOwner() == Thread.currentThread()) {
            super.freeBusyFlag();
            if (getBusyFlagOwner() == null) {
                Thread.currentThread().setPriority(currentPriority);
                notifyAll();
            }
        }
    }
}
```

Usage of the PriorityBusyFlag class is similar to usage of the BusyFlag class. The two differences are that the requesting thread will raise the priority of the thread that already owns the BusyFlag if the priority of the requesting thread is higher than the priority of the owning thread, and the original priority of the thread will be restored when the BusyFlag is freed.

This behavior is functionally identical to native-threading systems that support priority inheritance. However, in a virtual machine, these details are handled internally. The best that we can do is to use the PriorityBusyFlag class in a cooperative manner by using the setPriority() method. If another thread also changes the priority of threads, or the threads themselves are changing their priority, this cooperative technique will not work.

Thread-Unsafe Classes

In a perfect world, we would not have to write this section: in that world, every class that you used would be correctly synchronized for use by multiple threads running simultaneously, and you would be free from considering synchronization issues whenever you used someone else's Java classes.

Welcome to the real world. In this world, there are often times when you need to use classes that are thread unsafe—classes that lack the correct synchronization to be used by multiple threads. Just because we acknowledge that these circumstances exist does not mean that you are absolved from producing thread-safe classes in your own work: we urge you to make this a better world and correctly synchronize all of your own classes.

In this section, we'll examine two techniques that allow you to deal with classes that are not thread safe.

Explicit Synchronization

Since its inception, Java has had certain classes that are collection classes: the Hashtable class, the Vector class, and others provide aggregates of objects. These classes all have the advantage that they are thread safe: their methods contain the necessary synchronization such that two threads that simultaneously insert objects into a vector, for example, will do so without corrupting the internal state of the vector.

Java 2 formalized the notion of a collection by introducing a number of collection classes; these are classes that implement either the Collection or the Map interface. There are a number of these classes: the HashMap and ArrayList classes, for example, provide similar semantics to the original Hashtable and Vector classes. But there is a big difference: most of the new collection classes are not thread safe.

In fact, there is no rule about these classes: while most of them are not thread safe, some of them are (such as the original Hashtable class, which implements the Map interface). And most of the thread-unsafe classes have the capability of providing a thread-safe implementation, so that when you deal with an object that is only identified by a generic type (such as Map), you are unsure as to whether the object in question is thread safe.

Synchronized Collections

As an aside, we'll mention that the Collection class has several methods—`synchronizedCollection()`, `synchronizedMap()`, `synchronizedList()`, and `synchronizedSet()`—that turn a thread-unsafe collection object into a thread-safe collection object. The techniques that we're discussing here apply only to the unsafe versions of collections; we're really just using the collection classes to illustrate our larger point.

This all places a big burden on the developer, who must now figure out whether a particular Map object is thread safe, and, if not, must then ensure that the object is used correctly when multiple threads are present. The easiest way to do this is simply to explicitly synchronize all access to the object:

```
import java.util.*;

public class ArrayTest {
    private ArrayList al;

    public ArrayTest() {
        al = new ArrayList();
    }

    public void addItems(Object first, Object second) {
        synchronized(al) {
            al.add(first);
            al.add(second);
        }
    }

    public Object get(int index) {
        synchronized(al) {
            return al.get(index);
        }
    }
}
```

All accesses to the array list in this example are synchronized; now multiple threads can call the addItems() and get() methods of the ArrayTest without damaging the internal state of the array list.

Note that we've made the array list itself private. In order for this technique to work, we have to ensure that no one inadvertently uses the array list without synchronizing it, and the simplest way to do that is to hide the actual array list within the object that uses it. That way, we only have to worry about accesses to the array list from within our ArrayTest class.

The addItems() method shows one advantage of providing the collection classes as they are: we can add multiple items to the collection within a single synchronization block. This is more efficient than synchronizing the add() method of the ArrayList class. In our test class, we need only obtain the synchronization lock once; in the traditional Vector class, we'd have to obtain the synchronization lock twice. This efficiency comes at a high price, however: if you forget to synchronize the map correctly, you'll end up with a nasty race condition that will be very hard to track down. Which side you land on in this debate is a matter of personal preference.

This technique can be used with any thread-unsafe class provided that all accesses to the thread-unsafe objects are synchronized as we've shown. There are some thread-unsafe classes (such as the JFC [Swing] classes, which we'll look at later) for which this technique will not work, since those classes internally call other thread-unsafe classes and do not synchronize access internally to those unsafe objects. But for unsafe data structure classes, explicit synchronization is the technique to use.

Explicit synchronization and native code

You must use explicit synchronization when you need to call a native library that is not thread safe. This may be a frequent occurrence, since developers who use C or other programming languages often do not consider that their libraries may be used in a threaded environment.

However, there is a slight difference in this case. We cannot simply synchronize at the object level (as we did in the previous example), because every object is sharing the same native code: there is only one instance of the shared native library that is loaded into the virtual machine. Hence, we must synchronize at the class level, so that every object that uses the native library will share the same lock.

It's simple to perform this task:

```
public class AccessNative {
    static {
        System.loadLibrary("myLibrary");
    }
    public static synchronized native void function1();
    public static synchronized native void function2();
    ...
}
```

Here we simply make each method that calls into the native library both static and synchronized. This ensures that only one thread in the virtual machine can enter the native methods at any point in time, since they all would have to acquire the single lock associated with the AccessNative class.

There is one caveat here: if another class also loads the myLibrary library, threads executing objects of that class will be able to call into the same native library code concurrent with the threads executing methods of the AccessNative class.

This technique is similar to one that was used by the JDBC-ODBC bridge: in early versions of the bridge, it was assumed that the underlying ODBC drivers were not thread safe, and so the bridge serialized access to the native library. This greatly reduced the utility of the bridge, however, since threads could not concurrently access the database—which is a problem for most database applications, where threads that access the database are often blocked waiting for I/O.

In Java 2, versions of the JDBC-ODBC bridge now assume that the underlying ODBC driver is thread safe. If you have a thread-unsafe ODBC driver, it is your responsibility to make sure that access to the driver is synchronized correctly. This is easily achieved using a modification of the first technique that we examined: simply make sure that any access to the Connection object of the driver is synchronized. In this case, however, since you are dealing with native code, you must also ensure that only one Connection object that uses the ODBC driver is present within the virtual machine.

Single-Thread Access

The other technique to use with thread-unsafe classes is to ensure that only one thread ever accesses those classes. This is generally a harder task, but it has the advantage that it always works, no matter what those classes might do internally. This technique must be used whenever threads are present in a program that uses the Java Foundation Classes for its GUI. We'll first show you how to interact with the JFC specifically, and then generalize how that technique might be used with other classes (particularly with classes that you develop).

Using the Java Foundation Classes

The Java Foundation Classes are the largest set of classes in the Java platform, and they also bear the distinction of being one of the few sets of classes that are not thread safe. Hence, whenever these classes are used, we must take care that we access JFC objects only from one thread; in particular, we must ensure that we access JFC objects only from the event-dispatching thread of the virtual machine. This is the thread that executes any of the listener methods (such as `actionPerformed()`) in response to events from the user.

All JFC objects are thread unsafe, which means that if we have our own thread that wants to invoke a method on such an object, it cannot do so directly. A thread that attempts to read the value of a slider, for example, cannot do so directly, since as it is reading the value of the slider, the user might be simultaneously changing the value of the slider. Since access to the slider is not synchronized, both threads might access the internal slider code at the same time, corrupting the internal state of the slider and causing an error. Hence, our own thread must arrange for the event-dispatching thread of the virtual machine to read the value of the slider and pass that data back to the thread.

This example also illustrates why the previous technique of explicitly synchronizing access to objects will not work for JFC: our thread could synchronize access to the slider, but the event-processing thread does not synchronize its internal access. Remember that locks are cooperative; if all threads do not attempt to acquire the lock, then race conditions can still occur.

So the requirement to interact safely with Swing components is to access them only from the event-dispatching thread; since that effectively makes access to those components single-threaded, there will be no race conditions. JFC contains many methods that are executed by the event-dispatching thread:

- Methods of the listener interfaces in the `java.awt.event` package when those methods are called from the event-dispatching thread
- `invokeAndWait()`
- `invokeLater()`
- `repaint()`

We'll look at each of these in turn.

The event-dispatching thread and event-related method

First, let's delve into what we mean by the event-dispatching thread. When the Java virtual machine begins execution, it starts an initial thread. Later, when the first AWT-related class (including a JFC class) is instantiated, the GUI toolkit inside of the JVM is initialized. Depending on the underlying operating system, this creates one or more additional threads that are responsible for interacting with the native windowing system.

Regardless of the number of threads created, one of these threads is known as the event-dispatching thread. This thread is responsible for getting events from the user; when the user types a character, the event-dispatcher thread receives this event from the underlying windowing system. When the user moves the mouse or presses a mouse button, the event-dispatching thread receives that event as well. When it receives an event, it begins the process of dispatching that event: it figures out which AWT component the event occurred on and calls the event methods that are registered on that component.

So any method that is called in response to one of these events will be called in the event-dispatching thread. In normal circumstances, any of the event-related methods—`actionPerformed()`, `focusGained()`, `itemStateChanged()`, and any other method that is part of one of the listener interfaces in the `java.awt.event` package—will be called by the event-dispatching thread.

That's good news, since it means that most of the code that needs to access Swing components will already be called in the event-dispatching thread. So for most GUI code, you do not need to use one of the other methods in our list: you only need to use the `invokeAndWait()` or `invokeLater()` methods if you want to access Swing components from a thread other than the event-dispatching thread. In other words, if you add your own thread to a Swing-based program and that additional thread directly accesses a Swing component, you need to use either the invokeAndWait() or invokeLater() methods. Otherwise, you just write your event-related methods as you normally would.

There are two subtle points to make about event dispatching. The first is that methods of the JApplet class that seem to be event-related are not called in the event-dispatching thread. In particular, the start() and stop() methods of the JApplet class are called by another thread in the program, and you should not directly access any Swing components in these methods. This warning technically applies to the init() method as well. Since the init() method typically does make Swing calls (e.g., to the add() method), that might seem like an ominous development. However, browsers are responsible for calling the init() method only once, and for calling it in a manner in which the Swing classes can be used safely. If you write your own application that uses an instance of a JApplet within it, you must take care to do the same thing: do not call the show() method of any JFrame before you call the init() method of the JApplet class (or use the invokeAndWait() method to ensure that the init() method is itself run in the event-dispatching thread). And, of course, if your program calls the init() method, it should take care to ensure that it does so from the event-dispatching thread.

The second point is more complicated, and it stems from the fact that it is possible to call an event-related method from a thread other than the event-dispatching thread. Let's say that you have a thread in which a socket is reading data from a data feed; the socket gets an I/O error, and now you want to shut down the program. You might be tempted in this case to call the same actionPerformed() method that is called in response to the user selecting the button labeled "Close"—after all, that method has the necessary logic to shut the program down, and you wouldn't want to rewrite that logic. So in this case, the actionPerformed() method can be called by two different threads: the event-dispatching thread (in response to a user event) and the socket-reading thread (in response to an I/O error). To accommodate both threads, you must make access to any Swing components in the actionPerformed() method safe by using one of the invoke methods that we'll discuss next.

The point is that there's nothing inherent within the actionPerformed() method (or any other event-related method) that makes it safe to manipulate Swing components: either the method is being executed by the event-dispatching thread itself (safe), or it is being executed by another thread (not safe). The thread context determines whether or not it is safe to directly manipulate a Swing component, not the method itself.

Which invokeAndWait() Method?

In Java 2, the EventQueue class introduces three new static methods: `isEventDispatchThread()`, `invokeLater()`, and `invokeAndWait()`. These methods are functionally identical to their counterparts in the Swing-Utilities class. You may use either one depending upon your preference; using the methods of the SwingUtilities class will keep your program compatible with Java 1.1.

The invokeAndWait() method

The easiest way to ensure that access to Swing components occurs in the event-dispatching thread is to use the `invokeAndWait()` method. When a thread executes the `invokeAndWait()` method, it asks the event-dispatching thread to execute certain code, and the thread blocks until that code has been executed.

Let's see an example of this. The `invokeAndWait()` method is often used when a thread needs to get the value of certain items within the GUI. In the following code, we use the `invokeAndWait()` method to get the value of the slider:

```
import javax.swing.*;
import java.awt.*;

public class SwingTest extends JApplet {
    JSlider slider;
    int val;

    class SwingCalcThread extends Thread {
        public void run() {
            Runnable getVal = new Runnable() {
                public void run() {
                    val = slider.getValue();
                }
            };

            for (int i = 0; i < 10; i++) {
                try {
                    Thread.sleep(2000);
                    SwingUtilities.invokeAndWait(getVal);
                    System.out.println("Value is " + val);
                } catch (Exception e) {}
            }
        }
    }
}
```

```
public void init() {
    slider = new JSlider();
    getContentPane().setLayout(new BorderLayout());
    getContentPane().add("North", slider);
}

public void start() {
    new SwingCalcThread().start();
}
}
```

While simply the skeleton of a real program, this applet puts up a slider and then starts a secondary thread to perform a calculation. Let's look at how execution of this applet will proceed:

1. The applet will initialize itself (via the init() method), creating a GUI with a single element (a slider).

2. In the applet's start() method, a calculation thread is spawned.

3. The calculation thread will then begin executing (okay, it's just sleeping, but it could be doing something useful here). Periodically, the calculation thread needs to obtain the current setting of the slider. It does this by creating a runnable object (the getVal instance variable) and passing that object to the invokeAndWait() method. The calculation thread then blocks until the invokeAndWait() method returns.

4. Meanwhile, the invokeAndWait() method itself has arranged for the run() method of the get object to be invoked in the event-dispatching thread of the GUI. When that run() method is invoked, the value of the slider is stored into the val instance variable.

5. Once the run() method of the getVal object has returned, the invokeAndWait() method will return and the calculation thread can continue its next iteration.

There's a further complication here, however: you cannot call the invokeAndWait() method from the event-dispatching thread itself; doing so will cause an error to be thrown. If you want to execute the same code from an event callback method and from a user thread—e.g., the socket example we described a little earlier—then you cannot simply put all references to Swing components inside of a call to the invokeAndWait() method in the actionPerformed() method; you must instead use the SwingUtilities.isEventDispatchThread() method to see if you're in the event dispatch method and code the actionPerformed() method accordingly. A skeleton of this example would look like this:

```
public class TestSwing extends JApplet implements ActionListener {
class ReaderThread extends Thread {
```

```
            public void run() {
                try {
                    //... read the socket, process the data ...
                } catch (IOException ioe) {
                    actionPerformed(null);
                }
            }
        }

    public void init() {
        JButton jb = new JButton("Close");
        getContentPane().add(jb);
        jb.addActionListener(this);
    }

    public void actionPerformed(ActionEvent ae) {
        class doClose implements Runnable {
            public void run() {
                //... access Swing components here ...
                //... This code would normally be the body ...
                //... of the actionPerformed method ...
            }
        };
        doClose dc = new doClose();
        if (SwingUtilities.isEventDispatchThread())
            dc.run();
        else {
            try {
                SwingUtilities.invokeAndWait(dc);
            } catch (Exception e) {}
        }
    }
}
```

This restriction does not apply to the invokeLater() method.

The invokeLater() method

The invokeLater() method is similar to the invokeAndWait() method except
that it does not block. Because it does not wait for the target object's run()
method to complete, this method is inappropriate for those instances when you
need to retrieve data from JFC objects. However, this method can be used to set
data within a JFC object:

```
import javax.swing.*;
import java.awt.*;

public class SwingTest extends JApplet {
    JSlider slider;
```

```
JLabel label;
int val;

class SwingCalcThread extends Thread {
    public void run() {
        Runnable getVal = new Runnable() {
            public void run() {
                val = slider.getValue();
            }
        };
        Runnable setVal = new Runnable() {
            public void run() {
                label.setText("Last calc is " + val);
            }
        };

        for (int i = 0; i < 10; i++) {
            try {
                Thread.sleep(2000);
                SwingUtilities.invokeAndWait(getVal);
                SwingUtilities.invokeLater(setVal);
            } catch (Exception e) {}
        }
    }
}

public void init() {
    slider = new JSlider();
    label = new JLabel("Last calc is 0");
    getContentPane().setLayout(new BorderLayout());
    getContentPane().add("North", slider);
    getContentPane().add("Center", label);
}

public void start() {
    new SwingCalcThread().start();
}
}
```

In this case, there's no reason why the calculation thread needs to wait until the data in the label is actually set; it merely schedules the operation and then continues to calculate. There are circumstances in which this is inappropriate. In this example, the new value of the label will not be reflected immediately when the invokeLater() method is called. As a result, the threads may be scheduled such that one iteration of the intermediate feedback is lost to the user. But in general, the invokeLater() method is useful when the thread that invokes it does not care about the results of the run() method.

The repaint() method

The `repaint()` method is also a thread-safe method, even within the JFC. Hence, any thread can at any time call the `repaint()` method of a particular component. This is very useful, since a variety of Java applications depend on periodic repainting behavior.

The reason this works is that the `repaint()` method itself doesn't really accomplish a great deal: it merely arranges for the `paint()` method to be called by the event-dispatching thread. Hence, an applet can have a thread that stores data into the instance variables of the applet and then calls the applet's `repaint()` method; when the applet next paints itself, it will use the new data.

There are other techniques for dealing with threads and the JFC. There is a timer class within the JFC that hides the details of the `invokeLater()` method for you; you pass an ActionListener object to the timer and it arranges for the `actionPerformed()` method of that object to be called from the event-dispatching thread every time the timer fires.

Additionally, there is a SwingWorker class on Sun's web site that performs the opposite of the principles that we've shown here: it dispatches a new target thread and provides a way for code within the event-dispatching thread to poll the target thread for its results. In our opinion, this is backwards: how will the event-dispatching thread know when it should check for output from the worker thread? Still, if you're interested, check out Sun's web site for more details.

How unsafe are the Swing classes, anyway? In the examples we've just shown, we've essentially set and retrieved an integer—the value—from the JSlider class. Since reading or writing an integer is guaranteed to be an atomic action in Java, is it really necessary to use the invoke methods? There are probably cases where the answer is no, but those cases cannot be clearly described. So it's really safer to use the invoke methods to execute all Swing methods from a thread other than the event-dispatching thread. Even in our example where we seem to be performing a simple assignment, there's a lot going on that we're not aware of: the `getValue()` method has to call the `getModel()` method, and a new model may be in the middle of being installed. That may be okay, or it may cause the `getModel()` method to return a null object reference, which would cause a runtime exception; without a very careful examination of the Swing code, it's tough to be sure. And it's impossible to know what future implementations might be. It's far better just to use the invoke methods as we've shown.

Other thread-unsafe classes

The implementation of the `invokeAndWait()` method (as well as the other similar methods we've just examined) provides us with a clue on how to deal with other unsafe classes for which simple external synchronization is insufficient. We need to implement a similar mechanism for these classes.

This is typically done by establishing a queue somewhere that one thread—and only one thread—is responsible for acting on. The `invokeAndWait()` method itself is based on the fact that there is an existing event queue within the virtual machine: it simply creates some new events, posts them to the queue, and waits for the event-dispatching thread to process them (the `invokeLater()` method returns without waiting). The event-dispatching thread is then responsible for executing the `run()` method of the object passed to the `invokeAndWait()` method. Interestingly enough, the `invokeAndWait()` method does not create a new thread, nor does it cause one to be created: the `run()` method is executed by an existing thread (the event-dispatching thread), just as we did in Chapter 7 with our thread pool example.

This similarity tells us how to ensure that only a single thread accesses our unsafe classes: place all access to those classes within objects executing in a thread pool and initialize the thread pool to contain only a single thread. Now we can use the `addRequest()` and `addRequestAndWait()` methods of the thread pool just as we used the `invokeLater()` and `invokeAndWait()` methods earlier.

Summary

The strong integration of locks into the Java language and API is very useful for programming with Java threads. Nonetheless, despite their strength, Java's locking mechanisms are not suitable for every type of synchronization you might need for more complex Java programs. Fortunately, the built-in synchronization techniques provide good building blocks to create the more complicated, more intelligent locks you need in special situations.

Like other parts of Java, its built-in locking mechanism is designed to be simple in order to reduce errors in your Java programs. And, like other parts of Java, this simplicity is enough to carry you through all but the most complex programming situations. You should use the built-in techniques unless you really need the more complex behavior of the mechanisms described in this chapter.

Finally, for those times when you are faced with other code that is not thread safe, Java's locking facilities offer the ability to use that code safely within a multi-threaded program, either by explicitly locking such code or by ensuring that such code is only ever executed within a single thread.

9

Parallelizing for Multiprocessor Machines

So far in this book, we've examined threading as a programming technique that allows us to simplify programming: we have used threading to achieve asynchronous behavior or to perform independent tasks. Although we discussed how threads are scheduled on machines with multiple processors, by and large the techniques that we've shown so far are not affected by a machine with multiple processors, nor do they exploit the number of processors on a machine to make the program run faster.

Multithreaded applications have a special bond with multiprocessor systems. The separation of threads provides a clear and simple separation for the multiprocessor machine. Since the operating system can place different threads on different processors, the application will run faster.

In this chapter, we'll look at how to parallelize Java programs so that they will run faster on a machine with multiple CPUs. The processes that we'll examine are beneficial not only to newly developed Java programs, but also to existing Java programs that have a CPU-intensive loop, allowing us to improve the performance of those programs on a multiprocessor system.

How does the Java threading system behave in a multiprocessor system? There are no conceptual differences between a program running on a machine with one processor and a machine with two or more processors; the threads behave exactly the same in either case. However, as we discussed in Chapter 6, the key difference between a multiprocessor and a single-processor system is that there may be one currently running thread for each CPU on the host platform. The impact of this is that when our Java program runs on a machine with multiple processors, the following assumptions become very important:

- We can no longer assume that a currently running thread has the highest priority. A higher-priority thread may be running on a different processor.

- We can no longer assume that a low-priority thread will not run. There may be enough processors to give it execution time.

- We can no longer assume that threads of different priorities will not be running at the same time.

- We can no longer assume that certain race conditions can be ignored because it is "unreasonable" for a particular case to occur. Race conditions in a multiprocessor system are real, whereas race conditions in a single-processor system are more dependent on the scheduling engine of the Java virtual machine.

The point to understand here is that these assumptions were never guaranteed in the first place. However, on a single-processor machine (especially under the green-thread model), violation of these assumptions was rare. On a multiprocessor system, these assumptions are violated quite often.

Parallelizing a Single-Threaded Program

Without redesigning a program, the best area to parallelize—that is, the area in which to introduce multiple threads to increase the program's performance—is where the application is CPU bound. After all, there is no reason to bring in more processors if the first processor cannot stay busy. In many of the cases where the process is CPU bound—that is, the process is using all of the computer processors' cycles, while not using the disks or the network at full capacity—the speed of the application can increase with the addition of more processors. The process could be involved in a long mathematical calculation or, more likely, in large iterations of shorter mathematical calculations. Furthermore, these calculations probably involve a large control loop or even a large number of loops inside loops. These are the types of common algorithms that we will examine here. Consider the following calculation:

```
public class SinTable {
    private float lookupValues[] = null;

    public synchronized float[] getValues() {
        if (lookupValues == null) {
            lookupValues = new float [360 * 100];
            for (int i = 0; i < (360*100); i++) {
                float sinValue = (float)Math.sin(
                                    (i % 360)*Math.PI/180.0);
                lookupValues[i] = sinValue * (float)i / 180.0f;
            }
        }
        return lookupValues;
    }
}
```

We'll use this code as the basis of our example for the rest of this chapter. A single thread, and hence a single processor, will execute the loop as specified in the code and store the results in the `lookupValues` array. Assuming that the calculation of the `sinValue` variable is time-consuming, the whole loop may take a long time to execute. For some cases, this is acceptable. However, on a twelve-processor computer without any other application running, only one CPU will be working while the other eleven would be sitting idle. Considering the cost of a twelve-way machine, this is not acceptable.

Before we get started, let's define some terminology.* The variable `sinValue` has a few special properties. Obviously, it exists only during the duration of the loop. It is a temporary variable used to aid the calculation of the lookup table. It does not carry a value in one iteration of the loop that is used in another iteration of the loop, and the value of the variable is reassigned in the next iteration. We will define `sinValue` as a *loop-private variable*, that is, a variable that is initialized, calculated, and used entirely in a single iteration of the loop.

Examining further, we can state that the index variable `i` is also a loop-private variable: it is also used completely in an iteration of the loop. It can be considered as a special type of loop-private variable. Since it is never changed in the iteration and is directly tied to the iteration index, we can actually treat it as a constant during the iteration of a loop. However, for now, simply considering it as a loop-private variable is good enough.

We may try to break the parts of this loop among many threads as follows:

```java
public class SinTable implements Runnable {
    private class SinTableRange {
        public int start, end;
    }

    private float lookupValues[];
    private Thread lookupThreads[];
    private int startLoop, endLoop, curLoop, numThreads;

    public SinTable() {
        lookupValues = new float [360 * 100];
        lookupThreads = new Thread[12];
        startLoop = curLoop = 0;
        endLoop = (360 * 100);
        numThreads = 12;
    }

    private synchronized SinTableRange loopGetRange() {
```

---

* The terminology that we will be using in this section is somewhat based on the autothreading MP C compiler available for the Solaris operating system.

```java
        if (curLoop >= endLoop)
            return null;
        SinTableRange ret = new SinTableRange();
        ret.start = curLoop;
        curLoop += (endLoop-startLoop)/numThreads+1;
        ret.end = (curLoop<endLoop)?curLoop:endLoop;
        return ret;
    }

    private void loopDoRange(int start, int end) {
        for (int i = start; i < end; i += 1) {
            float sinValue = (float)Math.sin((i % 360)*Math.PI/180.0);
            lookupValues[i] = sinValue * (float)i / 180.0f;
        }
    }

    public void run() {
        SinTableRange str;
        while ((str = loopGetRange()) != null) {
            loopDoRange(str.start, str.end);
        }
    }

    public float[] getValues() {
        for (int i = 0; i < numThreads; i++) {
            lookupThreads[i] = new Thread(this);
            lookupThreads[i].start();
        }
        for (int i = 0; i < numThreads; i++) {
            try {
                lookupThreads[i].join();
            } catch (InterruptedException iex) {}
        }
        return lookupValues;
    }
}
```

The code in this new version is functionally the same as the previous version, albeit
with many modifications to its logic. First, instead of a loop that does the calculation, we now have a loop that starts off 12 (numThreads) different worker threads
and provides each worker thread with different parts of the mathematical loop to
calculate. The original mathematical calculation is moved to a new method,
loopDoRange(). In this method, the loop has been modified to work on only part
of the lookup table instead of the whole table. Each different thread is responsible for calculating only its portion of the table. Each thread must call the
loopGetRange() method to determine which portion they must calculate. The
original thread that started the 12 worker threads then simply waits for all 12
worker threads to finish. Since the long calculation is now accomplished by 12

threads instead of by a single thread, it is now possible for a multiprocessor-based operating system to place the different threads on different processors.

The calculation works for a number of reasons. First, the loop index variable i and the sinValue variable, which were originally classified as loop private, are now stack variables in each worker thread. The loopDoRange() method uses different copies of these two variables in each thread executing the loop. This means that each of the 12 worker threads has its own copy of these variables while completing its portion of the calculation.

Second, although the lookupTable array is not loop private, the individual members of the array can be considered loop private. Each individual member of the array is only accessed in a particular iteration. There is no race condition because each iteration affects one and only one member of the array, and although the different worker threads handle many iterations of the loop, no single iteration is handled by more than one thread.

The only synchronization we need is in the assignment of the different ranges. To prevent the worker threads from stepping on each other during this assignment, the loopGetRange() method is synchronized. In this example, since the loop is partitioned only in 12 ranges, the execution time for this method is insignificant when compared with the loop calculation itself.

The code for this new version is more complicated than our first version. This new code now has to start and track 12 separate threads. The worker threads had to be modified to handle parts of the loop whose ranges they have to determine. Although there is very little synchronization in this case, we could easily have had a complicated requirement for synchronization depending on the algorithm used in the mathematical calculation.

Given the complexity we introduced to handle this simple loop, it may become too hard to handle more complex loops. To help with this complexity, we'll move all the logic related to loop management into a separate class. We can then implement the loop by simply using the services provided by this class:

```
public class LoopHandler implements Runnable {
    protected class LoopRange {
        public int start, end;
    }
    protected Thread lookupThreads[];
    protected int startLoop, endLoop, curLoop, numThreads;

    public LoopHandler(int start, int end, int threads) {
        startLoop = curLoop = start;
        endLoop = end;
        numThreads = threads;
        lookupThreads = new Thread[numThreads];
    }
```

```
protected synchronized LoopRange loopGetRange() {
    if (curLoop >= endLoop)
        return null;
    LoopRange ret = new LoopRange();
    ret.start = curLoop;
    curLoop += (endLoop-startLoop)/numThreads+1;
    ret.end = (curLoop<endLoop) ? curLoop : endLoop;
    return ret;
}

public void loopDoRange(int start, int end) {
}

public void loopProcess() {
    for (int i = 0; i < numThreads; i++) {
        lookupThreads[i] = new Thread(this);
        lookupThreads[i].start();
    }
    for (int i = 0; i < numThreads; i++) {
        try {
            lookupThreads[i].join();
        } catch (InterruptedException iex) {}
    }
}

public void run() {
    LoopRange str;
    while ((str = loopGetRange()) != null) {
        loopDoRange(str.start, str.end);
    }
}
}
```

In our new LoopHandler class, we have implemented the logic that we applied on our SinTable class. The logic of creating, tracking, and joining back with the original thread has been moved to the newly created loopProcess() method. The logic of determining the ranges and processing the loop—originally coded in the run() and loopGetRange() methods of the SinTable class—remains nearly unchanged. The loop handler has also been modified to handle more generic loops and has a constructor that will assign the start of the loop, the end of the loop, and the number of threads. Just as in our earlier example, the algorithm will call the loopDoRange() method to handle the processing. However, in this case, the LoopHandler class has an empty implementation for this method.

Now our implementation of the SinTable class is much simpler:

```
public class SinTable extends LoopHandler {
    private float lookupValues[];
```

```
    public SinTable() {
        super(0, 360*100, 12);
        lookupValues = new float [360 * 100];
    }

    public void loopDoRange(int start, int end) {
        for (int i = start; i < end; i++) {
            float sinValue = (float)Math.sin((i % 360)*Math.PI/180.0);
            lookupValues[i] = sinValue * (float)i / 180.0f;
        }
    }

    public float[] getValues() {
        loopProcess();
        return lookupValues;
    }
}
```

In this case, we simply need to configure the ranges needed by the loop handler, provide the logic of the loop in the loopDoRange() method, and call the loopProcess() method to process the loop in a multithreaded fashion. While this is still more complicated than the first SinTable class implementation, it is now much more manageable and less complex than the previous implementation.

Loop Scheduling and Load Balancing

We define the process of distributing the iterations of the loop to the individual threads as *loop scheduling*. In our LoopHandler class, this is handled by the loop-GetRange() method. To maximize processor usage, we should distribute the work to the threads as evenly as possible, with the least amount of overhead in determining this distribution. This is defined as *load balancing*.

Here are the basic loop-scheduling types at our disposal:

Static or chunk scheduling

> Under static scheduling, each thread is assigned an equal number of iterations that depends on the number of threads available. If there are 1000 iterations in the loop that are to be distributed and 10 threads that are assigned to the task, then each thread will be assigned 100 iterations of the loop. This is the algorithm that is used by the LoopHandler class. The algorithm also adds 1 to the size to make sure that the distribution is rounded up. Otherwise, there might be an iteration left over and a worker thread would have to perform that single iteration after already performing the original chunk.

> The problem with this algorithm is that it assumes that each iteration of the loop takes the same amount of time. If this is not true, then one of the threads

will take more time than the other threads to complete. Since all the work is divided up at the beginning of the loop, the other threads will be idle while the final iterations are completed by the last remaining thread.

Self-scheduling

In self-scheduling, each worker thread grabs a small chunk of the iterations to execute. After completion of its assigned range, it grabs another small chunk. If there are 1000 iterations in the loop that are to be distributed and 10 threads are assigned to the task, then each worker thread will work on a small chunk—say 20—until all 1000 iterations are completed.

As with static scheduling, the different worker threads may not complete at the same time. However, since the chunks are small in the self-scheduling model, the idle time of the threads at the end of the process is also small. To make this idle time even smaller, we can make the individual chunks smaller. However, there is an overhead in obtaining the ranges to execute; this overhead will increase as the chunks get smaller.

Here's an implementation of this model:

```
public class SelfLoopHandler extends LoopHandler {
    protected int groupSize;

    public SelfLoopHandler(int start, int end, int size, int threads) {
        super(start, end, threads);
        groupSize = size;
    }

    protected synchronized LoopRange loopGetRange() {
        if (curLoop >= endLoop)
            return null;
        LoopRange ret = new LoopRange();
        ret.start = curLoop;
        curLoop += groupSize;
        ret.end = (curLoop<endLoop)?curLoop:endLoop;
        return ret;
    }
}
```

Implementation of a self-scheduling loop handler is straightforward. Our current LoopHandler class already has the logic of working until the loop has been completed. We simply need to modify the constructor to handle the chunk size requested, and modify the `loopGetRange()` method to return this fixed chunk size. In our implementation of the self-scheduler, we simply subclass from the original loop handler and implement only the changes.

Guided self-scheduling

Guided self-scheduling is a compromise between the static scheduler and the self-scheduler. In the beginning, the guided scheduler grabs a large number of iterations of the loop, which becomes progressively smaller near the end of the loop. There is also a minimum chunk size that the guided self-scheduler uses. Thus, it basically behaves like a static scheduler that slowly becomes a self-scheduler.

If 1000 iterations in the loop are to be distributed and 10 threads are assigned to the task, then the first worker thread gets one-tenth of the work—100 iterations. The second thread gets one-tenth of the remaining work—90 iterations. This slowly gets smaller and smaller until the minimum—say 10—is assigned; the minimum is assigned until all 1000 iterations are completed.

This algorithm seems to have the fewest problems. Unlike the self-scheduler, the extra overhead only appears at the end of the loop. And unless the individual iterations have drastically different execution periods from the longer-term iterations at the beginning, it doesn't have the problems that the static scheduler has.

Here's how to implement guided self-scheduling:

```
public class GuidedLoopHandler extends LoopHandler {
    protected int minSize;

    public GuidedLoopHandler(int start, int end, int min, int threads){
        super(start, end, threads);
        minSize = min;
    }

    protected synchronized LoopRange loopGetRange() {
        if (curLoop >= endLoop)
            return null;
        LoopRange ret = new LoopRange();
        ret.start = curLoop;
        int sizeLoop = (endLoop-curLoop)/numThreads;
        curLoop += (sizeLoop>minSize)?sizeLoop:minSize;
        ret.end = (curLoop<endLoop)?curLoop:endLoop;
        return ret;
    }
}
```

Implementation of a guided self-scheduling loop handler is also straightforward. We simply need to modify the constructor to handle the minimum size required, and modify the `loopGetRange()` method to return a portion of the remaining loop. In our implementation of the guided self-scheduler, we also subclass the original loop handler and implement only the changes.

User-defined scheduler

The implementation of the self-scheduler and the guided self-scheduler is simple for a reason: it was designed to be so. The original loop handler was designed to be subclassed so that the scheduler algorithm could be modified.

As good as the implementation of the guided self-scheduler may be, it is still designed for a generic loop. There will be cases where each of the different schedulers will work better than others. However, if enough information concerning the loop is known, and the effort is large enough, it may justify the implementation of yet another scheduler. This entails figuring out the appropriate logic and coding a new `loopGetRange()` method.

Here's how our original example can be modified to use one of the scheduling techniques we've just seen:

```
public class SinTable extends GuidedLoopHandler {
    private float lookupValues[];

    public SinTable() {
        super(0, 360*100, 100, 12);
        lookupValues = new float [360 * 100];
    }

    public void loopDoRange(int start, int end) {
        for (int i = start; i < end; i++) {
            float sinValue = (float)Math.sin((i % 360)*Math.PI/180.0);
            lookupValues[i] = sinValue * (float)i / 180.0f;
        }
    }

    public float[] getValues() {
        loopProcess();
        return lookupValues;
    }
}
```

To use the guided self-scheduler algorithm in our SinTable class, we simply subclass from the GuidedLoopHandler class and modify our constructor to pass the minimum chunk size. We could also have written the GuidedLoopHandler class to have an overloaded constructor that picks a default minimum. This would allow it to have a constructor with the same signature as the static loop handler.

Variable Classifications

In the implementation of the SinTable class, we classified the variables used in the original nonthreaded loop as loop-private variables, but other variable classifications exist. The reason for classifying variables at all is that different types of variables require different types of handling within and between threads, because many loops have a data dependency that occurs between different iterations. By classifying the variables, we are able to correctly update and modify them without any race conditions. Different types of variable classifications can be determined by their usage, and these classifications will determine how they are to be implemented or treated in the multithreaded loop handler.

Auto-Parallelizing Compilers

The terminology used in this chapter is based on the terminology used by the auto-parallelizing MP C compiler for the Solaris platform. Automatic parallelization is the same technique that we are describing in this chapter, but it is accomplished by the compiler instead of by the programmer. While auto-parallelization has been available for other languages, such as FORTRAN, for a long time, it is relatively new for the C language. This is due to the aliasing problems with the C language: with pointers and other aliasing issues, it is very difficult to classify the variables or the loop itself. Even with the current implementation, #pragmas are needed to help the compiler classify variables used in the loop.

In this regard, Java is closer to FORTRAN than to C. All variable references are tracked (for garbage collection), pointer arithmetic is not allowed, and variable types are enforced. There are fewer aliasing problems in Java than in C. This means that it should be much easier to develop an auto-parallelizing compiler for Java than it is for C. Until one exists, however, you need to apply these techniques by hand, as we've done in this chapter.

Loop-private variables

As mentioned, a loop-private variable is a variable that does not pass its value from one iteration of the loop to another iteration of the loop. It can actually be a variable that is declared in the loop itself, and it can also be an instance or publicly accessed variable that is accessed by only one iteration of the loop. This was the case with the lookupValues array variable, where each member of the array was only accessed by one iteration of the loop. Although the whole array was not loop private to any iteration, specific members were loop private to specific iterations.

As shown with the SinTable class, treatment of loop-private variables is often done with a local copy of the variable in each thread. Since each thread has a copy, no interference between the threads is possible. In the case of the lookupValues array, there is an understanding that the threads will respect the privacy of the other threads by only accessing their loop-private portions of the array.

Read-only variables

Read-only variables are variables that do not change in value during the duration of the loop. They can be true constants or simply variables that have been initialized and will not change until after the loop has been processed.

No special treatment of read-only variables is necessary. The worker threads do not need to have their own copies of the variables, and access to them does not require synchronization of any type.

Storeback variables

Storeback variables are basically loop-private variables that are needed after the loop has been completed. For example, say that the processing of the `lookupValues` array required some extra work to be done after the loop was finished:

```
public float[] getValues() {
    if (lookupValues == null) {
        float sinValue = 0;
        lookupValues = new float [360 * 100];
        for (int i = 0; i < (360*100); i++) {
            sinValue = (float)Math.sin((i % 360)*Math.PI/180.0);
            lookupValues[i] = sinValue * (float)i / 180.0f;
        }
        lookupValues[0] += sinValue;
    }
    return lookupValues;
}
```

In this slightly modified version of the SinTable loop, both the `sinValue` variable and the individual members of the `lookupValues` array are still loop-private variables. There is no data dependency between these two variables in different iterations of the loop. However, in this case the `sinValue` variable is also a storeback variable. Since the variable is important after the loop has completed, it must be set to the value as if the loop had run in the correct order. The members of the `lookupValues` array were always considered as storeback variables, but since no individual copies were kept, there was little need to make this extra distinction.

Here's how we can handle the storeback variable:

```
public class SinTable extends GuidedLoopHandler {
    private float lookupValues[];
    private float sinValue;

    public SinTable() {
        super(0, 360*100, 100, 12);
        lookupValues = new float [360 * 100];
    }

    public void loopDoRange(int start, int end) {
        float sinValue = 0;
        for (int i = start; i < end; i++) {
            sinValue = (float)Math.sin((i % 360)*Math.PI/180.0);
            lookupValues[i] = sinValue * (float)i / 180.0f;
        }
```

```
        if (end == endLoop)
            this.sinValue = sinValue;
    }

    public float[] getValues() {
        loopProcess();
        lookupValues[0] += sinValue;
        return lookupValues;
    }
}
```

The sinValue variable is still treated as a loop-private variable. However, since this variable is really a storeback variable, we need to store the "last" value of this variable. Since the algorithm is now executed in a multithreaded manner, the last iteration is not necessarily the last value assigned to the variable by a thread.

A thread must check that it has executed the last chunk of the loop before copying the value of its loop-private copy to the global copy. Also note that no synchronization is necessary. Since only the last iteration will be copied, only one thread will be executing the code, and no race condition is possible.

Reduction variables

Obviously, it is not possible to make every variable a loop-private variable, since there are cases where there are real data dependencies between different iterations of the loop. Because of these data dependencies, different threads executing different iterations might interfere with each other during execution. We will define these types of variables as *shared variables*, since they are shared between iterations of the loop.

Shared variables have many problems. The first is the race conditions that exist when different threads access the variable simultaneously. The second is that the value of a variable may depend on the order in which it is processed. In the first case, we can simply use synchronization techniques to prevent the race conditions from existing. The second case poses a much greater problem.

However, what if the order did not matter? We would be able to process the loop in any order and would simply have to synchronize access to the shared variable. For example, let us assume that we also need to calculate the sum of our SinTable:

```
public float[] getValues() {
    for (int i = 0; i < (360*100); i++) {
        sinValue = (float)Math.sin((i % 360)*Math.PI/180.0);
        lookupValues[i] = sinValue * (float)i / 180.0f;
        sumValue += lookupValues[i];
    }
    return lookupValues;
}
```

In this case, the sumValue variable is clearly not a loop-private variable. The value of sumValue is passed from one iteration to another, and the correct result requires this dependency to exist. However, the sumValue variable is only useful after the loop has completed. The iterations simply add to the running total—subtotals or other order-based requirements are not necessary. Furthermore, addition itself is order independent: it is possible to add a bunch of numbers in any order, and the final result will be the same.

Sometimes, Order Does Matter

In the examples of this section, we assume that we can perform the addition in any order that we like. Since addition is associative, this is supposed to work.

On a computer, however, addition is not necessarily associative. Because of the internal mechanism that the computer uses to store numbers of infinite precision in a fixed number of bits, some rounding error occurs in every mathematical calculation. Normally, these errors are small enough that we don't need to worry about them, and they often cancel each other out. But there are many cases where the propagation of this error will lead to vastly different results when the order of the operations is changed.

If you're performing sensitive numerical analysis, then be aware that the tricks of this section may lead to unacceptable error propagation and incorrect answers.

The sumValue variable is a reduction variable. It must still be shared among the threads, but since order does not matter, this sharing only requires synchronization to prevent race conditions:

```
public class SinTable extends GuidedLoopHandler {
    private float lookupValues[];
    public float sumValue;

    public SinTable() {
        super(0, 360*100, 100, 12);
        lookupValues = new float [360 * 100];
    }

    public void loopDoRange(int start, int end) {
        float sinValue = 0;
        for (int i = start; i < end; i++) {
            sinValue = (float)Math.sin((i % 360)*Math.PI/180.0);
```

```
        lookupValues[i] = sinValue * (float)i / 180.0f;
        synchronized (this) {
            sumValue += lookupValues[i];
        }
    }
}

public float[] getValues() {
    loopProcess();
    return lookupValues;
}
}
```

Race conditions in this example are prevented by using the synchronization lock of the SinTable instance. If we have many reduction variables that are not dependent on each other and we cannot store them all at the same time, it might be a better idea to have separate synchronization locks—or BusyFlags—for each reduction variable.

Furthermore, we are synchronizing with each iteration of the loop. This is not very efficient. It is better to assign the value to loop-private variables and only synchronize the final summed value of the range to the reduction variable. By doing this, we are removing most of the need for synchronization, which can drastically add to the parallelization of the threads:

```
public class SinTable extends GuidedLoopHandler {
    private float lookupValues[];
    public float sumValue;

    public SinTable() {
        super(0, 360*100, 100, 12);
        lookupValues = new float [360 * 100];
    }

    public void loopDoRange(int start, int end) {
        float sinValue = 0.0f;
        float sumValue = 0.0f;
        for (int i = start; i < end; i++) {
            sinValue = (float)Math.sin((i % 360)*Math.PI/180.0);
            lookupValues[i] = sinValue * (float)i / 180.0f;
            sumValue += lookupValues[i];
        }
        synchronized (this) {
            this.sumValue += sumValue;
        }
    }

    public float[] getValues() {
        loopProcess();
```

```
        System.out.println(sumValue);
        return lookupValues;
    }
}
```

In this new example, we are doing a two-stage reduction of the values. We are reducing the value of each iteration to the local copy of the sumValue variable, and then we are reducing this local copy to the actual reduction variable. Since the local copy of the sumValue variable is loop private, synchronization is not necessary. Synchronization is still necessary when adding to the reduction variable. However, this is now done once per range instead of once per iteration.

Finally, all reduction variables are storeback variables. There is no need to have special storeback handling logic for reduction variables.

Shared variables

Originally, all variables in the loop are shared variables, since all variables can be accessed by all the threads that are executing the loop. As we parallelize the loop, we can quickly classify the shared variables that are also read-only variables. We can also reclassify those variables that are loop-private variables. Of the remaining shared variables, it may be possible either to convert them to loop-private variables or to classify them as reduction variables.

Unfortunately, there will be cases where a shared variable cannot be classified as anything but a shared variable. This is where our technique fails to work. As much as we would like to convert any loop to run in a multithreaded environment, not all algorithms can be redesigned to run in a parallel environment.

The other problem with shared variables is the side effect. For example, if we needed to save each of the subtotals of the sumValue variable, it could not be treated as a reduction variable since the changes in the variable are also important. If we had to print the subtotals during the loop, not only would the intermediate results be out of order, but the intermediate results would be different.

When variable classification is not enough for parallelization, we have other techniques that can help. They may not solve every case, but with experience, more and more loops can be converted to run in a multithreaded environment.

Loop Analysis and Transformations

To assist our parallelizing techniques, we can analyze the algorithms of the loop itself instead of just analyzing the variables in the loop. In the majority of the cases, there is very little that we can do without redesigning the algorithm, but there are a few situations where we can quickly modify the code without a complete redesign. By implementing simple transformations on the original code, we may be able to use the techniques discussed so far to thread the loop.

Loop distribution

In many cases, only a small portion of a large complex loop contains code that must be executed sequentially. It may be possible to separate the large complex loop into two separate loops. Once the complex loop is separated into two loops—one loop containing the code that can be parallelized, the other containing the sequential code—we can then parallelize a portion of the original loop. We may even be able to run the sequential loop in parallel with the loop that can be threaded.

Returning to our SinTable example, let's assume that we need not only a total but also a running subtotal of the table that is to be generated:

```java
public float[] getValues() {
    for (int i = 0; i < (360*100); i++) {
        sinValue = (float)Math.sin((i % 360)*Math.PI/180.0);
        lookupValues[i] = sinValue * (float)i / 180.0f;
        if (i == 0) {
            sumValues[0] = lookupValues[0];
        } else {
            sumValues[i] = lookupValues[i] + lookupValues[i-1];
        }
    }
    return lookupValues;
}
```

The sumValues array variable is definitely a shared variable. The members of the sumValues variable are also shared in that some of them are accessed by two different threads. Furthermore, the order matters. It is not possible for one thread to start a chunk before the thread that is working on the previous chunk is finished.

We can solve that problem like this:

```java
public class SinTable extends GuidedLoopHandler {
    private float lookupValues[];
    public float sumValues[];

    public SinTable() {
        super(0, 360*100, 100, 12);
        lookupValues = new float [360 * 100];
        sumValues = new float [360 * 100];
    }

    public void loopDoRange(int start, int end) {
        float sinValue = 0.0f;
```

```
        for (int i = start; i < end; i++) {
            sinValue = (float)Math.sin((i % 360)*Math.PI/180.0);
            lookupValues[i] = sinValue * (float)i / 180.0f;
        }
    }

    public float[] getValues() {
        loopProcess();
        sumValues[0] = lookupValues[0];
        for (int i = 1; i < (360*100); i++) {
            sumValues[i] = lookupValues[i] + lookupValues[i-1];
        }
        return lookupValues;
    }
}
```

While it is not possible to parallelize the running subtotal without drastically changing the algorithm, we can quickly convert the loop into two separate loops. The first loop contains the threadable code, and the second processes the subtotal. Once this is accomplished, we can then thread the first loop without changing the second. In the new SinTable class, we have moved the running subtotal code to a separate loop. This separate loop runs on a single thread, and only after the first loop is processed.

Some comparisons should be taken when using this technique. Since a large portion of the loop may be running single threaded, the performance gain may not justify the effort involved. In most cases, calculations of the subtotal are small considering the effort of the main calculation, and the performance penalty may be small in comparison.

Loop isolation

Many applications do not contain a single large loop. Even if a particular loop is determined to be unparallelizable, there may be other loops in the application. Even if these other loops also cannot be parallelized, we may be able to run each separate loop in a different thread.

Although the many loops may be very complex, with large data dependencies between iterations, there may be few data dependencies between the different loops. It may be possible to isolate the individual loops themselves and run them each in a separate thread. With this technique, load balancing is no longer possible. After all, if the application contains four major loops and you were able to isolate them all, it is still impossible to distribute these four loops among twelve processors.

Loop interchange

Multilayered loops are a prime cause of CPU-bound applications that run for a large period of time. This could be loops that are directly inside of other loops or, more likely, loops that call methods that contain loops. This scenario is so common that we will examine inner-loop threading later in this chapter. For now, there is a simple case to look for:

```
public float[][] getValues() {
    for (int i = 0; i < 360; i++) {
        lookupValues[0][i] = 0;
    }
    for (int j = 1; j < 1000; j++) {
        for (int i = 0; i < 360; i++) {
            float sinValue = (float)Math.sin((i % 360)*Math.PI/180.0);
            lookupValues[j][i] = sinValue * (float)i / 180.0f;
            lookupValues[j][i] += lookupValues[j-1][i]*(float)j/180.0f;
        }
    }
    return lookupValues;
}
```

For multilayered loops, it is generally more profitable to thread the outer loop instead of the inner one. It is not necessary to thread both the inner and outer loop because threading either one should use all the processors. If the outer loop is threaded, threading the inner loop will not provide any further speedup since there are no more processors to run the extra threads (and vice versa). The reason we prefer to thread the outer loop is that there is an overhead in creating, destroying, and synchronizing among the many threads. By threading the outer loop, we create and destroy the threads once and only synchronize at a coarse level—less synchronization should be necessary.

In this new version of the table calculation, we are now working on a two-dimensional table. There are three loops used during this calculation. However, the first loop is merely setting the first row of values to zero. The next two loops are actually a pair of multilayered loops. The algorithm is looping the processing from row to row, executing the inner loop that is processing the values to be stored in the different columns.

The problem in this case is that there is a data dependency between the rows themselves. Because the calculation at any row is dependent on the calculation of the previous row, the members of any column in the lookupValues array cannot be considered loop private—or made loop private. The inner loop can be parallelized with no problems since there are no data dependencies between the iterations. The only requirement is that the inner loop must assume that the outer loop ran in the correct order; this requirement is fine since we are not threading the outer loop.

However, we can also rewrite our original code as follows:

```
public float[][] getValues() {
    for (int i = 0; i < 360; i++) {
        lookupValues[0][i] = 0;
    }
    for (int i = 0; i < 360; i++) {
        for (int j = 1; j < 1000; j++) {
            float sinValue = (float)Math.sin((i % 360)*Math.PI/180.0);
            lookupValues[j][i] = sinValue * (float)i / 180.0f;
            lookupValues[j][i] += lookupValues[j-1][i]*(float)j/180.0f;
        }
    }
    return lookupValues;
}
```

In this example, the loops are interchanged. Instead of working from row to row, we can work from column to column. The inner loop can then process the data from row to row. By interchanging the loops, the inner loop is now no longer threadable, since there is data dependency between the members of the columns in the `lookupValues` array. However, the outer loop is now threadable. Once the outer loop has been threaded, there will no longer be a reason to thread the inner loop. Since it is more profitable to thread an outer loop than an inner loop, this simple change prior to multithreading gives us a better return on our development time investment.

Unfortunately, although loops within loops are common, this example may not be. There is generally setup code for an inner loop, and there may be multiple loops that are run sequentially within the outer loop, or the inner loop may be inside another method that is called from the outer loop. And the data dependencies may be such that a loop interchange will not solve the problem.

Having an inner loop that is threadable in an outer loop that is not threadable is common. We will be examining inner-loop threading in more detail later in this chapter.

Loop reimplementation

As you may have noticed, the loop handler that we have developed is fairly restrictive. It only applies to `for` loops, the range of the loop must be known prior to execution, it only works with integers as its index, and it has an interval of only 1 between iterations. While some of these restrictions are caused by the fact that we have not implemented support for certain features in the loop handler, the main cause is that it is difficult, if not impossible, to implement an algorithm that can handle all generic loops.

If all else fails during loop transformation, programming experience is still very useful. A while loop or a do loop may be converted to a for loop. The start and end iterations may be calculated prior to loop execution. Code may be moved from or into a loop, or between loops, to allow other loop transformations to occur. Code changes can also cause variable classifications to change. A shared variable may be reclassified as loop private or as a reduction variable because of how it is used in a loop.

Unfortunately, success is never guaranteed. The goal is to balance the effort of development with the acceleration that may be gained. It may take days to implement a change that can only achieve another one or two percent acceleration. After all, if unlimited effort were allowed, we would redesign the whole application from scratch.

Inner-Loop Threading

The issues that we have discussed so far do not change when the loops are nested: if you apply the techniques only to the inner loop, they will work. However, there are some other, very subtle issues that may apply to inner loops. Let's return to our two dimensional SinTable. As mentioned, a loop interchange should allow the outer loop to be threaded. However, instead of the loop transformation, let's try to thread the inner loop:

```
public float[][] getValues() {
    for (int i = 0; i < 360; i++) {
        lookupValues[0][i] = 0;
    }
    for (int j = 1; j < 1000; j++) {
        for (int i = 0; i < 360; i++) {
            float sinValue = (float)Math.sin((i % 360)*Math.PI/180.0);
            lookupValues[j][i] = sinValue * (float)i / 180.0f;
            lookupValues[j][i] += lookupValues[j-1][i]*(float)j/180.0f;
        }
    }
    return lookupValues;
}
```

The first variable that we will classify is the outer-loop index variable, j. We must classify this variable since it is used inside the inner loop. In this case, j is classified as a read-only variable. At first glance, this does not make sense: how could an index variable be read-only? We must only look at the scope that we are attempting to thread. During the execution of the inner loop, the variable has a single value that does not change throughout the entire execution of the loop.

While the lookupValues array variable is a shared variable, the elements can be classified as loop private. Since each iteration of the loop accesses a different member of the array based on the loop index and the read-only variable j, its members may be considered loop private. The members of the lookupValues array are also considered as storeback variables. However, since we will not be creating a local copy of these variables, there is no need to store the variables back.

The last two variables—sinValue and i—are simply classified as loop-private variables, and separate copies are created for each thread. Neither of these variables is used after the loop has completed, so storeback handling is not necessary.

Choosing the loop scheduler is done by examining the algorithm inside the inner loop itself. In this case, there is nothing that should cause any iteration to execute longer than any other iteration. Choosing the default—static or chunk—scheduler is probably best. However, there should be no harm in choosing either the self- or guided self-scheduler.

Once these tasks are completed, threading the loop is done by using the loop handler as usual. However, there is a slight complication: compared with the outer loop, the inner loop will be executed many more times. This means a thread creation and destruction overhead is executed many more times. Furthermore, the loop handler is designed as a "one use" object. A new loop handler will have to be created for each iteration of the outer loop. Although using the loop handler will work without any problems, the overhead may be more significant than for threading a higher-level loop.

We can partially overcome this complication as follows:

```java
public class PoolLoopHandler implements Runnable {
    protected class LoopRange {
        public int start, end;
    }
    protected ThreadPool poolThreads;
    protected int startLoop, endLoop, curLoop, numThreads;

    public PoolLoopHandler(int start, int end, int threads) {
        numThreads = threads;
        poolThreads = new ThreadPool(numThreads);
        setRange(start, end);
    }

    public synchronized void setRange(int start, int end) {
        startLoop = start;
        endLoop = end;
        reset();
    }

    public synchronized void reset() {
        curLoop = startLoop;
    }
```

```
        protected synchronized LoopRange loopGetRange() {
            if (curLoop >= endLoop)
                return null;
            LoopRange ret = new LoopRange();
            ret.start = curLoop;
            curLoop += (endLoop-startLoop)/numThreads+1;
            ret.end = (curLoop<endLoop)?curLoop:endLoop;
            return ret;
        }

        public void loopDoRange(int start, int end) {
        }

        public void loopProcess() {
            reset();
            for (int i = 0; i < numThreads; i++) {
                poolThreads.addRequest(this);
            }
            try {
                    poolThreads.waitForAll();
            } catch (InterruptedException iex) {}
        }

        public void run() {
            LoopRange str;
            while ((str = loopGetRange()) != null) {
                loopDoRange(str.start, str.end);
            }
        }
    }
```

The fact that our original LoopHandler class can be used only once was merely a design flaw. The loop index can never be set back to the start of the loop, nor can the range of the loop be changed. To fix this, we simply add two new methods, reset() and setRange(), that will reset the index back to the start of the loop and specify new ranges for the loop. To avoid many thread creations and destructions, we will use the ThreadPool class that we implemented in Chapter 7. Instead of creating threads in the loopProcess() method, this method will now assign the tasks to the threads in a thread pool. We can then simply wait for all the threads in the pool to complete their assigned tasks. This all helps somewhat, but the synchronization that we have introduced into the calculation will have an effect on the ultimate acceleration of our program.

We can implement other scheduling models in the pool handler quite easily:

```
public class PoolSelfLoopHandler extends PoolLoopHandler {
    private int groupSize;
```

A Warning About Inner Loops

Prior to threading any loop, we should always examine that loop. There is no reason to thread the loop if the loop executes in a very short period of time. For these cases, the overhead in the setup and takedown of the threaded loop may be greater than any speed gained from threading the loop.

When moving from the outer loop to the inner loop, we must examine the inner loop. Just because the outer loop is a candidate for threading does not mean the inner loop is a candidate for threading. If the number of iterations in the outer loop is many times higher than the inner loop, the inner loop may execute only for a short period of time. There could also be method calls in the outer loop, and not in the inner loop that is taking a long period of time to execute.

```
public PoolSelfLoopHandler(int start, int end,
                                int size, int threads) {
    super(start, end, threads);
    setSize(size);
}

public synchronized void setSize(int size) {
    groupSize = size;
    reset();
}

protected synchronized LoopRange loopGetRange() {
    if (curLoop >= endLoop)
        return null;
    LoopRange ret = new LoopRange();
    ret.start = curLoop;
    curLoop += groupSize;
    ret.end = (curLoop<endLoop)?curLoop:endLoop;
    return ret;
}
}
```

What's interesting here is the similarity to our original SelfLoopHandler class. However, to be more configurable, we have modified the handler to allow the extra parameters, such as the chunk size, to be changed.

Here's how we use our new handler:

```
public class SinTable extends PoolLoopHandler {
    private float lookupValues[][];
    private int j;
```

```
public SinTable() {
    super(0, 360, 12);
    lookupValues = new float[1000][];
    for (int j = 0; j < 1000; j++) {
        lookupValues[j] = new float[360];
    }
}

public void loopDoRange(int start, int end) {
    float sinValue = 0.0f;
    for (int i = start; i < end; i++) {
        sinValue = (float)Math.sin((i % 360)*Math.PI/180.0);
        lookupValues[j][i] = sinValue * (float)i / 180.0f;
        lookupValues[j][i] += lookupValues[j-1][i]*(float)j/180.0f;
    }
}

public float[][] getValues() {
    for (int i = 0; i < 360; i++) {
        lookupValues[0][i] = 0;
    }
    for (j = 1; j < 1000; j++) {
        loopProcess();
    }
    return lookupValues;
}
}
```

To implement the SinTable class, we place the code from the inner loop in the loopDoRange() method and then call the loopProcess() method to process the inner loop. Since the j index variable is a read-only shared variable, it is now an instance variable of the SinTable class.

Having a loop handler that can be used more than once is also very important. If we were using the earlier version of the loop handler, we would have had to create a new instance of the loop handler for each inner loop that we executed. This means that the code for the outer loop and the inner loop could not have been in the same class. Furthermore, we would have had to pass a reference to the j variable and lookupValues array to each instance, since these are shared between the different inner loop handlers.

Loop Printing

The task of sending a string to a file or the display is an I/O-bound task. Using multithreaded techniques on a loop of output does not make sense. Since the operation is I/O-bound, the threads will spend most of their time waiting, and there is little difference in having one processor or twelve processors available to run waiting threads. Furthermore, the order of the output is important. Data that is written to a file or the display will eventually be read by a person or another application. The output must look the same whether the calculation is done as a single-threaded or multithreaded application.

However, what if the printing portion of the loop is small when compared with the mathematical calculation? If enough of the loop is CPU intensive, it might be silly to abandon an attempt at parallelizing the loop just because it contains a println() method call. The only problem that needs to be solved is the ordering of the output. This can be done by a two-step printing process. Instead of printing directly to the display or file, the application can print to a virtual, memory-based display along with an index that is used to order the output. When the processing of the loop has completed, the output can then be sent to the display or file, using the index information to ensure that the data is sent in the correct order.

Let's reexamine our SinTable loop:

```java
public synchronized float[] getValues() {
    if (lookupValues == null) {
        for (int i = 0; i < (360*100); i++) {
            float sinValue = (float)Math.sin((i % 360)*Math.PI/180.0);
            lookupValues[i] = sinValue * (float)i / 180.0f;
            System.out.println(" " + i + "       " + lookupValues[i]);
        }
    }
    return lookupValues;
}
```

In this new version of the getValues() method, we are also printing the table to standard output. Obviously, this is a simple example that can be transformed with a loop distribution to two separate loops. But let us assume that the printing process is highly integrated into the algorithm and the loop transformation is not possible.

To solve this problem, we'll use this class:

```java
import java.util.*;
import java.io.*;

public class LoopPrinter {
    private Vector pStorage[];
    private int growSize;

    public LoopPrinter(int initSize, int growSize) {
        pStorage = new Vector[initSize];
        this.growSize = growSize;
    }
```

```java
    public LoopPrinter() {
        this(100, 0);
    }

    private synchronized void enlargeStorage(int minSize) {
        int oldSize = pStorage.length;
        if (oldSize < minSize) {
            int newSize = (growSize > 0) ?
                oldSize + growSize : 2 * oldSize;
            if (newSize < minSize) {
                newSize = minSize;
            }
            Vector newVec[] = new Vector[newSize];
            System.arraycopy(pStorage, 0, newVec, 0, oldSize);
            pStorage = newVec;
        }
    }

    public synchronized void print(int index, Object obj) {
        if (index >= pStorage.length) {
            enlargeStorage(index+1);
        }
        if (pStorage[index] == null) {
            pStorage[index] = new Vector();
        }
        pStorage[index].addElement(obj.toString());
    }

    public synchronized void println(int index, Object obj) {
        print(index, obj);
        print(index, "\n");
    }

    public synchronized void send2stream(PrintStream ps) {
        for (int i = 0; i < pStorage.length; i++) {
            if (pStorage[i] != null) {
                Enumeration e = pStorage[i].elements();
                while (e.hasMoreElements()) {
                    ps.print(e.nextElement());
                }
            }
        }
    }
}
```

Implementation of a loop printer is done with a two-dimensional vector. The first dimension is used to separate the output. This output index could be related to the index of the actual loop, or to a chunk of the loop, or it could even be a combination of multiple loop indices. In any case, an output index should not be assigned to more than one thread, since the ordering inside an indexed vector is based on it. The second dimension holds the strings that will be sent to the output. Since the indices have already ordered the strings to be printed, this dimension is just used to store the many strings that will be sent to this index.*

Printing an object to the virtual display is done with the print() and println() methods. Along with the object to be printed, the application must supply an index as a reference of the printing order. These methods simply store a reference to the strings so that they may be printed at a later time. The second phase of the printing process is done by the send2stream() method. Once the loop has completed, a call to this method will print the result to the output specified.

Here's how to use the LoopPrinter class:

```
public class SinTable extends GuidedLoopHandler {
    private float lookupValues[];
    private LoopPrinter lp;

    public SinTable() {
        super(0, 360*100, 100, 12);
        lookupValues = new float [360 * 100];
        lp = new LoopPrinter(360*100, 0);
    }

    public void loopDoRange(int start, int end) {
        for (int i = start; i < end; i++) {
            float sinValue = (float)Math.sin((i % 360)*Math.PI/180.0);
            lookupValues[i] = sinValue * (float)i / 180.0f;
            lp.println(i, " " + i + " " + lookupValues[i]);
        }
    }

    public float[] getValues() {
        loopProcess();
        lp.send2stream(System.out);
        return lookupValues;
    }
}
```

The loop printer is created prior to the loop, all printing that was previously sent to a file or the display is sent to the loop printer, and the send2stream() method is called upon completion of the loop. Since the loop printer will send all the information to one target, multiple loop printers will have to be created if the loop prints to different streams.

---

* Technically, we could have done the same thing with a single-dimensional array of string buffers.

Also note that we constructed the loop printer with the index size as its initial size. The loop printer is written to expand to any size, so this extra definition is not necessary. We want to avoid expanding the size because this operation not only requires the method to be synchronized, but also, depending on the size, will take some time to execute. The `print()` and `println()` methods must also be synchronized. This serves two purposes: First, it allows the array size to be increased without a race condition. Second, it allows the methods to work—although the print order is no longer guaranteed—if an index is assigned to two threads. If the loop printer were modified so as not to allow the array to be enlarged, and if it were assumed that developers would not assign two threads to the same index, synchronization at this level would no longer be necessary.

Multiprocessor Scaling

Scaling is a term that is sometimes overused. It can apply to how many applications a computer can execute simultaneously, how many disks can be written to simultaneously, or how many cream cheese bagel orders can be processed by the local bagel shop's crew. When the output cannot be increased no matter how many resources are added, this limit is generally the value used to specify what something scales to. If the oven cannot produce more bagels per hour, it does not matter how many people are added to the assembly line: the rate of bagels cannot exceed the rate produced by the oven. The scaling limit can also be controlled by many other factors, such as the rate that the cream cheese can be produced, the size of the refrigerators, or even by the suppliers for the bagel shop.

In this chapter, when we refer to the scalability of a multithreaded application, we are referring to the limit on the number of processors we can add and still obtain an acceleration. Adding more than this limit will not make the application run faster. Obviously, how an application scales depends on many factors: the operating system, the Java virtual machine implementation, the browser or application server, and the Java application itself. The best an application can scale will be based on the scalability limits of all of these factors.

For perfect CPU-bound programs in a perfect world, we could expect perfect scaling: adding a second CPU would halve the amount of time that it takes the program to run, adding another CPU would reduce the time by another third, and so on. Even for the loop-based programs we've examined in this chapter, however, the amount of scaling that we will see is also limited by these important constraints:

Setup time

A certain amount of time is required to execute the code outside of the loop that is being parallelized. This amount of time is independent of the number of threads and processors that are available, because only a single thread will execute that code.

New synchronization requirements

In parallelizing the loops of this chapter, we've introduced some additional bookkeeping code, some of which is synchronized. Because obtaining a synchronization lock is expensive, this increases the time required to execute the code.

Serialization of methods

Some methods in our parallelized code must run sequentially because they are synchronized. Contention for the lock associated with these methods will also affect the scalability of our parallelized programs.

The Effect of the Virtual Machine

One of the factors that can affect the scalability of a particular program is the implementation of the virtual machine itself. Obtaining a synchronization lock, for instance, takes a certain amount of time, and the code in the virtual machine that actually implements the synchronization is often synchronized itself. Hence, two threads attempting to obtain different synchronization locks may still compete for a resource within the virtual machine. And there are other examples where the virtual machine or operating system will affect the scalability of a program.

The results that we present in this chapter are based on the 1.1.6 production release of the Solaris 2.6 VM from Sun Microsystems. Other virtual machines and operating systems will show different results: in fact, the 1.2 beta production release for Solaris shows much better scaling results than we've presented here, primarily due to increased efficiencies in obtaining synchronization locks (which is very important, given that the `loopGetRange()` method is synchronized). These results are likely to be obtained once the Java 2 Solaris production release is available as well.

If we view the setup time, synchronization time, and time required to execute the serialized methods as a percentage of the total running time, the remaining time is the amount of code that is parallelized. The maximum amount of scaling that we'll see is given by Amdahl's law:

$$S = (1 - F) + \frac{F}{N}$$

Here, *S* is the scaling we'll see, assuming that *F*% of code is parallelized over *N* processors. If 95% of the code is parallelized and we have eight processors available, the code will run in 16.8% of the original time required (.05 + .95/8). However, when we introduce code to calculate loop ranges (or any other code), we've actually increased the amount of serialized code, so *F* could potentially be a negative number. In that case, our parallelized code will take longer to run than our original code.

So what sort of scaling can we expect from the techniques of this chapter? In order to answer this question, we will test several implementations of our sample double loop:

```
public float[][] getValues() {
    for (int i = 0; i < 360; i++) {
        lookupValues[0][i] = 0;
    }
    for (int j = 1; j < 1000; j++) {
        for (int i = 0; i < 360; i++) {
            float sinValue = (float)Math.sin((i % 360)*Math.PI/180.0);
            lookupValues[j][i] = sinValue * (float)i / 180.0f;
            lookupValues[j][i] += lookupValues[j-1][i]*(float)j/180.0f;
        }
    }
    return lookupValues;
}
```

To make testing easier, we will use the following class and interface to build a system by which we may test various loop handlers. Since we're working with CPU-intensive threads, we've included the Solaris-specific code to set the number of LWPs, but this code will run on any operating system:

```
public interface ScaleTester {
    public void init(int nRows, int nCols, int nThreads);
    public float[][] doCalc();
}

import java.util.*;
import java.text.*;
import java.io.*;

public class ScaleTest {
    private int nIter = 200;
    private int nRows = 2000;
    private int nCols = 200;
    private int nThreads = 8;
    Class target;

    ScaleTest(int nIter, int nRows, int nCols, int nThreads,
              String className) {
```

```
            this.nIter = nIter;
            this.nRows = nRows;
            this.nCols = nCols;
            this.nThreads = nThreads;
            try {
                target = Class.forName(className);
            } catch (ClassNotFoundException cnfe) {
                System.out.println(cnfe);
                System.exit(-1);
            }
        }

    void chart() {
        long sumTime = 0;
        long startLoop = System.currentTimeMillis();
        try {
            ScaleTester st = (ScaleTester) target.newInstance();
            for (int i = 0; i < nIter; i++) {
                st.init(nRows, nCols, nThreads);
                long then = System.currentTimeMillis();
                float ans[][] = st.doCalc();
                long now = System.currentTimeMillis();
                sumTime += (now - then);
            }
        } catch (Exception e) {
            e.printStackTrace();
            System.exit(-1);
        }
        long endLoop = System.currentTimeMillis();
        long calcTime = endLoop - startLoop;
        System.err.println("Loop time " + sumTime +
                        " (" + ((sumTime * 100) / calcTime) + "%)");
        System.err.println("Calculation time  " + calcTime);
    }

    public static void main(String args[]) {
        if (args.length != 5) {
            System.out.println(
    "Usage: java ScaleTester nIter nRows nCols nThreads className");
            System.exit(-1);
        }
        ScaleTest sc = new ScaleTest(Integer.parseInt(args[0]),
                                Integer.parseInt(args[1]),
                                Integer.parseInt(args[2]),
                                Integer.parseInt(args[3]),
                                args[4]);
        CPUSupport.setConcurrency(Integer.parseInt(args[3]) + 5);
        sc.chart();
    }
}
```

When we use the ScaleTest class, we get two numbers: the number of milliseconds required to run the entire program (including initialization, which is single-threaded) and the number of milliseconds required to run just the loop calculation. We can then compare these numbers to determine the scalability of various implementations of our loop handling classes.

As a baseline, we'll take the measurement of this class:

```
public class Basic implements ScaleTester {
    private float lookupValues[][];
    int nCols, nRows;

    public void init(int nRows, int nCols, int nThreads) {
        this.nCols = nCols;
        this.nRows = nRows;
        lookupValues = new float[nRows][];
        for (int j = 0; j < nRows; j++) {
            lookupValues[j] = new float[nCols];
        }
    }

    public float[][] doCalc() {
        for (int i = 0; i < nCols; i++) {
            lookupValues[0][i] = 0;
        }
        for (int j = 1; j < nRows; j++) {
            for (int i = 0; i < nCols; i++) {
                float sinValue =
                            (float)Math.sin((i % 360)*Math.PI/180.0);
                lookupValues[j][i] = sinValue * (float)i / 180.0f;
                lookupValues[j][i] +=
                            lookupValues[j-1][i]*(float)j/180.0f;
            }
        }
        return lookupValues;
    }
}
```

This class contains no threading; it is the way that we would normally implement the basic calculation we're interested in testing. One of the implementations that we'll compare this class against is the following loop handler class:

```
public class GuidedLoopInterchanged implements ScaleTester {
    private float lookupValues[][];
    private int nRows, nCols, nThreads;

    private class GuidedLoopInterchangedHandler
                                extends GuidedLoopHandler {
        GuidedLoopInterchangedHandler(int nc, int nt) {
```

```
        super(0, nc, 10, nt);
    }

    public void loopDoRange(int start, int end) {
        for (int i = start; i < end; i++) {
            lookupValues[0][i] = 0;
        }
        for (int i = start; i < end; i++) {
            for (int j = 1; j < nRows; j++) {
                float sinValue =
                            (float)Math.sin((i % 360)*Math.PI/180.0);
                lookupValues[j][i] = sinValue * (float)i / 180.0f;
                lookupValues[j][i] +=
                            lookupValues[j-1][i]*(float)j/180.0f;
            }
        }
    }

    public void init(int nRows, int nCols, int nThreads) {
        this.nRows = nRows;
        this.nCols = nCols;
        this.nThreads = nThreads;
        lookupValues = new float[nRows][];
        for (int j = 0; j < nRows; j++) {
            lookupValues[j] = new float[nCols];
        }
    }

    public float[][] doCalc() {
        GuidedLoopInterchangedHandler loop =
                    new GuidedLoopInterchangedHandler(nCols, nThreads);
        loop.loopProcess();
        return lookupValues;
    }
}
```

This class uses our simple loop handler to process the loop; notice, however, that we've interchanged the loops in order to make the outer loop threadable.

Table 9-1 lists the results of the ScaleTest program when run with different implementations of the interchanged loop: we've used chunk, self-scheduled, and guided self-scheduling loop handlers in conjunction with the code we showed earlier. These tests were run on a machine with eight CPUs, using an iteration count of 200. We've normalized the running time for the baseline run to be 100 so that other numbers can be viewed as a percentage: the best that we do is run in 20.6% of the time required for the original run. The first number in each cell represents a run with 500 rows and 1000 columns, and the second number represents a run with 1000 rows and 500 columns.

Table 9-1. Scalability of Simple Loop Handlers

	Number of Threads	**Total Time**	**Loop Time**
Basic	1	100/100	96/96
Chunk scheduling	1	124.6/123.4	120.8/119.7
	2	64.5/63.1	61.2/59.3
	4	34.7/35.3	31.5/31.8
	8	23.7/23.0	20.3/19.3
	12	24.0/24.0	20.6/20.2
Self-scheduling	1	129.7/127.6	125.8/123.8
	2	71.9/70.3	69.0/66.8
	4	39.3/39.6	36.1/36.1
	8	23.1/24.1	19.8/20.5
	12	22.7/23.5	19.2/19.8
Guided self-scheduling	1	124.7/122.5	120.9/118.9
	2	64.0/63.6	60.8/60.5
	4	34.4/34.2	31.3/30.8
	8	20.6/21.8	17.3/18.1
	12	22.3/23.1	18.9/19.1

There are a few conclusions that we can draw from this table:

- The overhead of setting up the thread and loop handling class itself is significant: it requires 22% to 29% more time to execute that code when only a single thread is available. So we would never use this technique on a machine with only one CPU.

- The scaling of the loop calculation itself is good. Since the original loop accounted for 96% of the code, with eight CPUs the best that we can hope for (using Amdahl's law) is 16.8%. We've achieved 20.6%, which implies that 90% of the code is now parallelized: the 6% difference is accounted for by the serialized calls to the `loopGetRange()` method and by the fact that each thread is probably not doing exactly the same amount of work.

- Going past eight threads—that is, the number of CPUs available—yields a penalty. This is partially because we now have threads competing for a CPU, but it is also because of the synchronization around the additional calls to the `loopGetRange()` method.

- The guided self-scheduler is the best choice in this example. This is not surprising: calculations based on sine values do not always require the same amount of time, so the chunk scheduler can be penalized by having one particular thread that requires too much time. That contributes to a loss of scaling, since the threads do not end up performing equal amounts of work.

All in all, though, we've achieved very good scalability.

What effect does a storeback variable have in our testing? We can rewrite our tests so that every time we calculate a lookup value, we add that value to a `sumValue` instance variable. Using the reduction technique we showed earlier, the modified test generates the numbers given in Table 9-2.

Table 9-2. Scalability of Loop Handlers with Storeback Variables

	Number of Threads	**Total Time**	**Loop Time**
Basic	1	100/100	97/96
Chunk scheduling	1	123.3/121.9	119.6/118.3
	2	64.1/62.7	61.5/59.5
	4	36.4/35.2	33.4/32.0
	8	22.5/22.7	19.3/19.3
	12	24.1/23.7	20.9/20.1
Guided self-scheduling	1	123.3/121.6	119.6/117.9
	2	64.6/63.2	62.0/60.0
	4	36.0/34.3	33.1/31.2
	8	20.2/21.5	17.1/18.0
	12	22.1/22.3	19.0/18.7

Because there's only one storeback variable, the effect on the scaling is minor. In fact, in some cases we did better because the baseline now takes longer to execute. However, the effect of many storeback variables could potentially aggregate into something more noticeable.

What if we had threaded only the inner loop? This question is very interesting, since it demonstrates the effect of synchronization overhead versus the amount of savings we obtain if the inner loop is small. Rewriting our first test (with no storeback variable) so that no loop interchange is performed and the inner loop is threaded instead produces the results in Table 9-3.

Table 9-3. Scalability of Inner Loop Handlers

	Number of Threads	**Total Time**	**Loop Time**
Basic	1	100/100	97/96
Guided self-scheduling	1	138.0/159.7	133.8/155.0
	2	82.2/138.3	77.2/131.4
	4	66.7/164.1	60.0/154.2
	8	104.3/515.3	92.8/499.9
	12	1318.9/4466.3	1292.5/4421.7

So what has happened here? First, we've slightly modified our test parameters: the first number was produced with a run of 100 rows and 5000 columns, and the second number was produced with a run of 500 rows and 1000 columns. In the first case, we've achieved some scalability to a point of four CPUs, which allows us to run inner loops of about 250 calculations per CPU. By the time we get to eight CPUs, however, the inner loop has only 125 calculations, and the additional overhead of repeatedly calling the synchronized `loopGetRange()` method has overcome any advantage we received by running the small loops in parallel. Things get drastically worse as we add additional threads.

In the second case, the inner loop is so small that we end up calling the `loopGet-Range()` method so many times that there is never any scalability. In the best case (with two threads), we've added the equivalent of 43% more code than we've parallelized.

As we mentioned, threading of small loops—and particularly of small inner loops—is not necessarily worthwhile.

Finally, what if we add code to the loop that prints out the result of some calculations? We can still thread such a case using the LoopPrinter class that we developed earlier. However, remember that we ended our section on the LoopPrinter class with a discussion that would enable us to remove the synchronization from the Loop-Printer class. Because in this particular test we always know the size of the output array and we can ensure that the same index is not used by two different threads, we can rewrite the LoopPrinter class like this:

```java
import java.util.*;
import java.io.*;

// Non-thread-safe version of a loop printer
public class LoopPrinter {
    private Vector pStorage[];

    public LoopPrinter(int size) {
        pStorage = new Vector[size];
    }

    public void print(int index, Object obj) {
        if (pStorage[index] == null) {
            pStorage[index] = new Vector();
        }
        pStorage[index].addElement(obj.toString());
    }

    public void println(int index, Object obj) {
        print(index, obj);
        print(index, "\n");
    }
}
```

```
public void send2stream(PrintStream ps) {
    for (int i = 0; i < pStorage.length; i++) {
        if (pStorage[i] != null) {
            Enumeration e = pStorage[i].elements();
            while (e.hasMoreElements()) {
                ps.print(e.nextElement());
            }
        }
    }
}
```

With this new version of the loop printer, there is no longer any synchronized code, and hence it should have fewer problems scaling. However, with all the calls to the Vector class, even this version of our loop printer adds a significant amount of overhead to our multithreaded program. In addition, it still takes longer to add strings to these vectors and then dump them out than to simply call the System. out.println() method. However, the difference between our thread-safe and our thread-unsafe versions of this class is important. Table 9-4 lists the results that we obtained for both cases.

Table 9-4. Scalability of the LoopPrinter Classes

	Number of Threads	**Total Time**	**Loop Time**
Basic	1	100/100	96/98
Thread-safe loop printer	1	125.4/126.0	116.7/119.7
	2	79.0/97.8	70.3/91.9
	4	55.5/82.5	47.2/76.7
	8	46.6/84.2	38.2/78.3
	12	48.2/86.9	39.5/80.0
Thread-unsafe loop printer	1	125.1/121.0	116.3/111.3
	2	77.9/92.7	69.4/85.3
	4	55.3/79.0	47.0/67.1
	8	45.6/78.2	37.0/64.9
	12	47.7/78.2	39.1/64.9

The first set of numbers in this table results from running 200 iterations with 200 rows and 1000 columns and printing out every 100th row. The second set of results shows what happens when we print out every 20th row instead. By the time that we print out every 20th row, the amount of extra code prevents any reasonable scaling at all. This is clearly a case where careful design and use of an unsynchronized class can have a big benefit.

We realize that this technique is at odds with our previous admonishments to produce thread-safe code. We still recommend that you always start with thread-safe code. In cases like this, however, when you take the extra care necessary to ensure that you use the thread-unsafe code correctly, the scaling benefits may outweigh the extra effort required to code carefully enough to prevent any race conditions.

Summary

In this chapter, we examined techniques that allow us to utilize multiprocessor machines so that our Java programs will run faster on those machines. We examined loops—the most common source of CPU-intensive code—and developed classes that allow these loops to run in a multithreaded fashion. Along the way, we have classified variables, used various scheduling algorithms, and applied simple loop transformations to achieve this parallelization.

The goals here are to write fast programs from the start, to increase the performance of old algorithms without redesigning them from scratch, and to provide a rich set of options that can be used for cases where high performance is required.

10

Thread Groups

In this chapter, we will discuss Java's ThreadGroup class, which, as the name implies, is a class that handles groups of threads. Thread groups are useful for two reasons: they allow you to manipulate many threads by calling a single method, and they provide the basis that Java's security mechanism uses to interact with threads. In Java 1.0, the actual use of thread groups was really limited to writers of Java applications: within an applet, virtually no operations on thread groups were possible, due in part to security restrictions (but also due in part to bugs in the API). This has changed in later releases of Java, so that thread groups may be used in any Java program.

Thread Group Concepts

Say that you're writing a server using the TCPServer class we developed in Chapter 5. Each client that connects to the server runs as a separate thread. Now say that for each client, the server is going to create many other threads: perhaps a timer thread, a separate thread to read data coming from the client, another to write data to the client, and maybe some threads for a calculation algorithm. Well, you get the idea: the server has a lot of threads it needs to manage.

This is where the ThreadGroup class comes into play. Thread groups allow you to modify many threads with one call—making it easier to control your threads and making it less likely that you'll forget one.

Although we haven't yet mentioned thread groups, they've been around all along: all threads in the Java virtual machine belong to a thread group. Every thread you create automatically belongs to a default thread group the Java virtual machine sets up on your behalf. So all the threads that we've looked at so far belong to this existing thread group.

Thread groups are more than just arbitrary groupings of threads, however; they are related to each other. Every thread group (with the obvious exception of the first thread group) has a parent thread group, so the groups exist in a tree hierarchy. The root of this tree is known as the *system thread group*.

You can create your own thread groups as well; each thread group is the child of an existing thread group. In the TCPServer example we discussed earlier, the thread hierarchy might appear as shown in Figure 10-1.

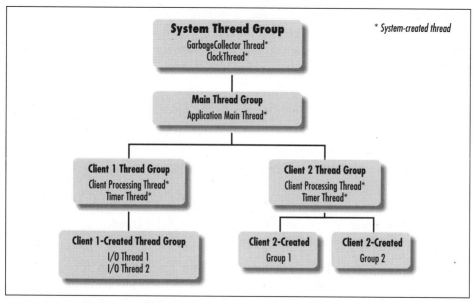

Figure 10-1. A thread group hierarchy

We'll end up with at least one thread group for each connected client; note that the thread groups have the option of creating other thread groups underneath them. Also note that the threads themselves are interspersed among the groups in the entire hierarchy: a thread group contains threads as well as (possibly) other thread groups.

Creating Thread Groups

There are two constructors that create new thread groups:

ThreadGroup(String name)
> Creates a thread group with the given name.

ThreadGroup(ThreadGroup parent, String name)

> Creates a thread group that descends from the given parent and has the given name.

In the case of the first constructor, the new thread group is a child of the current thread's thread group; in the second case, the new thread group is inserted into the thread group hierarchy with the given thread group as its parent. (Though it's probably bad design to do so, by default a thread group can be inserted anywhere in a Java application's thread group hierarchy.) In Java 1.0, only Java applications were allowed to create thread groups; this restriction no longer applies.

Each of these constructors creates an empty thread group—a thread group with no threads. There is no method to move a thread into a particular group; a thread is placed into a group only when the thread object is created. As this restriction implies, there are some additional constructors for the Thread class that specify the thread group to which the thread should belong:

Thread(ThreadGroup group, String name)

> Constructs a new thread that belongs to the given thread group and has the given name.

Thread(ThreadGroup group, Runnable target)

> Constructs a new thread that belongs to the given thread group and runs the given target object.

Thread(ThreadGroup group, Runnable target, String name)

> Constructs a new thread that belongs to the given thread group, runs the given target object, and has the given name.

Note that there is no constructor that takes just a ThreadGroup as a parameter, which seems to be an oversight. In the constructors we learned about in Chapter 2, the thread becomes a member of the same thread group to which the current thread belongs.

Similarly, there is no method by which a thread can be deleted from a thread group: a thread is a member of its thread group for the duration of its life. However, when the thread terminates, it is removed automatically from the thread group.

We can use these constructors to modify the TCPServer class so that each client is placed in a separate thread group as well as being run in a separate thread. Doing so is simple: we need only create the thread group immediately before creating the client thread, so that when the client thread is started, it is a member of the new thread group:

```
import java.net.*;
import java.io.*;
```

```
public class TCPServer implements Cloneable, Runnable {
    Thread runner = null;
    ServerSocket server = null;
    Socket data = null;
    volatile boolean shouldStop = false;
    ThreadGroup group = null;
    int groupNo = 0;

    public synchronized void startServer(int port) throws IOException {
        if (runner == null) {
            server = new ServerSocket(port);
            runner = new Thread(this);
            runner.start();
        }
    }

    public synchronized void stopServer() {
        if (server != null) {
            shouldStop = true;
            runner.interrupt();
            runner = null;
            try {
                server.close();
            } catch (IOException ioe) {}
            server = null;
        }
    }

    public void run() {
        if (server != null) {
            while (!shouldStop) {
                try {
                    Socket datasocket = server.accept();
                    TCPServer newSocket = (TCPServer) clone();

                    newSocket.server = null;
                    newSocket.data = datasocket;
                    newSocket.group =
                        new ThreadGroup("Client Group " + groupNo++);
                    newSocket.runner =
                        new Thread(newSocket.group, newSocket);
                    newSocket.runner.start();
                } catch (Exception e) {}
            }
        } else {
            run(data);
        }
    }
```

```
    public void run(Socket data) {
    }
}
```

Remember that the TCPServer is subclassed in order to provide functionality for the client; in the next section, we'll look at how this thread group makes it easier to program the code that handles the client.

Thread Group Methods

Other than some deprecated methods that we'll examine in the next section, the methods of the ThreadGroup class are mostly informative. We'll examine all the methods of the ThreadGroup class in this section.

Finding Thread Groups

There are often times when you'd like to call one of the thread group methods but don't necessarily have a thread group object. The Thread class has a method that returns a reference to the thread group of a thread object:

ThreadGroup getThreadGroup()
    Returns the ThreadGroup reference of a thread, for example:

```
// Find the thread group of the current thread.
ThreadGroup tg = Thread.currentThread().getThreadGroup();
```

You can also retrieve the parent thread group of an existing thread group with the getParent() method of the ThreadGroup class:

ThreadGroup getParent()
    Returns the ThreadGroup reference of the parent of a thread group.

Finally, you can test whether a particular thread group is an ancestor of another thread group with the parentOf() method of the ThreadGroup class:

boolean parentOf(ThreadGroup g)
    Returns true if the group g is an ancestor of a thread group.

Note that the parentOf() method is badly named; it returns true if the group g is the same as the calling thread group, or the parent of the thread group, or the grandparent of the thread group, and so on up the thread group hierarchy.

Enumerating Thread Groups

The next set of methods we'll explore allows you to retrieve a list of all threads in a thread group. Enumeration of threads is really the responsibility of the Thread-Group class: although the Thread class also contains methods that enumerate threads, those methods simply call their counterpart methods of the Thread-Group class.

There are two basic methods in the ThreadGroup class that return a list of threads:

int enumerate(Thread list[])
> Fills in the list array with a reference to all threads in this thread group and all threads that are in groups that descend from this thread group.

int enumerate(Thread list[], boolean recurse)
> Fills in the list array with a reference to all threads in this thread group and, if recurse is true, all threads that are in groups that descend from this thread group.

These calls fill in the input parameter list with a thread reference for each appropriate thread and return the count of threads that were inserted into the array. The appropriateness of a thread depends on the recurse parameter: if recurse is true, all threads of the given thread group are returned as well as all threads that are in thread groups that descend from the current thread group. Not surprisingly, calling the enumerate() method with recurse set to false returns only those threads that are actually members of the current thread group.

Calling the enumerate() method with recurse set to true on the system thread group returns all the threads in the virtual machine. You can find the system thread group by using the getParent() method we just examined (subject, of course, to the security model that may be in place).

Since arrays in Java are of a fixed size, the size of the list parameter must be determined before the enumerate() method is called (or you may not get a complete list). To find the correct size for the list array, use the activeCount() method:

int activeCount()
> Returns the number of active threads in this and all descending thread groups.

There is no recursion option available with this method; the activeCount() method always returns the count of all threads in the current and in all descending thread groups.

The following code fragment shows how to use these methods to display the threads in the current thread group. Changing the parameter in the enumerate() method displays the threads in this and all descending groups:

```
ThreadGroup tg = Thread.currentThread().getThreadGroup();
int n = tg.activeCount();
Thread list[] = new Thread[n];
```

```
int count = tg.enumerate(list, false);
System.out.println("Threads in thread group " + tg);
for (int i = 0; i < count; i++)
    System.out.println(list[i]);
```

You can also request an enumeration of ThreadGroup objects rather than Thread objects via the enumerate() method with these signatures:

int enumerate(ThreadGroup list[])

Retrieves all thread group references that are descendants of the given thread group. This method operates recursively on the thread group hierarchy.

int enumerate(ThreadGroup list[], boolean recurse)

Retrieves all thread group references that are immediate descendants of the given thread group and, if recurse is true, all descendants of the current thread group.

These methods are conceptually equivalent to the methods that we've just discussed. To determine the size of the list parameter, use the activeGroupCount() method:

int activeGroupCount()

Returns the number of thread group descendants (at any level) of the given thread group.

Recall that the Thread class also had an enumerate() method. The Thread class's enumerate() method always searches recursively; it is really shorthand for:

```
Thread.currentThread().getThreadGroup().enumerate(list, true);
```

Similarly, the Thread class's activeCount() method is really shorthand for:

```
Thread.currentThread().getThreadGroup().activeCount();
```

Finally, there is a method useful only for debugging:

void list()

Sends a list of all the threads in the current thread group to standard out.

Thread Group Priority Calls

Java thread groups carry with them the notion of a maximum priority. This maximum priority interacts with the priority methods of the Thread class: the priority of a thread cannot be set higher than the maximum priority of the thread group to which it belongs. By default, the maximum priority of a thread group is the same as the maximum priority of its parent thread group. As you might have guessed, the maximum priority of the system thread group is 10 (Thread.MAX_PRIORITY). The maximum priority of the applet thread group—the group to which all threads in an applet belong—is only 6.

There are two methods that handle a thread group's priority:

void setMaxPriority(int priority)
> Sets the maximum priority for the thread group.

int getMaxPriority()
> Retrieves the maximum priority for the thread group.

In the reference release of the Java virtual machine, the maximum priority of a thread group is enforced silently: if the thread group to which your thread belongs has a maximum priority of 6 and you attempt to raise your thread's priority to 8, your thread is silently given a priority of 6. In some browsers (and in Java 1.0), if you attempt to set an individual thread's priority higher than the maximum priority of the thread group, a SecurityException will be thrown.

Once the maximum priority of a thread group has been lowered, it cannot be raised.

These values are only checked when a thread's priority is actually changed. Thus, if you have a thread group with a maximum priority of 10 that contains a thread with a priority of 8, changing the thread group's maximum priority to 6 doesn't affect that thread: it continues to have a priority of 8 until that thread's set-Priority() method is called. However, the maximum priority of any nested thread groups is changed immediately: any thread groups that are contained within the target thread group will have their maximum priority lowered to the requested value. This change is propagated recursively throughout the thread group hierarchy.

Destroying Thread Groups

A thread group can be destroyed with the destroy() method:

void destroy()
> Cleans up the thread group and removes it from the thread group hierarchy.

The destroy() method is of limited use: it can only be called if there are no threads presently in the thread group. The destroy() method operates recursively, so it destroys not only the target thread group but all thread groups that descend from the target thread group. If any of these thread groups have active threads within them, the destroy() method generates an IllegalThreadState-Exception.

You can test to see if the destroy() method has been called on a particular thread group by using this method:

boolean isDestroyed() (Java 1.1 and above only)
> Returns a flag indicating whether the thread group has been destroyed.

This may seem somewhat confusing: if the thread group has been destroyed, how can we execute a method on it? The answer is that the destroy() method only removes the thread group from the thread group hierarchy; the actual thread group object will not be garbage collected until there are no valid references to it.

Daemon Thread Groups

The ThreadGroup class has the notion of a daemon thread group, which is similar to the notion of a daemon thread. The two are unrelated, however: daemon threads can belong to non-daemon thread groups, and a daemon thread group can contain non-daemon threads. The benefit of a daemon thread group is that it is destroyed automatically once all the threads it contains have exited and all the groups that it contains have been destroyed. Unlike a thread, a thread group's daemon status can be changed at any time:

void setDaemon(boolean on)
> Changes the daemon status of the thread group.

boolean isDaemon()
> Returns true if the thread group is a daemon group.

We should stress that a daemon thread group is destroyed only if all threads in the group have actually exited: if there are only daemon threads in a daemon thread group, the daemon thread group is not destroyed unless the daemon threads it contains are stopped first. This is because daemon threads serve user threads throughout the virtual machine, not just the user threads of a particular thread group.

Of course, the benefit of daemon threads in the first place is that the programmer never bothers to stop them explicitly. Thus, while the concept of a daemon thread group that automatically exits when it contains only daemon threads may be attractive, it does not work that way.

Miscellaneous Methods

There are three remaining methods of the ThreadGroup class that we will mention here for completeness:

String getName()
> Returns the name of the thread group.

void uncaughtException(Thread t, Throwable e)
> This method is called when a thread exits due to an uncaught exception; its default behavior is to print the stack trace of the thread to System.err. We'll say more about this method in Appendix A.

boolean allowThreadSuspension(boolean b) (Java 1.1 only)

> Sets the vmAllowSuspension flag of the thread group, returning the old value. When the virtual machine runs low on memory, some implementations of the virtual machine will seek to obtain memory by suspending threads in thread groups for which the vmAllowSuspension flag is set to true.

> However, since the suspend() method itself is deprecated in Version 2, the virtual machine can no longer suspend threads within a group that is marked to allow thread suspension, so this method is not terribly useful.

Manipulating Thread Groups

One of the really useful ideas behind a thread group is the ability to manipulate all of its threads at once. There are four methods in the ThreadGroup class that allow us to do just that; however, since three of them are now deprecated, this idea is not as useful as it once was:

void suspend() (deprecated in Java 2)

> Suspends all threads that descend from this thread group.

void resume() (deprecated in Java 2)

> Resumes all threads that descend from this thread group.

void stop() (deprecated in Java 2)

> Stops all threads that descend from this thread group.

void interrupt() (Java 2 and above only)

> Interrupts all threads that descend from this thread group.

These methods all function in the same way as their counterparts in the Thread class, but they affect all threads in the thread group as well as all threads that are contained in the thread groups that descend from this group. In other words, these methods operate recursively on all groups that descend from the specified group. In the case of our TCPServer thread group hierarchy, this means that if, for example, we interrupted the Client1 thread group, we interrupt all threads in that group as well as the I/O threads in the Client1-created thread group.*

We can use these calls to save some programming when we create the subclass of our TCPServer. In our ServerHandler subclass, we left out the processing that is performed on behalf of the client. This time, we'll assume that the server reads a set of commands from the client and runs each command in a separate thread; this allows the client to send commands asynchronously, without waiting for the

---

* We know you're anxious to try it yourself, but yes, if you suspend the system thread group in a Java application, every thread in the virtual machine will be suspended, effectively hanging the virtual machine. The same is not true of Java applets due to the security restrictions we discuss later.

server to finish the previous command. By placing all these threads in one group, we're able to modify all the threads running on behalf of the client in one call via the thread group mechanism.

In this example, we're using this mechanism to handle the case where the client closes the connection: with one call, we can interrupt all threads running on behalf of this client (this assumes that the threads will periodically check their interrupted state and exit if that state is true, as we showed in our example in Chapter 4).

We'll also set up another thread group, to which we'll add all the client threads that we create. The end result will be that we'll have these thread groups:

- The thread group of the TCPServer, containing the thread that is listening for client requests.

- A thread group for each client, containing the thread that is communicating with the client. This is the thread group that was set up in our TCPServer example earlier.

- A calculation thread group of the client, containing all the threads that are performing calculations on behalf of the client. This is the thread group we will create in the following code.

This is a useful technique: it's better to have a thread outside of the thread group actually manipulate the thread group. This is not an absolute requirement: you could, for example, interrupt the thread group to which you belong.

Here's our modified ServerHandler class with this additional thread group logic:

```java
import java.net.*;
import java.io.*;

class CalculateThread extends Thread {
    OutputStream os;
    CalculateThread(ThreadGroup tg, OutputStream os) {
        super(tg, "Client Calculate Thread");
        this.os = os;
    }
    public void run() {
        // Do the calculation, sending results to the OutputStream os.
        // Make sure to check the isInterrupted() flag often.
    }
}

public class ServerHandler extends TCPServer {
    public static final int INTERRUPT = 0;
    public static final int CALCULATE = 1;
    ThreadGroup tg;
```

```
        public volatile boolean shouldRun;

        private int getCommand(InputStream is) {
            // Read the command data from input stream and return the
            // command.
        }

        public void run(Socket data) {
            tg = new ThreadGroup("Client Thread Group");
            try {
                InputStream is = data.getInputStream();
                OutputStream os = data.getOutputStream();
                while (shouldRun) {
                    switch(getCommand(is)) {
                        case INTERRUPT:
                            tg.interrupt();
                            break;
                        case CALCULATE:
                            new CalculateThread(tg, os).start();
                            break;
                    }
                }
            } catch (Exception e) {
                tg.interrupt();
            }
        }

        public static void main(String args[]) throws Exception {
            TCPServer serv = new ServerHandler();
            serv.startServer(300);
        }
    }
```

Thread Groups, Threads, and Security

The various restrictions on applets that we've mentioned in this chapter are a product of Java's security mechanism. There are security mechanisms at several points in Java: in the language itself, in the virtual machine, and built into the Java API. As far as threads are concerned, only the security mechanisms of the API come into consideration, and we'll examine how those mechanisms affect both threads and thread groups in this section. The enforcement of security is a prime reason behind the ThreadGroup class.

Java's thread security is enforced by the SecurityManager class; security policies in a Java program are established when an instance of this class is instantiated and installed in the virtual machine. When certain operations are attempted on threads or thread groups, the API consults the security manager to determine if those operations are permitted. Prior to Java 2, there was no security manager in a Java application unless you wrote and installed one yourself; this is the reason that all the operations we've discussed are legal in Java applications. In a Java applet, there is typically a security manager in place that enforces particular restrictions.

Browsers and Security Managers

When you write a Java applet, you're not given the opportunity to do anything with the security manager: the security manager is instantiated and installed by the browser itself and, once installed, cannot be changed.

But the Java specification does not specify what policies the security manager should enforce. Instead, the security policies at this level are a product of the particular browser. Different browsers may implement different levels of security: for example, the Netscape browser does not permit Java applets to read any files from the user's local disk, but Sun's HotJava browser allows the user to specify a list of directories in which the applet can read files.

The rule of thumb here is that the author of any Java application ultimately determines what security policy is in place; in the case of a browser, the author of the browser is the author of the application. Hence, different browsers can and do have different security models and policies.

In Java 2, there is still typically a security manager in place that enforces restrictions on applets, but there is also a new way to launch an application such that the application may be subject to a default security manager. Of course, applications may still install their own security manager (or run without a security manager) by launching themselves in the traditional way.

There is one method in the SecurityManager class that handles security policies for the Thread class and one that handles security policies for the ThreadGroup class. These methods have the same name but different signatures:

void checkAccess(Thread t)
  Checks if the current thread is allowed to modify the state of the thread t.

void checkAccess(ThreadGroup tg)
  Checks if the current thread group is allowed to modify the state of the thread group tg.

Like all methods in the SecurityManager class, these methods throw a SecurityException if they determine that performing the operation would violate the security policy. As an example, here's the code that the interrupt() method of the

Thread class implements (this is actually a conflation of code contained in the Thread class):

```
public void interrupt() {
    SecurityManager s = System.getSecurityManager();
    if (s != null)
        s.checkAccess(this);     // this is Thread.currentThread();
    interrupt0();
}
```

This is the canonical behavior for thread security: the checkAccess() method is called, which generates a runtime exception if thread policy is violated by the operation. Assuming that no exception is thrown, an internal method is called that actually performs the logic of the method.

Security and the checkAccess() Method

Both the Thread and ThreadGroup classes have an internal method named checkAccess(); this method, by default, calls the security manager's checkAccess() method, passing either the thread or the thread group object.

The checkAccess() method within the Thread and ThreadGroup classes is public, so you can call it directly from any thread or thread group object if you want to check what security policy is in place.

The checkAccess() method within the ThreadGroup class is final; it may not be overridden. The checkAccess() method within the Thread class, however, is not final, meaning that you could override it and effectively change the security policy for your particular thread (but remember that this would only affect your thread class, and not other threads within the system).

Because there is only one method in the SecurityManager class that's available to the Thread class and only one method that is available to the ThreadGroup class, a thread security policy is an all-or-nothing proposition. If the security manager determines that a particular thread is prevented from interrupting other threads, that thread is also prevented from setting the priority of other threads. However, the security manager can (and usually does) take into account contextual information about the thread—including its thread group—in order to determine the policy for the thread.

Table 10-1 lists methods in the Thread and ThreadGroup class that call the security manager to determine if an operation is legal. Note that this group of methods includes all methods that create or otherwise change the state of a particular thread or thread group, but does not include any method that provides thread information (such as the enumerate() methods or the getPriority() method). Hence, no matter what security manager may have been installed by the application, any thread is able to examine all other threads in the virtual machine; threads are only (possibly) prohibited from changing each other's state.

Table 10-1. Thread and ThreadGroup Methods Affected by the Security Manager

Thread Methods	ThreadGroup Methods
Thread() [all signatures]	ThreadGroup() [all signatures]
stop() [both signatures]	stop()
suspend()	suspend()
resume()	resume()
interrupt()	interrupt()
setPriority(int priority)	setMaxPriority()
setDaemon(boolean on)	setDaemon()
setName(String s)	destroy()

Since the controls established by the security manager are completely at the discretion of the author of the Java application or Java-enabled browser, it is impossible to predict exactly what operations a thread might be able to perform. However, we'll list some of the best-known cases here:

Java 1.0.2 and 1.1 applications

By default, applications in these releases have no security manager at all, and all threads are permitted to perform any operation on any other thread. This is not the case, of course, if the author of the application decides to install a security manager.

Java 1.0.2-based browsers

This category includes the 1.0.2 appletviewer, Internet Explorer 3.0, and Netscape 3.0. In these browsers, each applet is created within its own thread group. An applet is allowed to create a thread within its own thread group, and although an applet is allowed to create another thread group, it may not actually add threads into that thread group. Hence, Applet 1 in Figure 10-2 would be able to create subgroups 1 and 2, but not threads C and D. The fact that applets cannot add threads to any other thread group makes the ability to create a thread group useless in this case.

Within the thread hierarchy, applet threads are allowed to modify any other thread group and any other thread as well, including threads in unrelated applets (e.g., thread A could modify thread B).

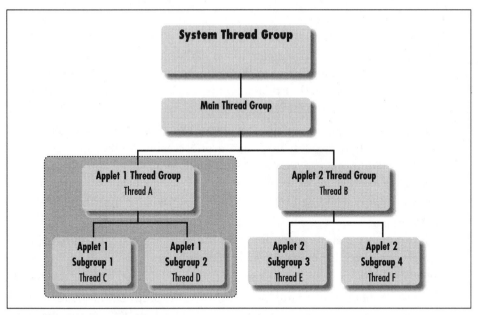

Figure 10-2. Possible threads in a Java-enabled browser

Java 1.1-based browsers

This category includes the 1.1 appletviewer, Internet Explorer 4.0, and Netscape 4.0. Although these browsers share a common reference base, there are differences in how they implement thread security. In the case of the appletviewer, each applet in these browsers is given a unique thread group, and the applet may create other thread groups that are installed into the thread group hierarchy under the applet's thread group. In Figure 10-2, the browser would have created the applet 1 thread group, and the applet itself is allowed to create subgroups 1 and 2. The shaded box delineates the thread groups that belong to applet 1.

Any thread within the shaded box in Figure 10-2 is able to access any other thread within that box. Hence, thread A can manipulate threads C and D, and thread C can also manipulate its parent thread (thread A) as well as threads in any sibling thread groups (thread D). However, applet threads are not allowed to access the system or main threads, nor are they allowed to access any threads outside of their own set of thread groups (thread C cannot access thread E). In Netscape, however, applet threads are allowed to access threads of their parent (i.e., the main thread group). Oddly enough, however, applets are able to access and manipulate any thread group, including the system and main thread groups.

In Internet Explorer 4.0, this basic idea of thread security is slightly modified. To begin, IE 4.0 does not allow an applet to call the getParent() method in order to find out about the system and main thread groups. This is a change to the core API, which, as we mentioned earlier, does not make such a security check. So an applet thread in IE 4.0 can manipulate any thread or thread group that it can access, but that access is restricted to the applet itself (e.g., the shaded box in Figure 10-2).

In Netscape 4.0, applets are still not allowed to create threads within thread groups other than the default thread group created by the browser for the applet. In addition, the enumerate() method in Netscape 4.0 does not retrieve the correct set of threads for thread groups other than the applet's thread group, so tracking down other threads outside the applet is impossible.

Java 2 applications

By default, Java 2 applications function the same way as 1.0.2- and 1.1-based applications: there is no security manager, and any thread is allowed to access any other thread.

If a Java 2 application is started with the -Djava.security.manager option, however, a default security manager is installed for it. In this security manager, permission to access another thread is strictly based on the thread hierarchy: any thread can manipulate any other thread that is below it in the hierarchy. Sibling threads may not manipulate each other, and a child thread may not manipulate its parent threads.

Java 2 also allows this default security manager to be configured via a series of policy files; normally these policy files include the files *${JAVAHOME}/lib/security/java.policy* and *${HOME}/.java.policy*. The policy files used by an application contain a mapping between the URLs where the application may obtain code and the permissions that the code loaded from those URLs should be granted. Hence, code loaded from a particular URL may be granted a permission of:

```
permission java.security.AllPermission
```

or a permission of:

```
permission java.security.RuntimePermission "thread"
```

Code that is granted one of these permissions will be able to access any other thread in the virtual machine.

In addition, in Java 2, the stop() method of the Thread class now performs an additional security check. In order to be able to call the stop() method on any thread, the URL from which the code was loaded must have been given a permission of:

```
permission java.lang.RuntimePermission "stopThread"
```

By default, this permission is granted to all code, but it's possible for an end user or system administrator to change the policy file so that the stop() method cannot be called arbitrarily.

Java 2-based browsers

As of this writing, there are no Java 2–based browsers available, so it is unclear what thread security policies they might adopt. The Java 2 appletviewer policy, however, follows the same policy as the 1.1 appletviewer. That policy, too, may be additionally configured through the policy files, so that code loaded from certain URLs may be given permission to access any thread in the virtual machine.

Summary

Here are the methods of the ThreadGroup class that we introduced in this chapter:

ThreadGroup(String name)

Creates a thread group with the given name.

ThreadGroup(ThreadGroup parent, String name)

Creates a thread group that descends from the given parent and has the given name.

void suspend() (deprecated in Java 2)

Suspends all threads that descend from this thread group.

void resume() (deprecated in Java 2)

Resumes all threads that descend from this thread group.

void stop() (deprecated in Java 2)

Stops all threads that descend from this thread group.

void destroy()

Cleans up the thread group and removes it from the thread group hierarchy.

void interrupt() (Java 2 and above only)

Interrupts all threads that descend from this thread group.

ThreadGroup getParent()

Returns the ThreadGroup reference of the parent of a thread group.

boolean parentOf(ThreadGroup g)

Returns true if the group g is an ancestor of a thread group.

int enumerate(Thread list[])

Fills in the list array with a reference to all threads in this thread group and all threads that are in groups that descend from this thread group.

int enumerate(Thread list[], boolean recurse)

> Fills in the `list` array with a reference to all threads in this thread group and, if `recurse` is true, all threads that are in groups that descend from this thread group.

int activeCount()

> Returns the number of active threads in this and all descending thread groups.

int enumerate(ThreadGroup list[])

> Retrieves all thread group references that are descendants of the given thread group. This method operates recursively on the thread group hierarchy.

int enumerate(ThreadGroup list[], boolean recurse)

> Retrieves all thread group references that are immediate descendants of the given thread group and, if `recurse` is true, all descendants of the current thread group.

int activeGroupCount()

> Returns the number of thread group descendants (at any level) of the given thread group.

void setMaxPriority(int priority)

> Sets the maximum priority for the thread group.

int getMaxPriority()

> Retrieves the maximum priority for the thread group.

void setDaemon(boolean on)

> Changes the daemon status of the thread group.

boolean isDaemon()

> Returns `true` if the thread group is a daemon group.

boolean isDestroyed() (Java 1.1 and above only)

> Returns a flag indicating whether the thread group has been destroyed.

String getName()

> Returns the name of the thread group.

void list()

> Sends a list of all the threads in the current thread group to standard out.

boolean allowThreadSuspension(boolean b) (Java 1.1 only)

> Sets the `vmAllowSuspension` flag of the thread group, returning the old value. When the virtual machine runs low on memory, some implementations of the virtual machine will seek to obtain memory by suspending threads in thread groups for which the `vmAllowSuspension` flag is set to `true`.

void uncaughtException(Thread t, Throwable e)

> This method is called when a thread exits due to an uncaught exception; its default behavior is to print the stack trace of the thread to `System.err`.

In addition, we introduced these new methods of the Thread class:

Thread(ThreadGroup group, String name)

> Constructs a new thread that belongs to the given thread group and has the given name.

Thread(ThreadGroup group, Runnable target)

> Constructs a new thread that belongs to the given thread group and runs the given target object.

Thread(ThreadGroup group, Runnable target, String name)

> Constructs a new thread that belongs to the given thread group, runs the given target object, and has the given name.

ThreadGroup getThreadGroup()

> Returns the ThreadGroup reference of a thread.

Finally, we introduced these methods of the SecurityManager class that operate on threads:

void checkAccess(Thread t)

> Checks if the current thread is allowed to modify the state of the thread `t`.

void checkAccess(ThreadGroup tg)

> Checks if the current thread group is allowed to modify the state of the thread group `tg`.

In this chapter, we filled in the final piece of Java's thread mechanism: a way to group threads together and operate on all threads within the group. Additionally, the ThreadGroup class forms a thread hierarchy on which security policies for Java's thread mechanism are based.

Like the other topics in the last few chapters, the ThreadGroup class is not one that is needed by the majority of programs; it's a special-use class for cases in which you need additional control over groups of threads. The ThreadGroup class is the last of the special-use mechanisms you need in order to complete your understanding of using threads in Java. Although we present some informative miscellaneous topics in the appendixes, the information we've presented in the body of this book should allow you to write productive and, if need be, very complex threaded programs in Java.

A

Miscellaneous Topics

Throughout this book, we have examined the various parts of the threading system. This examination was based on various examples and issues that commonly occur during program development. However, there were certain rather obscure issues that fell through the cracks; these are the topics we will examine in this appendix.

Thread Stack Information

The Thread class provides these methods to supply the programmer with information about the thread's stack:

int countStackFrames() (deprecated in Java 2)

> Returns the number of stack frames in the specified thread. The thread must be suspended in order for this method to work. This is a method of the Thread class and does not count the frames that are from native methods. Since the thread must be suspended, it is not possible to obtain the count for the current thread directly.

static void dumpStack()

> Prints the stack trace of the current thread to System.err. This is a static method of the Thread class and may be accessed with the Thread specifier. Only the stack trace of the currently running thread may be obtained.

Interestingly, we might conclude from these two methods that we can both count the number of stack frames and actually print the stack frames out. However, these two methods cannot be used together. Since the thread needs to be suspended in order to count the stack frames, it is not possible to count the frames of the current thread, and the dumpStack() method can only print the stack information of the current thread.

The information printed by the dumpStack() method is the same information provided by the printStackTrace() method of the Throwable class. The dumpStack() method is just a convenience method; it actually instantiates an Exception object and calls the printStackTrace() method.

General Thread Information

To print thread or thread group information, use the following methods:

String toString()

Returns a string that describes the Thread object. Originally a method of the Object class, it is overridden by the Thread class to provide the name of the thread, the priority of the thread, and the name of the thread group to which the thread belongs.

String toString()

Returns a string that describes the ThreadGroup object. Originally a method of the Object class, it is overridden by the ThreadGroup class to provide the name of the thread group and the maximum priority of the group.

The toString() method is overridden by the thread classes to allow a sensible conversion of the object into a string. Hence, the following code:

```
Thread t = new TimerThread(this, 500);
System.out.println(t);
```

yields the following output:

```
Thread[TimerThread-500,6,group applet-TimerApplet]
```

void list()

Prints the current layout of the thread group hierarchy, starting with the thread group on which the method is invoked. This is a method of the ThreadGroup class and simply prints the information to System.out. This method operates recursively on the thread group.

The information that is printed by the list() method is the information returned by the toString() methods. A sample list() of an applet may be as follows:

```
java.lang.ThreadGroup[name=system,maxpri=10]
    Thread[clock handler,11,system]
    Thread[Idle thread,0,system]
    Thread[Async Garbage Collector,1,system]
    Thread[Finalizer thread,1,system]
    java.lang.ThreadGroup[name=main,maxpri=10]
        Thread[main,5,main]
        Thread[AWT-Input,5,main]
```

```
Thread[AWT-Motif,5,main]
Thread[Screen Updater,4,main]
AppletThreadGroup[name=group applet-Ticker,maxpri=6]
    Thread[thread applet-Ticker,6,group applet-Ticker]
    Thread[SUNW stock reader,5,group applet-Ticker]
    Thread[APPL stock reader,5,group applet-Ticker]
    Thread[NINI stock reader,5,group applet-Ticker]
    Thread[JRA stock reader,5,group applet-Ticker]
    Thread[ticker timer thread,4,group applet-Ticker]
```

Default Exception Handler

We examined the start() method to the extent of saying that "the start() method indirectly calls the run() method," but let's examine exactly what happens. The start() method does start another thread of control, but the run() method is not the "main" routine for this new thread. There are other bookkeeping details that must be taken care of first. The thread must be set up in the Java virtual machine before the run() method can execute. This process is shown in Figure A-1.

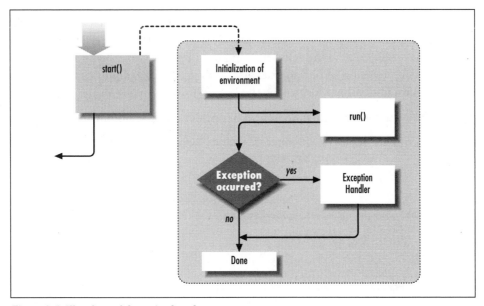

Figure A-1. Flowchart of the main thread

All uncaught exception conditions are handled by code outside of the run() method before the thread terminates. It is this exception handling that we will examine here.

Why is this exception handler interesting to us? The default exception handler is a Java method; it can be overridden. This means that it is possible for an application to write a new default exception handler. This method looks like this:

void uncaughtException(Thread t, Throwable o)
> The default exception handler method, which is called as a final handler to take care of any exceptions not caught by the thread in the run() method. This is a method of the ThreadGroup class.

The default exception handler is a method of the ThreadGroup class. It is called only when an exception is thrown from the run() method. The thread is technically completed when the run() method returns, even though the exception handler is still running in the thread.

But just what is done by the default exception handler? Practically nothing. The only task accomplished by the default exception handler is to print out the stack trace recorded by the Throwable object. This is the stack trace of the thread that threw the object in the first place. (The only exception to this is if the throwable object is a ThreadDeath object, in which case nothing happens. We'll discuss that situation next.)

Let's return to the banking example from Chapter 3. We know that any uncaught exception in our ATM system is unacceptable, so we must handle every exception. But certain problems, like the ATM running out of money, may be encountered in more than one location in our algorithm. Handling the out-of-money condition in the default exception handler may be the best solution.

Let's examine a possible implementation of our default exception handler:

```
public class ATMOutOfMoneyException extends RuntimeException {
    public ATMOutOfMoneyException() {
        super();
    }

    public ATMOutOfMoneyException(String s) {
        super(s);
    }
}

public class ATMThreadGroup extends ThreadGroup {
    public ATMThreadGroup(String name) {
        super(name);
    }

    public void uncaughtException(Thread t, Throwable e) {
        if (e instanceof ATMOutOfMoneyException) {
            AlertAdminstrator(e);
        } else {
```

```
                super.uncaughtException(t, e);
        }
    }
}
```

You can implement a default exception handler by overriding the uncaught-Exception() method. This requires that you subclass the ThreadGroup class, instantiate an instance of that subclass, and create all your threads so that they belong to that instance. The method is passed an instance of the Thread class that threw the object, along with the actual object that was thrown. In our case, we are only concerned with the out-of-money condition. Every other object that is thrown is passed to the original default handler.

The ThreadDeath Class

The ThreadDeath class is a special Throwable class that is used to stop a thread. This class extends the Error class and hence should not be caught by the program. In theory, there is no reason to catch and handle any Throwable object that is not an object of the Exception class, and that usually applies to the ThreadDeath class as well.

How does throwing an object actually stop a thread? As we mentioned, the thread cleans up after itself when the run() method completes. Of course, there are two ways for the run() method to complete: it can complete on its own by simply returning, or it can throw or fail to catch an exception (including an Error or Throwable object).

By default, if the run() method throws an exception, the thread prints an error message, along with the stack trace of the exception. However, a special case is made for the ThreadDeath object. If a ThreadDeath object is thrown from the run() method, the uncaughtException() method simply returns.

The ThreadDeath object is normally used only in conjunction with the stop() method. When you call the stop() method on a particular thread, a Thread-Death object is created and then thrown by the target thread. Since the stop() method is deprecated, the utility of this technique is minimal.

Is it possible to catch the ThreadDeath object? It is possible to catch any Throwable object; however, it is not advisable to use this technique to prevent the death of the thread. After all, if we did not want the thread to die, why was the stop() method called? And what about other threads that expect the target thread to stop? The thread that has called the target thread's stop() method might then attempt to join the target thread; if you catch ThreadDeath, the join will never complete.

One possible use of this technique is to handle cleanup conditions when the thread is being stopped. In this case, we would catch the ThreadDeath object, execute the cleanup code, and then rethrow the object. However, even in this case it is hard to justify catching the ThreadDeath object; we could accomplish the same thing by using the `finally` clause. The `finally` clause is *always* executed, though, and you may conceivably only want the code to be executed if the thread is stopped.

It's interesting to note that the ThreadDeath class is what caused the `stop()` method to become deprecated in the first place: if the exception is thrown in the middle of a synchronized method or block, the thread will immediately return from that method, (possibly) leaving the critical data of the object in an inconsistent state. You could judiciously catch the ThreadDeath exception and clean up your code correctly to make the `stop()` method safer, but that will only protect your own code, not the code in critical sections of the virtual machine or the code within the Java API itself.

However, the ThreadDeath class may be useful in one limited circumstance as a replacement for the `stop()` method. Say that a thread encounters an error and wants to terminate itself, but the error is not egregious enough that it wants the user to see the error. One way to do this is for the thread simply to return from its `run()` method, but it may be difficult for the thread to unwind all of its methods in order to do that. A second way is for the thread to call the `stop()` method on itself. And a final way is for the thread to throw a ThreadDeath error. This will unwind the thread's stack and cause the thread to exit its `run()` method, but since the ThreadDeath error is handled by the virtual machine in the special manner, the end user will be unaware that the thread has exited: there will be no stack trace printed to the Java console.

Even so, a thread that wants to terminate itself cannot simply throw a ThreadDeath object willy-nilly: the thread must throw this object only when it is sure that it has not left any data in a possibly inconsistent state (e.g., when it is not presently holding any locks). If you've programmed your thread very carefully and are sure that the thread has left all data in a consistent state, it is safe to throw the ThreadDeath object to make your thread exit immediately. This is really the same thing as calling the `stop()` method on yourself: the only difference is that the compiler will complain if you call the `stop()` method (even if a thread calls it on itself when it knows it is safe to do so), whereas the compiler won't complain about throwing a ThreadDeath object. Still, you have to be very careful only to do this when it's absolutely safe to do so.

Inheriting from the ThreadDeath Class

The ThreadDeath object is used in conjunction with a new stop() method:

void stop(Throwable o) (deprecated in Java 2)
    Terminates an already running thread. The thread is stopped by throwing the specified object.

The stop() method is overloaded with a signature that allows the developer to unwind the stack with any Throwable object. Until now, there was little reason to stop the thread with any object but a ThreadDeath object. But we can now override the default exception handler; if we wanted a thread to die due to a particular reason and handle the special reason, we might create a new Throwable type and handler as follows:

```
public class ATMThreadDeath extends ThreadDeath {
    public int reason;
    public ATMThreadDeath(int reason) {
        this.reason = reason;
    }
}

public class ATMThreadGroup extends ThreadGroup {
    public ATMThreadGroup(String name) {
        super(name);
    }

    public void uncaughtException(Thread t, Throwable e) {
        if (e instanceof ATMThreadDeath) {
            HandleSpecialExit(e);
        }
        super.uncaughtException(t, e);
    }
}
```

Assuming that there are special exit-handling conditions that need to be taken care of, we can create a new version of the ThreadDeath class that contains the reason for the death. Given this new version of the ThreadDeath class, we can then create a special handler to take care of the exit conditions. Of course, we must now use the other stop() method to send our ATMThreadDeath object:

```
runner.stop(new ATMThreadDeath(3));
```

Can we use the stop() method to deliver a generic exception to another thread? It will work, but it is not advisable. There are many reasons against doing so. Depending on the exception and when the stop() method is called, we might throw an exception that violates the semantics of the throws keyword. The compiler requires that you handle exceptions it knows will be thrown, but the compiler will not, in this case, know about the generic exception you are causing the other thread to throw. If you execute the code:

```
runner.stop(new IOException());
```

the runner thread may be executing code that is not prepared to handle an IOException. This is confusing at best.

We could list more reasons against using this technique, but that will not stop certain developers from using this technique as a signal delivery system.* Simply put, stop() was not designed as a signal delivery system, and using it as such may yield unexpected or platform-specific results.

More on Thread Destruction

By calling the stop() method and using the exception mechanism to exit the run() method, we caused the run() method to exit prematurely and, hence, allowed the thread to terminate. We could also have killed the thread using the destroy() method, which, in turn, terminates the execution of the run() method. The difference is the way the run() method exits: the first case allows the run() method to terminate, and hence kills the thread. The second mechanism kills the threads, which terminates the run() method.

By allowing the run() method to terminate, the stack for the thread is allowed to unwind. This means that the finally clauses are all allowed to execute as the stack is unwound. This allows a better state to exist in the program when the thread terminates; it also allows synchronization locks to be released as the stack is unwound. Because of these benefits, the thread is always allowed to unwind rather than just to terminate. Of course, the problem is that since the thread death exception may be thrown at any time, there may not be a finally clause to execute, which again leads us to the problem that requires the stop() method to be deprecated.

In order to be complete in our discussion, we'll now examine the destroy() method, which allows the thread to be destroyed without unwinding the stack. This method would be used as a last resort:

void destroy() (not implemented)

Destroys a thread immediately. This method of the Thread class does not perform any cleanup code, and any locks that are locked prior to this method call will remain locked.

Why would you want to not clean up after a thread? There should be no case where you do not want to clean up after a thread. However, there may be cases where the

---

* Or from using the exception system as a callback mechanism.

cleanup code may not work. For example, with the wait and notify mechanism, it may not be possible to immediately unwind the stack due to an unavailable lock: a thread that is stopped while it is executing the `wait()` method may not terminate for quite a while. If the thread deadlocks while trying to reacquire the lock, then the thread will never exit. A waiting period to unwind may not be acceptable.

However, we should regard this as a bug in the program and fix the code rather than leave possibly unreleased locks. As it stands now, it doesn't really matter: the `destroy()` method is not actually implemented in the reference JDK and simply throws a NoSuchMethodError.

The Volatile Keyword

As we mentioned in Chapter 3, the act of setting the value of a variable (except for a long or a double) is atomic. That means there is generally no need to synchronize access simply to set or read the value of a variable.

However, Java's memory model is more complex than that statement indicates. Threads are allowed to hold the values of variables in local memory (e.g. in a machine register). In that case, when one thread changes the value of a variable, another thread may not see the changed value. This is particularly true in loops that are controlled by a variable (like the `shouldRun` variable that we use to terminate threads): the looping thread may have already loaded the value of the variable into a register and will not necessarily notice when another thread sets that variable to false.

There are many ways to deal with this situation. You can synchronize on the object that contains the control variable—or better yet, you can provide accessor methods for the control variable (such as we do with the `busyflag` variable in our `BusyFlag` class). Or you can mark the variable as `volatile`, which means that every time the variable is used, it must be read from main memory.

In versions of the VM through 1.2, the actual implementation of Java's memory model made this a moot point: variables were always read from main memory. But as VMs become more sophisticated, they will introduce new memory models and optimizations, and observing this rule will be increasingly important.

B

Exceptions and Errors

So far we have discussed the Thread class and its related classes with little attention to error conditions. One of the reasons for this is the lack of actual error conditions, because the threading system does not depend on external hardware. Classes that deal with the disk or network have to handle all possible error conditions that exist due to the failure of the hardware. Databases or the windowing system need an error system, which allows the programmer better control over the interaction between application, data structures, and user.

But what is necessary to deal with threading? Threading is a processor resource. Starting another thread means simply setting up data structures that allow the processor to run code and that configure the processor to switch between the different threads. As we discussed in Chapter 6, threading may involve the operating system; it may involve more than one processor. But in any case, the only hardware involved is the processor(s) and possibly additional memory. The synchronization system also only involves memory: there is not much that can go wrong when there is little hardware involved. We can get processor or memory errors, but these errors generally affect the entire virtual machine and not an individual thread.

The only errors that we need to be concerned with, then, are programmer errors. It is possible for the programmer accidentally to configure the threads incorrectly or to use threads or the synchronization mechanism incorrectly.

How are error conditions reported? As with any other classes provided with the Java system, the thread classes use the concept of throwing exceptions and errors. Let's examine some of the exceptions and errors that are thrown from the threading system.

InterruptedException

The InterruptedException is probably the most common exception condition we have encountered in this book. It indicates that the method has returned earlier than expected. While we have chosen to catch and ignore these exceptions in most of our examples, we didn't have to: depending on the program, it may be possible to handle the exception condition. (The solution may be as simple as calling the method again.)

Let's examine the interrupted exception conditions that we have encountered in this book:

The join() method

> The Thread class provides the `join()` method, which allows a thread to wait for another thread to finish or be terminated (see Chapter 2). If this exception is thrown, it simply means that the other thread may not have finished. The `join()` method is also overloaded with two other method signatures that allow the program to specify a timeout. If the exception is thrown with these methods, it means that neither the termination of the other thread nor the timeout condition has been satisfied.

The sleep() method

> The Thread class provides the `sleep()` method, which allows a thread to wait a specified time period (see Chapter 2). When this exception is thrown, it simply means that the `sleep()` method has slept for less than the specified amount of time.

The wait() method

> The Object class provides the `wait()` method, which allows a thread to wait for a notification condition (see Chapter 4). When this exception is thrown, it means that the `wait()` method has not received the notification. The `wait()` method is also overloaded with two other method signatures that allow the program to specify a timeout. If the exception is thrown with these methods, it means that neither the notification nor the timeout condition has been satisfied.

An InterruptedException is generated via the `interrupt()` method of the Thread class.

InterruptedIOException

Some methods of various I/O classes will throw an InterruptedIOException in response to the `interrupt()` method: if the target thread was blocked on an I/O operation, then the InterruptedIOException will be thrown. On green-thread implementations, this is implemented incompletely: some I/O methods are interruptible and some are not. This feature is not implemented at all on Windows. On Solaris native-thread virtual machines, this is implemented somewhat inconsistently: in Java 1.1, some operations will throw a standard exception (e.g., SocketException), and in Java 2 they will throw an InterruptedIOException.

In the future, this implementation will be consistent, but it is unclear what direction that will take, and it's possible that this exception will be deprecated. In the meantime, developers who need to interrupt I/O should close the stream on which the I/O is being performed, and interrupted I/O should not be considered restartable, even on platforms that support it.

NoSuchMethodError

When the Thread class was designed, certain methods were not immediately supported. To avoid changing the interface to the Thread class, most of these methods were simply written to throw the NoSuchMethodError. As more functionality has been added, fewer of these methods now throw this error condition. As of this writing, the only method that throws this error object is the `destroy()` method of the Thread class (see Appendix A).

Exceptions or Errors

What is the difference between an error and an exception? As far as the virtual machine is concerned, there is little difference between the two: they are simply objects that are thrown to report a condition. It is possible to catch an Error object just like an Exception object. In practice however, the usage of the two types of conditions is different.

Error conditions are faults in the Java virtual machine. In general, they are a sign of a problem that cannot be solved by the program. This can be caused by an out-of-memory condition, stack overflow, or problems in loading or resolving the classes in the program. The reason they are separated is to allow a catch-all of general exceptions. A program may catch all exception conditions by catching the Exception object, but a program should have little reason to catch an Error object.

RuntimeException

The RuntimeException is not thrown directly by any of the methods in the thread classes; it is simply a base class that specifies a special group of exceptions. Runtime exceptions are considered so basic that it would be too tedious to check for every possible runtime exception that could be thrown (another reason is that these exceptions are generally bugs in the program). Unlike other exceptions, the compiler does not require that you handle a RuntimeException.

All of the following exceptions are runtime exceptions.

IllegalThreadStateException

The IllegalThreadStateException is thrown by the thread classes when the thread is not in a state where it is possible to fulfill the request. This is caused by an illegal request made by the program and generally indicates a bug in the program. The following are the possible cases in the thread system where the IllegalThreadState-Exception is thrown:

The start() method

The Thread class provides the `start()` method, which starts a new thread (see Chapter 2). As we mentioned, a thread should be started only once. However, if a program calls the `start()` method of an already running thread, the IllegalThreadStateException is thrown.

The setDaemon() method

The Thread class provides the `setDaemon()` method, which specifies whether the thread is a daemon thread (see Chapter 6). As we mentioned, the daemon status of a thread must be set before the thread is started. If the `setDaemon()` method is called when the thread is already running, the Illegal-ThreadStateException is thrown.

The countStackFrames() method

The Thread class provides the `countStackFrames()` method, which determines how deep in the call stack the thread is currently executing (see Appendix A). A thread must be suspended in order for this count to take place. If the thread is not suspended when this method is called, the Illegal-ThreadStateException is thrown.

The destroy() method

The ThreadGroup class provides the `destroy()` method to allow the thread group to be destroyed (see Chapter 10). A ThreadGroup instance can only be destroyed when the group does not contain any threads and does not contain any groups that contain threads. If the `destroy()` method is called on a group that contains threads or is already destroyed, the IllegalThreadStateException is thrown.

The Thread constructors

The Thread class contains certain constructors that allow the thread to be placed into a specific thread group (see Chapter 10). The thread group that is passed to these constructors must not have been destroyed; if the constructor is passed a thread group that has been destroyed, the IllegalThreadStateException is thrown.

IllegalArgumentException

It is possible to call methods of the thread classes with incorrect parameters. When this is done, an IllegalArgumentException is thrown. Only one method related to the Thread classes throws the exception:

The setPriority() method
> The Thread class provides the `setPriority()` method, which controls the priority assigned to the thread (see Chapter 6). The priority that is assigned must fall between the system minimum and maximum priorities. If the priority requested is not within this range, an IllegalArgumentException is thrown. (The `setPriority()` method may also throw a security exception; see the section "SecurityException," later in this appendix.)

The IllegalThreadStateException is actually a subclass of the IllegalArgumentException class; if you attempt to catch objects of type IllegalArgumentException, you will also catch objects of type IllegalThreadStateException.

IllegalMonitorStateException

The IllegalMonitorStateException is thrown by the Thread system when an operation on a wait monitor is attempted and the state of the monitor is not valid for the operation to take place. Currently, the only operation that involves this exception is the wait and notify mechanism; grabbing or releasing the lock itself is not a method call and hence cannot throw an exception.

The wait() method
> The Object class provides the `wait()` method, which allows a thread to wait for a notification condition (see Chapter 4). The `wait()` method must be called while the synchronization lock for the object is held. The `wait()` method is also overloaded with two other method signatures that allow the program to specify a timeout. If any of these methods is called without owning the synchronization lock, the IllegalMonitorStateException is thrown.

The notify() and notifyAll() methods
> The Object class provides the `notify()` method, which allows a thread to send a notification signal to any threads waiting (see Chapter 4). The `notify()` method must be called while the synchronization lock for the object is held. The Object class also provides the `notifyAll()` method, which wakes up all the waiting threads. If either of these methods is called without owning the synchronization lock, the IllegalMonitorStateException is thrown.

NullPointerException

The thread classes throw this exception in the following cases:

The stop() method

The Thread class provides a version of the stop() method that allows the user to specify the object used to stop the thread (see Appendix A). Normally, programs do not use this method; however, if a program does use this method and passes a null object to stop a thread, the NullPointerException is thrown.

The ThreadGroup constructor

The ThreadGroup class provides a version of its constructor that allows the application to specify the parent group (see Chapter 10). If null is specified for the parent group, the NullPointerException is thrown.

In addition, the NullPointerException can be thrown by the Java virtual machine itself while it is executing code within the thread classes.

SecurityException

Most methods of the Thread and ThreadGroup classes can throw a Security-Exception. The SecurityException can be thrown by the following methods:

The checkAccess() method

The Thread class provides the checkAccess() method, which simply calls the security manager to determine if the thread can be accessed by the current thread group (see Chapter 10). A SecurityException is thrown if access is not permitted. For a complete list of methods that call the checkAccess() method, see Table 10-1.

The checkAccess() method

The ThreadGroup class provides the checkAccess() method, which simply calls the security manager to determine if the thread group can be accessed by the current thread group (see Chapter 10). A SecurityException is thrown if access is not permitted. For a complete list of methods that call the checkAccess() method, see Table 10-1.

The setPriority() method

The Thread class provides the setPriority() method, which sets the scheduling priority of the thread. The priority requested must be less than the maximum priority of the thread group to which the thread belongs. If the priority is greater than this maximum priority, a SecurityException may be thrown (see Chapter 10).

The stop() method

> The stop() method of the Thread class may throw a security exception under Java 2 and later releases if the stopThread permission has not been granted to the code that is calling the stop() method (see Chapter 10).

Arbitrary Exceptions

Arbitrary runtime exceptions may be thrown by the following method:

The run() method

> The run() method of the Thread class executes user-specific code and, hence, can throw any runtime exception the user code does not catch. Exceptions that the run() method throws are caught in the manner we describe in Appendix A.

Index

About the Authors

Scott Oaks is a Java Technologist at Sun Microsystems, where he has worked since 1987. While at Sun, he has specialized on many disparate technologies, from the SunOS kernel to network programming and RPCs to the X Window System to threading. Since early 1995, he has primarily focused on Java and bringing Java technology to end users; he writes a monthly column on Java solutions for *The Java Report*. Around the Internet, Scott is best known as the author of *olvwm*, the OPEN LOOK window manager. He is also the author of *Java Security* (O'Reilly & Associates).

Scott holds a Bachelor of Science degree in mathematics and computer science from the University of Denver and a Master of Science degree in computer science from Brown University. Prior to joining Sun, he worked in the research division of Bear, Stearns.

In his other life, Scott enjoys music (he plays flute and piccolo with community groups in New York), cooking, theater, and traveling with his husband, James.

Henry Wong is a senior systems engineer at Sun Microsystems, where he has worked since 1989. Originally hired as a consultant to help customers with special device drivers, kernel modifications, and DOS interoperability products, Henry has also worked on Solaris ports, performance tuning projects, and multithreaded design and implementations for benchmarks and demos. Since early 1995, Henry has been involved in developing Java prototypes, and supporting customers who are using Java.

Prior to joining Sun, Henry earned a Bachelor of Science degree in chemical engineering from The Cooper Union in 1987. He joined a small software company in 1986, working on SCSI device drivers, image and audio data compression, and graphics tools used for a medical information system.

When not in front of a computer, Henry is an instrument-rated private pilot, who also likes to dabble in archery, cooking, and traveling to different places with his wife, Nini.

Colophon

Our look is the result of reader comments, our own experimentation, and feedback from distribution channels. Distinctive covers complement our distinctive approach to technical topics, breathing personality and life into potentially dry subjects.

The image of a top on the cover of *Java Threads, Second Edition,* is from the CMCD PhotoCD Collection. It was manipulated by Edie Freedman using Adobe Photoshop 3.0 and Adobe Gallery Effects filters. The cover layout was produced with Quark-XPress 3.3 using the Bodoni Black font from URW Software. Whenever possible, our books use RepKover™, a durable and flexible lay-flat binding. If the page count exceeds RepKover's limit, perfect binding is used.

Madeleine Newell was the production editor for *Java Threads, Second Edition.* Cindy Kogut of Editorial Ink copyedited this edition. Quality control was provided by Jane Ellin, Melanie Wang, and Sheryl Avruch. Seth Maislin wrote the index.

The inside layout was designed by Nancy Priest. Text was formatted in FrameMaker 5.5 by Mike Sierra. The heading font is Bodoni BT; the text font is New Baskerville. The illustrations that appeared in the first edition of this book were created in Macromedia Freehand 5.0 by Chris Reilley; for this edition, the illustrations were created and updated by Rob Romano using Macromedia Freehand 8 and Adobe Photoshop 5.

Java

Java Cryptography

By Jonathan B. Knudsen
1st Edition May 1998
362 pages, ISBN 1-56592-402-9

Java Cryptography teaches you how to write secure programs using Java's cryptographic tools. It includes thorough discussions of the java.security package and the Java Cryptography Extensions (JCE), showing you how to use security providers and even implement your own provider. It discusses authentication, key management, public and private key encryption, and includes a secure talk application that encrypts all data sent over the network. If you work with sensitive data, you'll find this book indispensable.

Java Distributed Computing

By Jim Farley
1st Edition January 1998
384 pages, ISBN 1-56592-206-9

Java Distributed Computing offers a general introduction to distributed computing, meaning programs that run on two or more systems. It focuses primarily on how to structure and write distributed applications and discusses issues like designing protocols, security, working with databases, and dealing with low bandwidth situations.

Java Network Programming

By Elliotte Rusty Harold
1st Edition February 1997
442 pages, ISBN 1-56592-227-1

The network is the soul of Java. Most of what is new and exciting about Java centers around the potential for new kinds of dynamic networked applications. *Java Network Programming* teaches you to work with Sockets, write network clients and servers, and gives you an advanced look at the new areas like multicasting, using the server API, and RMI. Covers Java 1.1.

Java Security

By Scott Oaks
1st Edition May 1998
474 pages, ISBN 1-56592-403-7

This essential Java 2 book covers Java's security mechanisms and teaches you how to work with them. It discusses class loaders, security managers, access lists, digital signatures, and authentication and shows how to use these to create and enforce your own security policy.

Java I/O

By Elliotte Rusty Harold
1st Edition March 1999
596 pages, ISBN 1-56592-485-1

All of Java's Input/Output (I/O) facilities are based on streams, which provide simple ways to read and write data of different types. Java I/O tells you all you need to know about the four main categories of streams and uncovers less-known features to help make your I/O operations more efficient. Plus, it shows you how to control number formatting, use characters aside from the standard ASCII character set, and get a head start on writing truly multilingual software.

Java Virtual Machine

By Jon Meyer & Troy Downing
1st Edition March 1997
452 pages, Includes diskette
ISBN 1-56592-194-1

This book is a comprehensive programming guide for the Java Virtual Machine (JVM). It gives readers a strong overview and reference of the JVM so that they may create their own implementations or write their own compilers that create Java object code.

Java

Java Fundamental Classes Reference

By Mark Grand & Jonathan Knudsen
1st Edition May 1997
1114 pages, ISBN 1-56592-241-7

The *Java Fundamental Classes Reference*
provides complete reference documentation
on the core Java 1.1 classes that comprise the
java.lang, java.io, java.net, java.util, java.text,
java.math, java.lang.reflect, and java.util.zip

packages. Part of O'Reilly's Java documentation series, this edition
describes Version 1.1 of the Java Development Kit. It includes
easy-to-use reference material and provides lots of sample code
to help you learn by example.

Java Language Reference, 2nd Edition

By Mark Grand
2nd Edition July 1997
492 pages, ISBN 1-56592-326-X

This book helps you understand the subtle
nuances of Java – from the definition of
data types to the syntax of expressions and
control structures – so you can ensure
your programs run exactly as expected.

The second edition covers the language features that have been
added in Java 1.1, such as inner classes, class literals, and
instance initializers.

Developing Java Beans

By Robert Englander
1st Edition June 1997
316 pages, ISBN 1-56592-289-1

Developing Java Beans is a complete
introduction to Java's component architecture.
It describes how to write Beans, which are
software components that can be used in
visual programming environments. This book

discusses event adapters, serialization, introspection, property
editors, and customizers, and shows how to use Beans within
ActiveX controls.

Java AWT Reference

By John Zukowski
1st Edition April 1997
1074 pages, ISBN 1-56592-240-9

The *Java AWT Reference* provides complete
reference documentation on the Abstract
Window Toolkit (AWT), a large collection of
classes for building graphical user interfaces
in Java. Part of O'Reilly's Java documentation

series, this edition describes both Version 1.0.2 and Version 1.1
of the Java Development Kit, includes easy-to-use reference
material on every AWT class, and provides lots of sample code.

Exploring Java, 2nd Edition

By Pat Niemeyer & Josh Peck
2nd Edition September 1997
614 pages, ISBN 1-56592-271-9

Whether you're just migrating to
Java or working steadily in the forefront
of Java development, this book gives a clear,
systematic overview of the language. It covers
the essentials of hot topics like Beans and

RMI, as well as writing applets and other applications, such as
networking programs, content and protocol handlers, and security
managers.

Java Power Reference

By David Flanagan
1st Edition March 1999
64 pages, Features CD-ROM
ISBN 1-56592-589-0

Java Power Reference is a searchable,
browser-based resource that documents all
the packages and classes of the Java 2(TM)
platform on a single CD-ROM. Based on the
clear, concise quick-reference style of the

bestselling *Java in a Nutshell*, the *Java Power Reference* provides
a unique view of the functionality of the Java APIs. In addition to
the CD-ROM, the package contains a concise printed overview
of the newly released Java 2 platform.

O'REILLY®

TO ORDER: **800-998-9938** • *order@oreilly.com* • *http://www.oreilly.com/*
OUR PRODUCTS ARE AVAILABLE AT A BOOKSTORE OR SOFTWARE STORE NEAR YOU.
FOR INFORMATION: **800-998-9938** • **707-829-0515** • *info@oreilly.com*

Java

Java Servlet Programming

By Jason Hunter with William Crawford
1st Edition November 1998
528 pages, ISBN 1-56592-391-X

Java servlets offer a fast, powerful, portable replacement for CGI scripts. *Java Servlet Programming* covers everything you need to know to write effective servlets. Topics include: serving dynamic Web content, maintaining state information, session tracking, database connectivity using JDBC, and applet-servlet communication.

Java Swing

By Robert Eckstein, Marc Loy & Dave Wood
1st Edition September 1998
1252 pages, ISBN 1-56592-455-X

The Swing classes eliminate Java's biggest weakness: its relatively primitive user interface toolkit. *Java Swing* helps you to take full advantage of the Swing classes, providing detailed descriptions of every class and interface in the key Swing packages. It shows you how to use all of the new components, allowing you to build state-of-the-art user interfaces and giving you the context you need to understand what you're doing. It's more than documentation; *Java Swing* helps you develop code quickly and effectively.

Enterprise JavaBeans

By Richard Monson-Haefel
1st Edition June 1999
336 pages, ISBN 1-56592-605-6

Enterprise JavaBeans is a thorough introduction to EJB for the enterprise software developer. It shows how to get started developing enterprise Beans, how to deploy those Beans in a server, and how to use those Beans to create applications that do useful tasks. The end result is a highly flexible system built from components that can easily be reused and that can be changed to suit your needs without upsetting other parts of the system.

Java 2D Graphics

By Jonathan Knudsen
1st Edition May 1999
366 pages, ISBN 1-56592-484-3

Java 2D Graphics describes the 2D API from top to bottom, demonstrating how to set line styles and pattern fills as well as more advanced techniques of image processing and font handling. You'll see how to create and manipulate the three types of graphics objects: shapes, text, and images. Other topics include image data storage, color management, font glyphs, and printing.

In a Nutshell Quick References

Java in a Nutshell, 2nd Edition

By David Flanagan
2nd Edition May 1997
628 pages, ISBN 1-56592-262-X

This second edition of the bestselling Java book describes all the classes in the Java 1.1 API, with the exception of the Enterprise APIs. And it still has all the great features that have made this the Java book most often recommended on the Internet: practical real-world examples and compact reference information. It's the only quick reference you'll need.

Java Examples in a Nutshell

By David Flanagan
1st Edition September 1997
414 pages, ISBN 1-56592-371-5

From the author of *Java in a Nutshell*, this companion book is chock full of practical real-world programming examples to help novice Java programmers and experts alike explore what's possible with Java 1.1. If you learn best by example, this is the book for you.

O'REILLY®

TO ORDER: **800-998-9938** • *order@oreilly.com* • *http://www.oreilly.com/*
OUR PRODUCTS ARE AVAILABLE AT A BOOKSTORE OR SOFTWARE STORE NEAR YOU.
FOR INFORMATION: **800-998-9938** • **707-829-0515** • *info@oreilly.com*

In a Nutshell Quick References

Java Enterprise in a Nutshell

By David Flanagan, Jim Farley,
William Crawford & Kris Magnusson
1st Edition September 1999
622 pages, ISBN 1-56592-483-5

The Java Enterprise APIs are essential building blocks for creating enterprise-wide distributed applications in Java. *Java Enterprise in a Nutshell* covers the RMI, Java IDL, JDBC, JNDI, Java Servlet, and Enterprise JavaBeans APIs, providing a fast-paced tutorial and compact reference material on each of the technologies. Covers Java 2.

Java Foundation Classes in a Nutshell

By David Flanagan
1st Edition September 1999
748 pages, ISBN 1-56592-488-6

Java Foundation Classes in a Nutshell provides an in-depth overview of the important pieces of the (JFC), such as the Swing components and Java 2D. It also includes compact reference material on all the GUI- and graphics-related classes in the numerous javax.swing and java.awt packages. Covers Java 2.

Java in a Nutshell, Deluxe Edition

By David Flanagan, et al.
1st Edition June 1997
628 pages, Includes CD-ROM & book
ISBN 1-56592-304-9

Java in a Nutshell, Deluxe Edition brings together on CD-ROM five volumes for Java developers and programmers, linking related info across books. *Exploring Java, 2nd Edition* covers Java basics. *Java Language Reference, 2nd Edition*, *Java Fundamental Classes Reference*, and *Java AWT Reference* provide a definitive set of documentation on the Java language and the Java 1.1 core API. *Java in a Nutshell, 2nd Edition*, our bestselling quick reference, is included both on the CD-ROM and in a companion desktop edition. This deluxe library is an indispensable resource for anyone doing serious programming with Java 1.1.

Web Programming

Writing Apache Modules with Perl and C

By Lincoln Stein & Doug MacEachern
1st Edition March 1999
746 pages, ISBN 1-56592-567-X

This guide to Web programming teaches you how to extend the capabilities of the Apache Web server. It explains the design of Apache, mod_perl, and the Apache API, then demonstrates how to use them to rewrite CGI scripts, filter HTML documents on the server-side, enhance server log functionality, convert file formats on the fly, and more.

Webmaster in a Nutshell, 2nd Edition

By Stephen Spainhour & Robert Eckstein
2nd Edition June 1999
540 pages, ISBN 1-56592-325-1

This indispensable book takes all the essential reference information for the Web and pulls it together into one volume. It covers HTML 4.0, CSS, XML, CGI, SSI, JavaScript 1.2, PHP, HTTP 1.1, and administration for the Apache server.

DocBook: The Definitive Guide

By Norman Walsh & Leonard Muellner
1st Edition October 1999
652 pages, Includes CD-ROM
ISBN 1-56592-580-7

DocBook is a Document Type Definition (DTD) for use with XML (the Extensible Markup Language) and SGML (the Standard Generalized Markup Language). DocBook lets authors in technical groups exchange and reuse technical information. This book contains an introduction to SGML, XML, and the DocBook DTD, plus the complete reference information for DocBook.

Web Programming

JavaScript Application Cookbook

By Jerry Bradenbaugh
1st Edition September 1999
478 pages, ISBN 1-56592-577-7

JavaScript Application Cookbook literally hands the Webmaster a set of ready-to-go, client-side JavaScript applications with thorough documentation to help them understand and extend the applications. By providing such a set of applications, *JavaScript Application Cookbook* allows Webmasters to immediately add extra functionality to their Web sites.

Practical Internet Groupware

By Jon Udell
1st Edition October 1999
524 pages, ISBN 1-56592-537-8

This revolutionary book tells users, programmers, IS managers, and system administrators how to build Internet groupware applications that organize the casual and chaotic transmission of online information into useful, disciplined, and documented data.

How to stay in touch with O'Reilly

1. Visit Our Award-Winning Web Site

http://www.oreilly.com/

★ "Top 100 Sites on the Web" —*PC Magazine*
★ "Top 5% Web sites" —*Point Communications*
★ "3-Star site" —*The McKinley Group*

Our web site contains a library of comprehensive product information (including book excerpts and tables of contents), downloadable software, background articles, interviews with technology leaders, links to relevant sites, book cover art, and more. File us in your Bookmarks or Hotlist!

2. Join Our Email Mailing Lists

New Product Releases

To receive automatic email with brief descriptions of all new O'Reilly products as they are released, send email to:
listproc@online.oreilly.com
Put the following information in the first line of your message (*not* in the Subject field):
subscribe oreilly-news

O'Reilly Events

If you'd also like us to send information about trade show events, special promotions, and other O'Reilly events, send email to:
listproc@online.oreilly.com
Put the following information in the first line of your message (*not* in the Subject field):
subscribe oreilly-events

3. Get Examples from Our Books via FTP

There are two ways to access an archive of example files from our books:

Regular FTP

- ftp to:
  ftp.oreilly.com
  (login: anonymous
  password: your email address)
- Point your web browser to:
  ftp://ftp.oreilly.com/

FTPMAIL

- Send an email message to:
  ftpmail@online.oreilly.com
  (Write "help" in the message body)

4. Contact Us via Email

order@oreilly.com
To place a book or software order online. Good for North American and international customers.

subscriptions@oreilly.com
To place an order for any of our newsletters or periodicals.

books@oreilly.com
General questions about any of our books.

software@oreilly.com
For general questions and product information about our software. Check out O'Reilly Software Online at **http://software.oreilly.com/** for software and technical support information. Registered O'Reilly software users send your questions to: **website-support@oreilly.com**

cs@oreilly.com
For answers to problems regarding your order or our products.

booktech@oreilly.com
For book content technical questions or corrections.

proposals@oreilly.com
To submit new book or software proposals to our editors and product managers.

international@oreilly.com
For information about our international distributors or translation queries. For a list of our distributors outside of North America check out:
http://www.oreilly.com/www/order/country.html

O'Reilly & Associates, Inc.
101 Morris Street, Sebastopol, CA 95472 USA
TEL   707-829-0515 or 800-998-9938
          (6am to 5pm PST)
FAX   707-829-0104

TO ORDER: **800-998-9938** • **order@oreilly.com** • **http://www.oreilly.com/**
OUR PRODUCTS ARE AVAILABLE AT A BOOKSTORE OR SOFTWARE STORE NEAR YOU.
FOR INFORMATION: **800-998-9938** • **707-829-0515** • **info@oreilly.com**

Titles from O'Reilly

WEB

Advanced Perl Programming
Apache: The Definitive Guide,
    2nd Edition
ASP in a Nutshell
Building Your Own Web Conferences
Building Your Own Website™
CGI Programming with Perl
Designing with JavaScript
Dynamic HTML:
    The Definitive Reference
Frontier: The Definitive Guide
HTML: The Definitive Guide,
    3rd Edition
Information Architecture
    for the World Wide Web
JavaScript Pocket Reference
JavaScript: The Definitive Guide,
    3rd Edition
Learning VB Script
Photoshop for the Web
WebMaster in a Nutshell
WebMaster in a Nutshell,
    Deluxe Edition
Web Design in a Nutshell
Web Navigation:
    Designing the User Experience
Web Performance Tuning
Web Security & Commerce
Writing Apache Modules

PERL

Learning Perl, 2nd Edition
Learning Perl for Win32 Systems
Learning Perl/TK
Mastering Algorithms with Perl
Mastering Regular Expressions
Perl5 Pocket Reference, 2nd Edition
Perl Cookbook
Perl in a Nutshell
Perl Resource Kit—UNIX Edition
Perl Resource Kit—Win32 Edition
Perl/TK Pocket Reference
Programming Perl, 2nd Edition
Web Client Programming with Perl

GRAPHICS & MULTIMEDIA

Director in a Nutshell
Encyclopedia of Graphics
    File Formats, 2nd Edition
Lingo in a Nutshell
Photoshop in a Nutshell
QuarkXPress in a Nutshell

USING THE INTERNET

AOL in a Nutshell
Internet in a Nutshell
Smileys
The Whole Internet for Windows95
The Whole Internet:
    The Next Generation
The Whole Internet
    User's Guide & Catalog

JAVA SERIES

Database Programming with
    JDBC and Java
Developing Java Beans
Exploring Java, 2nd Edition
Java AWT Reference
Java Cryptography
Java Distributed Computing
Java Examples in a Nutshell
Java Foundation Classes in a Nutshell
Java Fundamental Classes Reference
Java in a Nutshell, 2nd Edition
Java in a Nutshell, Deluxe Edition
Java I/O
Java Language Reference, 2nd Edition
Java Media Players
Java Native Methods
Java Network Programming
Java Security
Java Servlet Programming
Java Swing
Java Threads
Java Virtual Machine

UNIX

Exploring Expect
GNU Emacs Pocket Reference
Learning GNU Emacs, 2nd Edition
Learning the bash Shell, 2nd Edition
Learning the Korn Shell
Learning the UNIX Operating System,
    4th Edition
Learning the vi Editor, 6th Edition
Linux in a Nutshell
Linux Multimedia Guide
Running Linux, 2nd Edition
SCO UNIX in a Nutshell
sed & awk, 2nd Edition
Tcl/Tk in a Nutshell
Tcl/Tk Pocket Reference
Tcl/Tk Tools
The UNIX CD Bookshelf
UNIX in a Nutshell, System V Edition
UNIX Power Tools, 2nd Edition
Using csh & tsch
Using Samba
vi Editor Pocket Reference
What You Need To Know:
    When You Can't Find Your
    UNIX System Administrator
Writing GNU Emacs Extensions

SONGLINE GUIDES

NetLaw   NetResearch
NetLearning   NetSuccess
NetLessons   NetTravel

SOFTWARE

Building Your Own WebSite™
Building Your Own Web Conference
WebBoard™ 3.0
WebSite Professional™ 2.0
PolyForm™

SYSTEM ADMINISTRATION

Building Internet Firewalls
Computer Security Basics
Cracking DES
DNS and BIND, 3rd Edition
DNS on WindowsNT
Essential System Administration
Essential WindowsNT
    System Administration
Getting Connected:
    The Internet at 56K and Up
Linux Network Administrator's Guide
Managing IP Networks with
    Cisco Routers
Managing Mailing Lists
Managing NFS and NIS
Managing the WindowsNT Registry
Managing Usenet
MCSE: The Core Exams in a Nutshell
MCSE: The Electives in a Nutshell
Networking Personal Computers
    with TCP/IP
Oracle Performance Tuning,
    2nd Edition
Practical UNIX & Internet Security,
    2nd Edition
PGP: Pretty Good Privacy
Protecting Networks with SATAN
sendmail, 2nd Edition
sendmail Desktop Reference
System Performance Tuning
TCP/IP Network Administration,
    2nd Edition
termcap & terminfo
The Networking CD Bookshelf
Using & Managing PPP
Virtual Private Networks
WindowsNT Backup & Restore
WindowsNT Desktop Reference
WindowsNT Event Logging
WindowsNT in a Nutshell
WindowsNT Server 4.0 for
    Netware Administrators
WindowsNT SNMP
WindowsNT TCP/IP Administration
WindowsNT User Administration
Zero Administration for Windows

X WINDOW

Vol. 1: Xlib Programming Manual
Vol. 2: Xlib Reference Manual
Vol. 3M: X Window System
    User's Guide, Motif Edition
Vol. 4M: X Toolkit Intrinsics
    Programming Manual,
    Motif Edition
Vol. 5: X Toolkit Intrinsics
    Reference Manual
Vol. 6A: Motif Programming Manual
Vol. 6B: Motif Reference Manual
Vol. 8 : X Window System
    Administrator's Guide

PROGRAMMING

Access Database Design and
    Programming
Advanced Oracle PL/SQL
    Programming with Packages
Applying RCS and SCCS
BE Developer's Guide
BE Advanced Topics
C++: The Core Language
Checking C Programs with lint
Developing Windows Error Messages
Developing Visual Basic Add-ins
Guide to Writing DCE Applications
High Performance Computing,
    2nd Edition
Inside the Windows 95 File System
Inside the Windows 95 Registry
lex & yacc, 2nd Edition
Linux Device Drivers
Managing Projects with make
Oracle8 Design Tips
Oracle Built-in Packages
Oracle Design
Oracle PL/SQL Programming,
    2nd Edition
Oracle Scripts
Oracle Security
Palm Programming:
    The Developer's Guide
Porting UNIX Software
POSIX Programmer's Guide
POSIX.4: Programming
    for the Real World
Power Programming with RPC
Practical C Programming, 3rd Edition
Practical C++ Programming
Programming Python
Programming with curses
Programming with GNU Software
Pthreads Programming
Python Pocket Reference
Software Portability with imake,
    2nd Edition
UML in a Nutshell
Understanding DCE
UNIX Systems Programming for SVR4
VB/VBA in a Nutshell: The Languages
Win32 Multithreaded Programming
Windows NT File System Internals
Year 2000 in a Nutshell

USING WINDOWS

Excel97 Annoyances
Office97 Annoyances
Outlook Annoyances
Windows Annoyances
Windows98 Annoyances
Windows95 in a Nutshell
Windows98 in a Nutshell
Word97 Annoyances

OTHER TITLES

PalmPilot: The Ultimate Guide
Palm Programming:
    The Developer's Guide

O'REILLY®

TO ORDER: **800-998-9938** • **order@oreilly.com** • **http://www.oreilly.com/**
OUR PRODUCTS ARE AVAILABLE AT A BOOKSTORE OR SOFTWARE STORE NEAR YOU.
FOR INFORMATION: **800-998-9938** • **707-829-0515** • **info@oreilly.com**

International Distributors

UK, EUROPE, MIDDLE EAST AND AFRICA (EXCEPT FRANCE, GERMANY, AUSTRIA, SWITZERLAND, LUXEMBOURG, LIECHTENSTEIN, AND EASTERN EUROPE)

INQUIRIES
O'Reilly UK Limited
4 Castle Street
Farnham
Surrey, GU9 7HS
United Kingdom
Telephone: 44-1252-711776
Fax: 44-1252-734211
Email: josette@oreilly.com

ORDERS
Wiley Distribution Services Ltd.
1 Oldlands Way
Bognor Regis
West Sussex PO22 9SA
United Kingdom
Telephone: 44-1243-779777
Fax: 44-1243-820250
Email: cs-books@wiley.co.uk

FRANCE

ORDERS
GEODIF
61, Bd Saint-Germain
75240 Paris Cedex 05, France
Tel: 33-1-44-41-46-16 (French books)
Tel: 33-1-44-41-11-87 (English books)
Fax: 33-1-44-41-11-44
Email: distribution@eyrolles.com

INQUIRIES
Éditions O'Reilly
18 rue Séguier
75006 Paris, France
Tel: 33-1-40-51-52-30
Fax: 33-1-40-51-52-31
Email: france@editions-oreilly.fr

GERMANY, SWITZERLAND, AUSTRIA, EASTERN EUROPE, LUXEMBOURG, AND LIECHTENSTEIN

INQUIRIES & ORDERS
O'Reilly Verlag
Balthasarstr. 81
D-50670 Köln
Germany
Telephone: 49-221-973160-91
Fax: 49-221-973160-8
Email: anfragen@oreilly.de (inquiries)
Email: order@oreilly.de (orders)

CANADA (FRENCH LANGUAGE BOOKS)

Les Éditions Flammarion ltée
375, Avenue Laurier Ouest
Montréal (Québec) H2V 2K3
Tel: 00-1-514-277-8807
Fax: 00-1-514-278-2085
Email: info@flammarion.qc.ca

HONG KONG

City Discount Subscription Service, Ltd.
Unit D, 3rd Floor, Yan's Tower
27 Wong Chuk Hang Road
Aberdeen, Hong Kong
Tel: 852-2580-3539
Fax: 852-2580-6463
Email: citydis@ppn.com.hk

KOREA

Hanbit Media, Inc.
Sonyoung Bldg. 202
Yeksam-dong 736-36
Kangnam-ku
Seoul, Korea
Tel: 822-554-9610
Fax: 822-556-0363
Email: hant93@chollian.dacom.co.kr

PHILIPPINES

Mutual Books, Inc.
429-D Shaw Boulevard
Mandaluyong City, Metro
Manila, Philippines
Tel: 632-725-7538
Fax: 632-721-3056
Email: mbikikog@mnl.sequel.net

TAIWAN

O'Reilly Taiwan
No. 3, Lane 131
Hang-Chow South Road
Section 1, Taipei, Taiwan
Tel: 886-2-23968990
Fax: 886-2-23968916
Email: taiwan@oreilly.com

CHINA

O'Reilly Beijing
Room 2410
160, FuXingMenNeiDaJie
XiCheng District
Beijing, China PR 100031
Tel: 86-10-66412305
Fax: 86-10-86631007
Email: beijing@oreilly.com

INDIA

Computer Bookshop (India) Pvt. Ltd.
190 Dr. D.N. Road, Fort
Bombay 400 001 India
Tel: 91-22-207-0989
Fax: 91-22-262-3551
Email: cbsbom@giasbm01.vsnl.net.in

JAPAN

O'Reilly Japan, Inc.
Kiyoshige Building 2F
12-Bancho, Sanei-cho
Shinjuku-ku
Tokyo 160-0008 Japan
Tel: 81-3-3356-5227
Fax: 81-3-3356-5261
Email: japan@oreilly.com

ALL OTHER ASIAN COUNTRIES

O'Reilly & Associates, Inc.
101 Morris Street
Sebastopol, CA 95472 USA
Tel: 707-829-0515
Fax: 707-829-0104
Email: order@oreilly.com

AUSTRALIA

WoodsLane Pty., Ltd.
7/5 Vuko Place
Warriewood NSW 2102
Australia
Tel: 61-2-9970-5111
Fax: 61-2-9970-5002
Email: info@woodslane.com.au

NEW ZEALAND

Woodslane New Zealand, Ltd.
21 Cooks Street (P.O. Box 575)
Waganui, New Zealand
Tel: 64-6-347-6543
Fax: 64-6-345-4840
Email: info@woodslane.com.au

LATIN AMERICA

McGraw-Hill Interamericana
Editores, S.A. de C.V.
Cedro No. 512
Col. Atlampa
06450, Mexico, D.F.
Tel: 52-5-547-6777
Fax: 52-5-547-3336
Email: mcgraw-hill@infosel.net.mx

O'REILLY®

O'REILLY™

O'Reilly & Associates, Inc.
101 Morris Street
Sebastopol, CA 95472-9902
1-800-998-9938

Visit us online at:
http://www.ora.com/
orders@ora.com

O'REILLY WOULD LIKE TO HEAR FROM YOU

Nineteenth century wood engraving
of a bear from the O'Reilly &
Associates Nutshell Handbook®
Using & Managing UUCP.

POST CARD

BUSINESS REPLY MAIL

FIRST CLASS MAIL   PERMIT NO. 80   SEBASTOPOL, CA

Postage will be paid by addressee

O'Reilly & Associates, Inc.
101 Morris Street
Sebastopol, CA 95472-9902